16

THE
FATHERLESS
DAUGHTER
PROJECT

THE
FATHERLESS
DAUGHTER
PROJECT

Understanding Our Losses and Reclaiming Our Lives

Denna D. Babul, RN, and
Karin Luise, PhD

AVERY

an imprint of Penguin Random House

New York

AVERY

an imprint of Penguin Random House LLC
375 Hudson Street
New York, New York 10014

Copyright © 2016 by Denna D. Babul and Karin Luise
Penguin supports copyright. Copyright fuels creativity, encourages diverse voices,
promotes free speech, and creates a vibrant culture. Thank you for buying an authorized
edition of this book and for complying with copyright laws by not reproducing, scanning,
or distributing any part of it in any form without permission. You are supporting writers
and allowing Penguin to continue to publish books for every reader.

Most Avery books are available at special quantity discounts for bulk purchase
for sales promotions, premiums, fund-raising, and educational needs.
Special books or book excerpts also can be created to fit specific needs.
For details, write SpecialMarkets@penguinrandomhouse.com.

Library of Congress Cataloging-in-Publication Data

Babul, Denna D., author.
The fatherless daughter project : understanding our losses and reclaiming
our lives / Denna D. Babul, RN, and Karin Luise, PhD.
p.   cm.
Includes bibliographical references and index.
ISBN 978-1-59463-369-0
1. Fathers and daughters.   2. Children of single parents.   3. Parent and adult child.
4. Loss (Psychology).   I. Luise, Karin, author.   II. Title.
HQ755.86.B323   2016   2015025161
306.874'2—dc23

Printed in the United States of America
1   3   5   7   9   10   8   6   4   2

Book design by Ellen Cipriano

Some names and identifying characteristics have been changed
to protect the privacy of the individuals involved.

To Karin's and Denna's younger selves
(One day you'll write a book.)

DENNA:

For my two sweet love bugs, Sophie Bleu and Weston Grey.
For my husband, Jon, thank you for going on this journey with me.
For my mother and best friend, Mary Dobbins.

KARIN:

For the three soul miracles in my life, West, Elise, and Hoyte.
For my mother and inspiration, Rev. Lisa L. Graves.

In memory of:
Joan Babul
James Dobbins
Nancy Gay Smithson

The real purpose of books is to trap the mind

into doing its own thinking.

~CHRISTOPHER MORLEY

CONTENTS

INTRODUCTION

This book is so meaningful to us. We believe this book can be so meaningful for *you*. We have been where you have been. We want to help you to better understand the impact the loss of your father had on your life and how you can heal from that loss. We have, through personal experience and exploration of this issue, become passionate about sharing our knowledge and helping women better understand why they may be acting and feeling the way that they do—because they are fatherless.

As we were preparing the material for this book, we knew that we needed something living alongside it to help women further see themselves through the stories of others. We are creating a thirty-minute documentary, *The Fatherless Daughter Project*, that contains intimate and compelling interviews with a diverse group of fatherless daughters to showcase their resilience and how they've created success in their lives.

Beyond the documentary, we wanted to write this book to share our stories, the stories of women who have lost their fathers, and most important, successful strategies for coping, surviving, and thriving despite the loss. Each woman's story is unique to her own circumstances, but fatherless daughters also share some commonalities.

Karin's losses were the consequences of divorce, adoption, and dysfunction; Denna's losses were because of divorce and death.

Karin's Story

While writing this book, Denna and I spent countless hours talking about our own journeys. Because we were both willing to search our own lives, amazing, life-changing moments have come along the way. It was during our first major rewrite that I realized I needed to have a conversation with my father—my natural father. He was not the dad who raised me, but he was the father who created me and had now become increasingly present in my life. As the years passed, we got together more regularly, and he has become a wonderful grandpa to my three children. Although my children got their grandpa, I still felt a void. We had never talked about what all of those years of his absence did to my life, and I continued to struggle with it.

On a sunny June morning Dad was paying us his regular Friday visit. He knew I was writing a book on fatherlessness, but we had not spoken about it at length. We had talked about a lot of *things*; we just never talked about *us*. I think I had avoided the sensitive topic because I knew the conversation would be difficult.

There were several reasons for his absence during my childhood, including his giving me up for adoption to my "new father." His and my mother's stories about the past were different, which left me confused. Without understanding the story, I had felt abandoned by him most of my life. Being disconnected from my adopted father twenty years later added stinging salt to the wound. Still, I didn't want my truth to run my birth father off and leave me abandoned again. Although I was waiting for the ideal moment for The Conversation, I did not know that it was going to happen that morning.

He caught me off guard when the children left the room to play. As the room quieted, he walked slowly around the breakfast table, putting his hand atop the curve of one of the chairs. He said something I could tell he had been waiting to say: "Karin, I was looking at your father-less daughters research study online." He smirked and shook his head, pausing, his eyes fixed on the white tablecloth. Heart pounding, I stopped still at the kitchen counter and waited. The Conversation was happening.

"Do you think you are *fatherless*? I mean, I *am* your father, and I am right *here*." We stood still for a moment as the challenge hung in the air between us, him looking at me, and me looking everywhere for a safety net. *Oh my God, what do I say? I'm not ready. . . . I can't do this. . . . I'm scared of the words I want to use.* My heart's thumping was making me feel faint, so I took a deep breath. I had to overcome my decades-old insecurity to speak as I scrambled to find honesty and my first sentence. Silently, I told myself, "You have what it takes, Karin. You need to *just say it*." I had to push through this scary place to get rid of the fears that had re-sided in me for too long. I steadied myself and looked him in the eye.

"Dad, let me start by saying I am so glad that you are here now. I don't want to lose this. I am so grateful that you are in our lives and that my kids are getting their grandpa." I paused, reaching deep inside for a new boldness to continue. "But, Dad, I *did* lose my father when I was a little girl. You *did* give me up for adoption. You let another man raise me, and he and I are now estranged too. You don't know what I went through. I lost a close connection with you for a long time. There is so much to the story that we have never talked about. Things were bad, and I was in a lot of pain for a lot of years." I took a break, as I could feel he wanted to interject.

"You think it was bad for *you*?" he said. "Do you know how hard that was for *me*?"

I felt that familiar spike of cortisol flood my bloodstream, as he changed the subject from me to him. I wanted *my* turn today. "Yes, I know it was hard for you, Dad, and I am sorry. I am sorry for all of it. But it happened. It happened to *me*. *I* was a little girl. I was the daughter, and you were the father. *You* were the adult. I did not know what to do. I was a *child*."

He continued with his truth. He wanted me to know how much he had wished to be involved in my life, but that he felt he had no choice. I had heard the story many times before and did not want to get into the details again. I wanted to be heard.

I needed to let my dad know about the lost years, the depression, and the negative consequences that played out over my life. I talked about the cutting, the tears, and the traumas I rarely call by name. As I cried, he seemed to watch me in confusion. I could tell he was lost in my retelling, but I was not going to let him change the subject to avoid what I wanted to say. I was getting this out. Right here. I took a very deep breath and told him something I had never said before.

"Dad, please stop changing the subject. I need to talk about *this*—I need to talk about *me*—and I need you to *listen*. I need you to be here right now and *hear* me. I have to tell you this. You did not protect me. You did not come in and fight off the bad guys, even after I tried to tell you what was happening. I needed you to be there. I needed you to stand up for me. I needed *someone* to stand up for me. Even now, we are standing here, and I am crying and telling you all of this, and you are avoiding me." He stood very still, surprised by my forthrightness. But he was listening. And then, in a very vulnerable leap of faith, I asked for exactly what I needed.

"Dad." I trembled. "I . . . I need you to say to me, 'I am sorry. I am sorry I wasn't there. I am sorry this happened.' And then I need you to hug me." I waited.

As I stood wiping away my tears, my dad did something different. He got quiet too. He closed his eyes. Then he stepped forward and hugged me. He kept himself in the room and in the moment and with me. Then, he said slowly into my ear, "Karin, I am sorry I wasn't there." And with those seven words I got a gift that I had been waiting to receive for forty years. Recognition. An apology. A hug. As we embraced, I felt the gaping hole between us beginning to fill.

Denna's Story

I lost my Dad twice. The first loss was at the age of three when my parents divorced. The second loss was when I was thirteen, and he was killed. It wasn't until 2008, when I was thirty-seven, that I had a major breakthrough about how I could use my story—my life—to help other fatherless women.

After getting a divorce and moving to another state to start my life anew, I started feeling like my old life was infiltrating my new life. My fear of abandonment had come back in full swing now that I had walked away from everyone I knew and loved. My new relationship was not working. I was hanging on for dear life, trying to avoid facing my past. After our third and final break-up, devastated, I finally realized that changing area codes was not going to fix me. In order to "fix me" I would have to do the inevitable . . . get alone and into therapy. Until then, I had not known how upset I was about my dad. I thought the source of my problems was more about finding and losing love—not about the biggest love that I had lost.

Before long I had thrown my entire self into the process of sifting through my past. Tear by tear, I was putting the pieces back together. On a particularly emotional day, my therapist said something that rattled me to my core. He leaned in and said poignantly, "Denna, the only thing you seem to know for sure about your dad is how he *died*. What you need to fill in are the gaps on how he *lived*. Who was he as a person? Who was he as a father?"

I was shocked, but he was right. I had no idea who my dad was beyond that he was a sharp dresser, did occasional magic tricks, and had a glass of chocolate milk every morning instead of coffee. The rest I had gathered from a photo album and the occasional story I had heard. I knew that asking a lot of questions about him would upset my mom, and so I learned to listen instead of explore. My dad was a taboo subject. The older I got, the more I seemed to miss this man named Jim who was my father. I was desperate to know him. I was desperate to know the other half of me and who I had come from.

Because my mother and father had been through a tumultuous divorce, I already knew that my mom would not be my go-to person to fill in all of the blanks. Believe me, I had tried. After a lot of deep thought, I decided to reach out to my dad's brother, my uncle Bill. We had always been in touch. He sent me money on all of the major holidays and always said "I love you" when we spoke, yet we never spoke about my father— his brother—at length.

When I was sixteen, I got up the nerve to write Uncle Bill a letter asking some very generic questions: What was my dad's favorite color? Did he like to fish? But what I really wanted to know was, did he love me? Did he like being a father? Did I remind my uncle of my father? Did he know who had killed him? My uncle wrote back and answered all of my generic questions. My dad's favorite color was blue, and yes, he enjoyed fishing. I wanted to know so much more, yet I was too afraid to ask. Life moved on.

After years of soul searching I decided to write a book to fill in the holes of my own story. I needed to see my own story in writing to understand it. I thought that by going back and talking through all of the highs and lows I could help not only myself but perhaps others. In order to be accurate about the details of my story I spent almost every weekend for the next year with my uncle Bill in Charleston, South Carolina. We walked on the beach. We held hands. We laughed. We cried. He painstakingly helped me put my dad's story together and filled me up with love and acceptance along the way.

I wrote day and night, reading excerpts to my uncle, family, and therapist. It took me about five years to finish the book. The process was both healing and extremely difficult. I was exceedingly better as a person and as my father's daughter. My coping skills had been replaced with new and improved ways of handling my past and future. My mind was no longer jumbled and confused. I was free from my past and excited for my future. Now came the hard part. I had to put myself and my story out there if I was going to help other fatherless daughters.

Sitting at my computer one day, I came across information on an upcoming show about family secrets on the *Today Show*'s website. Instinctively, as I typed my life's secret into a single paragraph, I knew that I was about to change my life. There would be no turning back, and I knew that I was ready. My gut told me that I would be on that show, sitting on that couch, being interviewed by Meredith Vieira for the entire world to see.

Within weeks, the producers came to Atlanta to interview me, along with the rest of my family. My uncle respectfully declined to be interviewed. One by one, we were exposing the truth as we talked about something that before had been kept private: how I became fatherless.

In a weird way, the secret that I held tightly for all of those years was slowly bringing my dad's death to the forefront. My family and I spoke more about my dad in those forty-eight hours than we had in the twenty-four years since he had passed. A few days later, when one of the producers called, I heard a sentence that would change the course of my life: "We want you to come be on the show live to tell your story." It was really happening. I did not know whether to scream out loud or vomit. What I did know was that I was finally ready to face whatever was coming—head-on.

The next Monday morning, I found myself in New York, in front of cameras, in a tailored blue dress, with my palms sweating. "Oh God," I thought, "I've done this to myself." I sat still and watched along with the rest of the world as my story was told on the screen right in front of me like a family home video.

One thought ran wild circles through my mind: "Now twenty million people will know why I am fatherless. . . . Twenty million people . . . I am fatherless because someone out there killed him. Oh my God. Is this really happening?" But to tell the truth, despite the twenty-four-year-old fear, deep down in my soul, I didn't want to hide anymore. Somehow, I had found the courage to tell the truth.

For years I'd been telling everyone that my dad died of a heart attack when I was thirteen. It was my go-to story. But on live television, I spoke what always had been unspeakable in my family: the real story. My dad had been killed. We don't know why. We never found out who did it. We never talked about it. Until now. And the secret was out, right there as I sat across from Meredith Vieira talking about the past, trying to be the strong woman I had taught myself to be. I was finally taking charge of my past and fulfilling my destiny. I thought, "My story is going to help someone. Right now I am talking to all of the fatherless daughters out there who want so badly to feel better about their situations. I am showing them that I am one of them, and I am OK."

The irony was that once I shared my secret, I instantaneously felt free. More free than I had ever felt! In fact, it was one of the single most powerful days in my life. I had (*gulp*) told the world my fatherless story. Then I waited. And guess what? Nothing horrible happened. I didn't fall into a deep depression. I was not shunned from my social groups. I did not curl up into a thumb-sucking ball on the floor.

In fact, the opposite happened. I had actually found my calling and myself. I had inklings that this was my purpose all along. Although I tucked that secret deep inside of my past, something inside of me had always known that I would one day help other women who had gone through losing their dads. I couldn't deny the persistent nudge inside of me to keep looking, keep listening, and keep searching for others who were like me. My fatherless-daughter radar was always on high alert, *beep-beep-beeping* in my head everywhere I went.

I was the girl at the dinner party who sat huddled at the end of the table into the midnight hour, talking with a broken-hearted young woman about her recent breakup, which ultimately ended up being a conversation about why she was really hurting so deeply—her father. Seriously. It always came down to fatherlessness when women opened up to me.

Every week, I would watch CBS's *Sunday Morning* and, if the person they were featuring mentioned being fatherless, I would jot down the name and research more about her story. I distinctly recall being mesmerized, curled up on my couch, watching Patricia Cornwell talking about being abandoned by her father. Everywhere I turned there was another daughter with another story. With each one, the meaning of the stories started to bring more clarity and purpose to my own life. I listened intently to the words that Bethenny Frankel used when describing her own fatherless story to her therapist on her reality show. Demi Moore's story had me emotional as I read about how her father abandoned her before she was born. Any time Caroline Kennedy spoke about her father, I was taking notes, intrigued at the journey of her life. I felt a connection with these women.

My passion for fatherless daughters was all-consuming. I started keeping a running list of women and statistics that I found noteworthy. I wrote on napkins, in notebooks, and on my computer. I tucked the facts into my brain, and often it seemed the stories were all I heard on days filled with so much other white noise. It became what some might call my obsession, but I believe it to be my calling.

I felt that calling from deep within when I spoke to anyone who was fatherless. I was driven by it. People had told me for years to try to just let it go. I wondered if they were right. And so I tried. I questioned many times if I was stuck. If the pain of losing my dad was just something that

I would never be able to completely shake. But everything had led me to this. It was who I was.

As I walked off the *Today Show* set that brisk fall morning, it hit me like a ton of bricks. It was not what happened to my *father*. It was what happened to *me* because I did not have my father. Therefore, I would have to go back to the drawing board. I would need to write a book that spoke of all of our stories, not just my own. That was my revelation. That was my breakthrough. The more I let go of the secret and shame of my own father's desertion and death, the more my destiny became clear. I wanted to help every single fatherless daughter out there let go of being stuck in the past, shed the shame, and take control of her own destiny. Fatherlessness does not have to define you. In fact, it can redefine who you want to become.

Your Story

It's not uncommon to be asked about your parents. Each time someone asks about your father, you probably have a brief story that you have kneaded and molded into a form that you can handle—and that others can handle—as you pushed through the significant years of your life without the security of a father–daughter bond. We need to protect our histories and our hearts from being hurt again in the retelling of what happened to our fathers. At the same time, we have felt compelled to protect those who are asking for an answer that might make them uncomfortable. We can become wary over time of the need to take care of someone after we have spilled a painful answer onto his or her lap, so we reshape the story and try out different versions to find one that works. The gift in this retelling is that we learn how to be creative storytellers.

First, you have the real story about what really happened in his life, to your parents, and to you. You hold the real story close to your chest because telling it could reveal a wound that you usually keep covered. The real story might be immensely private and one you have likely divulged to only a handful of trustworthy people in your life.

Those who hear your real story—your confidants—are the friends or family you trust enough to call when the pain comes crashing down on Father's Day. They know that you can become emotionally sidelined by the sound of your uncle's hoarse voice because it echoes your father's. They know that your jewelry box still holds the jeweled peacock that your dad gave you on your tenth birthday. It is the one that you pull out every year just to feel its familiar edges in your fingers and be taken back to a moment when that sparkling gift made you feel like the most special girl in the world.

You have shown your confidants that grief has no expiration date and is as individual as the person experiencing it. And they understand. In turn, they have shown you that they do not expect you to "get over it," even when society tells you to. So you have slowly trusted them with your story. Many of them have also lost a loved one and understand the process. You trust that they will not judge you but will hold your story as sacred as you do. You trust that they will understand when you are being triggered by something as fleeting as a commercial showing a father giving his daughter a piggyback ride or something as slow and painful as heartbreak. We were not surprised to find in our research that over half of fatherless daughters' best friends are also fatherless. They get it, and they get *you*.

The other story you carry around is your go-to story, briefly explaining what happened to your dad in a few quick sentences. In most situations, you keep the go-to story emotion-free and quick, so as not to raise a flag during the conversation. You might dismiss your tragedy—if you experienced one—or lessen the feeling of emotional loss inside so that you can move on to another topic. If you are ashamed of the reason you are fatherless, you might have a half-truth version to explain where he is, why he left, or how he died. You have come to peace with this version because it simplifies things, has a less tragic tone, and does not leave much room for questions. You can move on without raising tears or concern, protecting yourself and the person you are speaking with from details that could become uncomfortable.

No matter what you have told people along the way, you know what your real story is, and you have learned to protect it. To tell things exactly as they happened, you have to be ready on many levels. You have to be able to handle the truth yourself before sharing it completely with another person. You need to feel safe enough to be vulnerable with the details and emotions. Grief is not predictable. You never know how the other person will be affected by what you reveal or, moreover, how *you* will feel after divulging it. Thus fatherless daughters are tasked with carrying the burden of when to tell, when not to tell, how much to tell, and how much to keep to themselves.

Over the years, as adult fatherless daughters, we usually condition ourselves to play a part—to present a tough-as-nails exterior. While grieving our loss, we go through a metamorphosis that is unique. We try to take charge of everything on the outside, although we might be hurting on the inside, and we decide that if our original superhero is not going to save us, we are going to have to do it on our own. Sometimes we have the strength to be our own Supergirl or Superwoman, but sometimes we are too weak to put on that cape. In an interview with the *International Design Times*, Charlize Theron said it best when talking about her decision to open up about her father's 1991 murder: "Everything changed for me that day my father died. Years ago I used to cover it all up and say he died in a car accident. I have now come to terms with it and have been able to move on."

We may all have different histories and come from varying walks of life, but the one thing we have in common is the loss of our fathers.

While some of our pain may show up a little differently, in the end, what we really want is the same—to feel better.

This book explores the multifaceted lives of fatherless daughters. Through groundbreaking research, women's stories, and countless interviews, we have gathered new insight that will help you understand your own fatherless story in a fresh and inspiring way. In reading this book you will soon realize the impact losing your dad has had on your life. We have included some exercises to encourage self-reflection and growth. We want you to take a minute (or two) and think about your own personal narrative. What does your inner voice tell you? How do you view the world and those around you based on your story? To start this journey, get out your laptop or a notebook and take some time for yourself to write your fatherless story. Keep in mind that there is no right or wrong way to do this. It can be as short as a single paragraph or fill up multiple pages. In it, write down how you feel about your story and what you believe your future holds. Put it to the side. We will come back to your story at the end of this book.

We are about to get honest and talk about how you have lived in the past, what you are doing now, and what could happen later. As Dr. Brené Brown so poignantly wrote in her best seller *The Gifts of Imperfection*, "If we want to live and love with our whole hearts, and if we want to engage with the world from a place of worthiness, we have to talk about the things that get in the way—especially shame, fear, and vulnerability."

Amen. Let's keep talking.

CHAPTER 1

You Have Lost Your Father

The loss of my father was the defining moment in my life.
~Denna Babul, *The Fatherless Daughter Project: The Documentary*

Are you fatherless? If so, you are not alone. You are also not alone in wondering how it has impacted your relationships, behavior, and more. Being a fatherless daughter puts you in a sisterhood. We have been there too, and because of major turning points in our lives, we decided it was time to take a close look at what being fatherless means for us both. We have closely examined our own pasts to see what went wrong and what went right. Both of us chose professions that are focused on helping others. Denna worked as a critical care nurse for over ten years and has continued her love of patient care in her current career working with medical devices. She has spent years counseling families through both tragedy and triumph. Denna also works as a full-time life coach and motivational speaker, inspiring people everywhere to let go of the past in order to jump into their own jet streams in life. Karin was an elementary and middle school teacher before pursuing her doctorate in counseling education and practice to work with adults. She now applies her training and life experience helping others as a spiritual counselor, inspirational speaker, and educator. We have each used our own pasts as a springboard to dive deeper into what it means to be a fatherless daughter. Our personal experiences drew us together, our professional expertise deepened our collective knowledge and inspired us to share what we knew with other fatherless daughters.

Together, while developing our documentary, *The Fatherless Daughter Project*, we interviewed over a thousand fatherless daughters both formally and informally. We spoke with women in so many unexpected places over the last ten years, including grocery lines, funeral homes, nail salons, day care centers, and other random places—all because women carry around the need to express their experiences and feel validated. Our quantitative research was conducted over a year's time, bringing in results from more than five thousand women, and counting, worldwide. Our participants ranged from age fifteen to almost eighty, from a variety of ethnic backgrounds, levels of education, career paths, and socioeconomic standings. While the bulk of our respondents were from the United States, we were able to access an international response through social media. We were interested to discover that fatherless daughters were referring each other to take the survey. They were learning about themselves along the way and wanted to help others do the same.

In the year before our survey was launched, we researched other books written on this subject, as well as other websites and forums that address this issue, and we found something was missing. We wanted to find the answers to questions that we wished someone had asked us. For example, we asked the daughters how they thought father loss affected their lives relationally, sexually, and professionally. We wanted to highlight the positive attributes developed from being fatherless and not just focus on the negative. We formulated a survey that would show a daughter's perception of her own experiences and further explore the heart of where she came from, what she has been through, and where she wants to go in her life. Personally, we had a vested interest in exploring the experiences of fatherless daughters in specific areas of their lives: with their mothers, fathers' families, siblings, significant others, colleagues, and friends. We wanted to find out what coping mechanisms were used and were effective in helping them live a more vibrant life. Our minds were blown by the results of our research, as we discovered how fatherlessness plays out in a woman's life. These results are shared throughout the book. If you would like to, go to FatherlessDaughterProject.com and take the survey as a step toward your own self-awareness.

Fatherless daughters had a lot of similarities in some areas of their lives; however, major differences surfaced, depending on the way a daughter lost her father. From death to emotional absence, we cover the primary reasons for father loss.

Our research showed that most women who grew up fatherless, no matter how they got there, seemed to have challenges in some of the same places—usually in their relationships. They might get stuck between not knowing how to give love and not knowing how to receive love. They often see the opposite sex as a mystery because they may not have had enough time with their own fathers to develop a much-needed foundation for intimate relationships. Because the bond with their dad was cut short, they may not have learned what it truly feels like to love, and be loved, by a man. For many of us, our boundaries were not set, our comfort levels did not settle in, and our understanding about real love failed to fully develop. For many fatherless daughters, relationship standards may have been pieced together by things we witnessed growing up, both good and bad.

Daughters learn by watching, especially if they are not given clear instructions by those who are supposed to teach them. For example, Tina described how she learned to envision the perfect father. "To be honest, as a girl I learned the most about father–daughter relationships by watching the show *Full House* and seeing how those girls were loved and guided by their father and other men who stepped in to help. In many ways, they fathered me through the television in my living room."

Think about your relationship history. Have you veered off track multiple times, leaving you confused about why heartache keeps happening to you? Do you wonder why you keep falling down in the same places? Are you frustrated with how much you struggle in intimate relationships? Although you seem to know deep down what you truly want, what keeps getting in the way of your receiving it? Have you started seeing a pattern in your choice of partners? Through our extensive research on fatherless daughters, including our own clinical work, surveys, interviews, and exhaustive review of other studies, we have discovered patterns of behavior we think would be healing for other fatherless daughters to see and understand. We have worked with countless women who are confused over the recurring issues in their lives, which sit alongside unresolved pain from losing their fathers too soon. The source of your relationship struggles could be related to unmet needs in your life due to the absence of your father.

If you are married, do you punish your husband when he does not get it right? Do you expect him to father you or do find yourself mothering him? Perhaps you try to control the situation by expecting him to jump through hoops to reinforce his dedication to you. Do you crave equality in your marriage but feel lost on how to create that?

Have you become a mother and seen yourself repeating some of the same coping patterns that your mom used when you were younger? Maybe you expect your daughter to be tougher than her friends or expect your son to be your main source of male attention. Do you live with an overwhelming fear that something might happen to one of your children, your husband, or you? As a fatherless daughter, you might have learned how to be a phenomenal caretaker, but too often you walk around with an overwhelming anxiety that something is about to go wrong.

If you are single, do you get spooked by the slightest sign of rejection and become overly emotional because of it? When you sense conflict, do you tend to push people away before they can do the same to you? If so, you might be reacting because of fatherless anxiety in order to avoid getting hurt. Walking away may seem like a better alternative than being left behind.

In friendships, fatherless daughters often become the caretaker (or mother) among their friends, and everyone comes to them with his or her issues. Depending on what happened in your home, you are likely accustomed to handling conflict, listening to the issues, and providing support. Helping others gives you a sense of purpose and value. You have a resiliency because of your survival, whether you realize it or not, and it is one of your strongest traits. You may need to ask yourself, Are you giving too much? Are you getting the support you need in return?

Because your mother is also deeply affected by your father's absence, fatherless daughters can have challenging relationships with their moms. Are you still carrying around conflicting feelings like sympathy, anger, or mommy guilt? Do you have a deep-rooted need to take care of your mom? Most fatherless daughters can relate. Although you may have many questions for your mom, the last thing you want to do is stir up the emotions of the past, so you may leave any questions you have for her about your father unasked. Because fatherless daughters typically find their way in the world on their own, each has quietly developed a self-made survival handbook in her mind. She has written her own rules according to what she has seen, heard, and experienced and privately flips through the pages to figure out how to maneuver certain situations and manage her emotions. Unfortunately, many of her formulas are defective, keeping her cycling through unfulfilling patterns, leaving her confused and frustrated.

In our study, we discovered that 42 percent of fatherless daughters have mothers who were fatherless, and over a third of them were in turn raising fatherless daughters themselves. We often repeat what we have seen and perpetuate the cycle of fatherlessness because of learned coping mechanisms, relationship choices, and faulty perceptions of ourselves. We can then pass these behaviors and attitudes down to our daughters. We have to get on with our healing to stop these negative generational patterns, not only for ourselves but for those who come after us.

So Many Questions

In May 1994, Hope Edelman published the wildly successful book *Motherless Daughters: The Legacy of Loss*, which spent twenty-four weeks on the *New York Times* best-seller list. Paige, one of the fatherless women we interviewed, said she carried Edelman's book around like the Bible after the loss of her father. When we asked why she was reading a book about being *motherless* when she was indeed *fatherless*, she said, "There was no book that spoke about father loss due to his choice. I am embarrassed about it, and it seems like mother loss is more of an accepted form of grief to be reading about."

By "loss due to his choice," Paige is referring to loss due to addiction rather than death. Her dad was an alcoholic, and he has come in and out of her life unpredictably. In her late teens, after much angst, she cut off all contact with him and told him he could come back when, and if, he was sober. She is now thirty-eight, and she has no idea if he is dead or alive.

Sharing with us the stigma she feels for being fatherless, Paige continues to explain her mixed emotions. "I don't know what to say. People look at me perplexed when I say that I don't know where he is or what he does for a living anymore. It is complicated. Sometimes I think if he would have died, it would have been easier." Paige's story echoes the experiences of many other fatherless daughters.

Father loss can be the result of many different situations. It can happen by choice, by circumstance, or by catastrophe. It can happen when you are a child, a teen, or an adult. It can happen privately or publicly, as a family tragedy or a national headline. Each of us has her own story. Each of us has her own questions.

If your father left you by choice, you might ask yourself, "What did I really mean to him?" Far too often father loss can be a casualty of separation and divorce. Geography, in-fighting, and lack of communication can all contribute to the father's increased disengagement. What happens if, after the divorce, the mother or father decides to move to another state? Can a father truly be integrated in a child's life hundreds of miles away, four days a month, or occasionally on Skype? Parental alienation happens far too often in this country, creating victims out of everyone involved. Obviously every case is different. While not all daughters of divorce suffer from broken relationships after the dissolution of their parents' marriage, it is a heartbreaking fact that many do.

The loss of a parent is incomprehensible. We are who we are largely because of our parents: their DNA and their influence on our lives. Losing that piece of ourselves can leave us feeling abandoned, alone, and unsure of our place in the world. We miss them because we love them. Whether we miss what we had or we miss what we wish we would have had, we experience life while carrying an immense sense of loss.

Where You Can Gain Even When You Have Lost

On the other side of the coin, there are many amazing traits that fatherless daughters can develop as a result of their loss and survival. We heard about their resilience when we spoke to women as we researched this book. They are not only tough, they are resourceful. Fatherless daughters don't just bounce back; they can thrive. When they are on their A game, they come back and conquer whatever is trying to bring them down. In a crisis, they push to find purpose in pain. They are a fiercely loyal group who treat their best friends like family. Because they have suffered great loss, they tend to be magnificent emotional caregivers. They will sit with you, pray with you, or even move in with you, if that is what it takes.

When they love, they really love. When they make a promise, they keep it. When they set a goal, they will almost always exceed it. They are hard workers who will work tirelessly to not only prove themselves but to out-do themselves. They are experts in self-survival, having used their greatest challenge in life to find their own insurmountable strengths. Lauren, eighteen, said it best: "I didn't have a dad around to help me through the tough times. I had to learn to grow up really fast. I guess that is what being a fatherless daughter really is—it's becoming wise beyond your years."

While father loss has shown to be a significant experience during childhood and adolescence, usually having a major impact on a woman's adulthood, we believe that the pain can be channeled into a positive pathway. By making the decision to do and see things differently, you can transform your life, your children's lives, and the lives of other women. You may not even be aware of how your father loss has played out in your life. Many of the women we spoke to found it confusing that their current issues could be directly linked back to their father loss. Some feel like they have already dealt with it or that they simply do not care enough about their father to relive their pasts. Others know something is wrong, but they have no idea it is linked to their father loss. Because fatherless daughters can be so good at marching on, it takes a keen eye to know the signs. I guess you could say, it takes one to know one. So here it is . . . the pain is still there. We know it and somewhere deep down you do too. It might be affecting you in more ways than you have imagined and not just on Father's Day. The pain can spill over into your relationships, career, and well-being. It can also isolate you, making you think you are better off alone. This book will help you explore, understand, and improve your life. By reading other fatherless daughters' stories, you may find similarities to your own experiences. This is part of your growth process, as it encourages you to look at your own life from a new perspective. Pay attention to your interactions with others as you read this book. Learn from what has worked for others. Issues are bound to become apparent that were once hidden, and you are sure to know yourself better along the journey.

What Is Fatherlessness?

In 2014, we conducted national surveys of almost five thousand women. We created an online questionnaire that looked into the stages and varying dimensions of women's lives, seeking to find out how father loss may or may not have had an effect on their development and decisions. Participants ranged from age fifteen to almost eighty, with the majority being in their twenties, thirties, and forties. Our respondents were from a range of ethnic backgrounds, educational levels, and socioeconomic situations. Participation was fully voluntary and confidential, and the surveys still remain open at SurveyMonkey (surveymonkey.com).

In analyzing our results, we found something that made our hearts skip a beat: Over 50 percent of women reported that they felt they were fatherless. The following are the ways that women reported becoming fatherless, with many citing multiple reasons:

- 28 percent to parents' divorce or separation
- 26 percent to complete emotional absence
- 19 percent to death
- 15 percent to desertion
- 13 percent to addiction

- 12 percent to abuse
- 6 percent never met their father
- 4 percent to incarceration

We describe fatherlessness as the loss of a bond between a daughter and her father from a range or combination of circumstances, including death, desertion, divorce, incarceration, abuse, addiction, and emotional absence. Maybe your father died after a long bout with heart disease or suddenly passed in a tragic accident. Perhaps he just picked up and left one Tuesday night when you were eight years old and never returned. It could be that he is in jail, addicted to drugs, or so checked out from you emotionally that it feels like he is absent even when he is present. Your parents may have divorced and your dad rarely showed up to see you on weekends. If he remarried, he may spend most of his time with his new family. Or you may have lost your father in more than one way at different times in your life.

No matter how you lost your dad, you may feel as if things should have gone differently, and your heart has been broken because you lost him far too soon. If your father left by choice, there might be a voice inside of you that wonders if you are unlovable even if others try to tell you differently. If your father passed away, you may walk around with an internal void, grappling for answers, feeling like you were cheated out of something other girls received. There can be shame, guilt, anger, low self-confidence, and a fear of suffering the same pain of loss in other relationships. You often do what you can to protect the vulnerability inside of you. Even if it means building a wall around you so you won't get hurt again.

Fatherlessness changes the course of your life. There can be a heavy emotional cost, a profound feeling of loss, and a deep-rooted need for survival that is unlike other losses. The repercussions of this loss can show up at different times in life in the form of difficult relationships or confusing emotions; most women are usually unaware of how often these experiences relate directly back to their fatherlessness. To survive, you might have long ago chosen to bury the pain, tucking it inside a secret room in your heart. You may have convinced yourself that you are long over it but something happens, and now you are not so sure. Maybe you can feel the presence of that secret pain more clearly than before, and you are ready to gently move toward it with compassion and courage to better understand how it affected you.

Getting to the other side of grief requires more than just living and breathing through the pain. Surviving trauma reaches past simply learning how to exist and hide from what is overwhelming to look at; it means finding the time and space to touch, hear, and feel the emotions that need their own validating and healing. Otherwise, it is possible to become lodged in a stagnant place. Stuck in old patterns, reenacting the same scenarios, and repeating those dysfunctional old coping skills that no longer work.

Being fatherless may be playing out in your life in a variety of ways, many of which lead to a common need for independence so that a fatherless daughter never gets hurt or let down. The need to stay in control is one of the hallmarks of a fatherless daughter. Take a look at the list of fatherless daughter characteristics below and place a check mark beside any trait that you feel describes you.

— You may be unaware of the unhealthy patterns in your relationships although others have tried to point them out.
— You may hold on to relationships for far too long or cut people off before they can leave you.
— You might engage in a "go away/please stay" relationship dynamic, which can become exhausting and unfulfilling.

— It may take you a lot longer than others to let go of a failed relationship.

— You may be carrying around pain and anger that is years (or decades) old.

— You may have been overly sexual at a point in your life or pulled away from intimacy and avoided sex all together.

— You may have a warrior exterior but on the inside have broken parts that no one can see.

— You may feel like it is you against the world but are determined that you can do it on your own.

— You may try to be totally independent so you can never be let down by others.

— You may have tried to stay in total control in your relationships.

— You may be an overachiever, feeling the need to prove your value over and over again.

— You might battle anxiety and depression related to your feelings of self-worth or your fear of losing people you love.

— You may be intensely (but secretly) fearful that you will be abandoned again.

— You might wonder what it feels like to be in a "normal relationship" and what type of standards you should be setting.

In our research, it became abundantly clear that these are the issues that a fatherless daughter is likely to run into over and over again in her life until she slows down, takes inventory of her own patterns, and decides to change her role in the recurring dynamics. The majority of fatherless women we surveyed reported struggling emotionally, mentally, and relationally as they matured as a result of the fears and maladaptive beliefs they had developed about themselves. In order to change these patterns, a fatherless daughter will have to get ready to feel many of the feelings directly associated with father loss that she may have been postponing.

Fatherless daughters tend to habitually push their own feelings to the side in order to focus on other external issues, like relationship drama, friends in need, or even problematic bosses.

In her work as a therapist, Karin has witnessed tremendous personal growth in therapy sessions that typically began with the female fatherless client feeling trapped and hopeless. Karin facilitates redirecting her client's focus from the external to the internal, guiding her into a place of self-compassion and gentle acceptance for what is and what has been in her life. The fatherless woman can reach toward a place of higher self-awareness and trust in the strength and wisdom of her own spirit. The voice (or the *absence* of the voice) of the father is extremely loud in a girl's life. It can either build up and encourage her or diminish her by communicating that she is not worthy of love or commitment. She usually believes it deeply until she decides that she is more than her loss and that this original belief system is getting in the way of her living her life.

When women are willing to step back from daily stressors and see why their personal pain flares up at specific moments, they can become more keenly aware of themselves and create change. They can become their own emotional captains. For example, Karin's client Meg came to her complaining of a tumultuous relationship that cycled her between feeling completely smothered by her boyfriend to feeling painfully detached from him. Meg immediately became engrossed in the drama and blamed him and herself for all that was wrong with them. But to heal, it became necessary for her to step away from the drama and try to decipher what was good or bad and instead look at why things were the way they were. What happened to teach them to treat each other this way?

Meg was raised in a home filled with conflict, shameful secrets, and a lack of steady love. Watching her own mother push and pull at her father as he binged, dried out, and binged again, coming and going for sometimes months at a time, Meg survived by being hypervigilant to vulnerability and intimacy. Her childhood experiences created her "normal": living in a constant state of fear, insecurity, and unworthiness. She learned over the years something she assumed to be fact: love was chaotic, difficult, and intermittent. She wanted it more than anything, but she believed she would have to earn it daily.

In therapy, Meg discovered newfound courage and was able to talk about her deepest desires for love and affection. However, because of her fear of intimacy, she kept herself at a seemingly safe, but painful, distance from true closeness with her boyfriend, accusing him of being "too clingy" or "smothering" if he got too close. The double-edged sword was that she constantly resented him for not chasing her affection, figuring out what she needed, and saving her from the world. The day the lightbulb went off, Meg realized what she never saw before. "I never knew how much of this I was actually creating myself because of what happened with my mom and dad."

A beautiful thing happened in Meg's story. Her boyfriend responded positively to her changes and agreed to join her in couples counseling. In the second session, he began to cry himself, relieved to finally feel safe enough to talk about the craziness between them as well as his own loss. She had never known how abandoned he felt by his father. Realizing that they were drawn to each other because they actually understood each other on deeper levels, they saw their relationship very differently. Meg found a great compassion for him, as he did for her, and while they are still a work in progress, they became exponentially closer once they were able to own and express their own emotions and needs with each other. They had to agree to work on their issues independently, without expecting to heal, correct, or erase the fatherless pain for the other.

Over time, fatherless daughters can learn how to transform their usual cycle of unhealthy behavior and teach themselves how to stop reacting to sensitive triggers and, instead, witness their own emotional experience, without judgment or negative responses. This practice can bring immense healing to people, giving them greater peace, healthier functioning, and overall improved happiness and meaning. You have to be prepared to look within yourself and not at everyone else's problems around you. Recognizing and owning your pain will allow you to grow. Learning new ways of coping can be frustrating and painstakingly hard. Many of the fatherless daughters we spoke to said that when they made monumental life changes like leaving home, changing jobs, or ending a relationship, they finally found the opportunity to look within and deal with their past. The breakthrough they needed showed up, and instead of looking for the next thing, they sat still and started their heart work.

Many things can keep us from trusting our readiness to face these issues. We may not have been emotionally capable as children to face the situation placed in front of us and might remain unsure of when we truly can. Friends and family can hold us back from dealing with the pain of sifting through the truth of what happened in our life. We might hear internal messages telling us that we are not strong enough to cope with the challenge, so we stick to what we know even if our gut is telling us to jump forward and deal. Addictive substances and behaviors can keep us medicated in order for us not to really feel what is tucked away inside of us. But at some point, we will be given an open door, whether it is in the gentle words of a best friend, an oh-my-God-this-is-about-me quote in a book, or a surprising revelation while jogging. Growth comes knocking. When our old coping skills no longer work, something else is changing in our lives. It is then that we can decide to stop stumbling over the same speed bumps, take charge of our direction, and choose a new path.

Where Do You Fit In?

Fatherlessness does not discriminate. While it affects all races, religions, and socioeconomic backgrounds, certain populations are clearly more at risk than others for fatherlessness. Research has shown the following U.S. statistics of fatherless homes:

- 67 percent of African American families
- 54 percent of American Indian families
- 43 percent of multiracial families
- 42 percent of Latino or Hispanic families
- 25 percent of white families

According to the Population Reference Bureau, a 2012 analysis of data from the U.S. Census Bureau found that 80 percent of single-parent families are father-absent households. Mothers are much more likely to be left behind to carry the household alone, and the consequences can be quite serious. In our research, we found that over one-third of fatherless daughters' households fell to the poverty level when their fathers were gone. Only 18 percent of our respondents reported being financially stable after their father loss, and 25 percent remembered their mothers working multiple jobs to make ends meet.

It might be time to start your own conversation. Whether your father is around to hear it or not, you can find a place of clarity and courage deep inside of you to start talking things out, and despite the fears, you can begin your journey of healing.

Different Losses, Different Reactions

There is a difference in how we process the various types of loss. Daughters who lose their fathers due to divorce or abandonment statistically have the most anger toward their fathers. Anger is understandable and often necessary, but if prolonged, it can hold us back from the life we were meant to lead and, in the case of fatherless daughters, mask the real emotions behind their abandonment.

Anger usually arises when denial and isolation wane and the reality of what one has lost or suffered is realized. We want to direct blame somewhere, and so we do. Maybe you are angry that he left and you resent him for it. Or you are angry that underneath it all you are still a little girl who misses her dad. Perhaps you direct your blame on someone else in the family. At some point, you need to take a good look at your anger, especially why and when it comes up.

Heather, forty-one, admits that her anger toward her boyfriend often gets out of hand. "I get so mad when he isn't totally dependable. He has a habit of telling me he will be home at a certain time but then he comes in hours later than he promised. I get so angry, and we end up having these huge shouting matches because he doesn't think it's a big deal. It *is* a big deal. I can't trust him. My dad did that to me growing up. He would promise that he was going to come get me for the weekend and never show up. Things got very heated during a recent argument between my boyfriend and me. He wasn't listening to me and was acting as if I were being irrational. I couldn't take it anymore. I jumped out of his car and slammed the door, trapping my purse on the inside. I yanked on the handle and was screaming at him in this parking lot how much I hated him. I totally lost it. He put the car in reverse, breaking my purse strap. He slammed on the brakes, and before I knew it, I was kicking the passenger's side door so hard that I dented it. I am so embarrassed that I acted like that, but sometimes I can't control myself."

As we listen to stories like Heather's, we want to help women modify their reactions and start to do things in a new way. Reacting can get in the way of your restoring yourself. In such a situation, Heather could have taken a deep breath, explained her pain without yelling, and talked about the real root of it. She can still hold her partner accountable, but she can also help him realize it isn't all about him. Her opening up and being vulnerable offers a chance for them to become closer. A way to have conflict resolution here is to set some ground rules that both partners will be comfortable with. Considering a check-in time when they are apart could set healthier expectations to lessen future conflict in the area of accountability and trust. By decreasing disputes, they will avoid a dented door and ongoing damage to the relationship.

While anger is one of the hallmark emotions of daughters who have dads who left by choice, we see a different story for girls whose fathers passed away. Girls who lose their fathers to death tend to have the most positive concept of their fathers, while also feeling the strongest sadness about their being gone. While these daughters can have bouts of rage, their rage is usually directed at "what could have been." It is rooted in sadness for what they are never going to experience or share with their fathers. They may also feel that the world owes them something in return for taking their dad.

Many daughters whose fathers have died have a hard time reconciling the truth about who their dads really were. It can be seen as cruel or morbid to speak unkindly about the deceased, so a woman who lost her father to death often idealizes him. She may not want to hear about his faults, mistakes, or negative qualities. Imagining that he was perfect validates the enormity of her loss. Of course, each of us is flawed, and as long as daughters are unable to hear or accept who their fathers were (warts and all), they remain stuck in an unrealistic place of loss. Idealizing can become a subconscious stalling tactic that stops them from feeling the real pain of their loss because sometimes the truth brings on emotions that force them to see their fathers in a new way.

For a time, even for years, it is completely normal (and sweet) for a girl to think of her dad as being perfect while recovering from his passing. However, as a daughter moves into adulthood and learns that she can tolerate the world's imperfections, a time should come when exploring the story of her dad's life can be healing. Sitting down and looking at the truth as a grown woman—perhaps when she is a wife and a mother—can actually bring her closer to her dad, as she realizes that he likely struggled with some of the same things that she might be challenged by.

Other costs of fatherlessness relate directly to the cause and the age of the loss and where those two intersect. For example, a girl whose father was incarcerated may be carrying an insurmountable burden of shame and resentment about him in addition to dealing with the truth privately and publicly. If addiction or abuse has caused a daughter to lose her bond with her father, she may experience the confusion of humiliation mixed with guilt because of her father's unpredictable behavior.

Emotionally absent fathers can leave lifelong wounds on girls' hearts, such as the fear of being unlovable and unworthy of a man's attention. For the fatherless daughter who has suffered trauma, deep roots of pain can take hold in her life along with the formation of negative psychological issues, including anxiety, depression, and substance abuse. The scars can be long lasting and impair her development if she doesn't have the right support. Research shows that the amount of time spent with or without the father's attention has a tremendous impact on daughters. In fact, 95 percent of the fatherless daughters we surveyed reported that they were emotionally affected by their fathers' absence. Fathers matter.

From Girls to Women

Father loss can come at any age, and the pain is always traumatic. But keep in mind that children mourn differently from adolescents, and adolescents mourn differently from young women.

The loss of a father can mean the loss of a playmate, protector, coach, toughen-upper, and first love. That is too much loss for any girl to wrap her mind around completely. Gone are the lessons a daughter is supposed to learn from her daddy: feeling worthy of love because she is unique, gaining confidence to succeed in a competitive world, and finding a secure understanding of how male–female relationships work.

She can be left to face the world with a load too big for her pockets to carry. So she finds a way to stuff it all somewhere, somehow, and although the burden is heavy, she carries on. Nevertheless, over time the stuff finds its way out and begins to work itself slowly into her life— her self-confidence, her coping skills, her relationships, and eventually (if she chooses these paths) her marriage and mothering.

As she ages, she will begin to see patterns and cracks in her heavy armor. Maybe she continues having the same issues in her relationships or the echoing fear of abandonment lingers, continuously putting her in the front car of an emotional roller coaster. Perhaps she has recurring dreams, taking her back to places and faces that have kept her stuck. If she is holding her emotions in, unable to speak her truth, she may find herself unable to communicate in her dreams—she tries to scream but nothing will come out. If she is still angry, she may try to fight for herself in her dreams, because there she is safe to feel and act on her deep emotions. Perhaps her dad comes back to her in her dreams, and when she awakens, the feelings of loss flood her all over again.

As a mother, a fatherless daughter might see her issues showing up in unpredictable places. She may snap at her children over minuscule things and within minutes wonder why her reactive anger can be so intense. She may pull away from her husband, subconsciously hoping he will rescue her. Her family will be the place where she can feel new hope for security, but it can also be the place where her emotions can be the most vulnerable, making her act out suppressed experiences and emotions from her youth all over again.

The Truth About Not Having a Dad

Warning: We are going to tell the truth. We are going to dig into places that may be uncomfortable, and we ask that you do the same. By delving into our own stories and those of the women we have interviewed, we have discovered a richness of emotion, experience, and resilience. Our research revealed some prevalent truths among fatherless daughters. Of course, these truths may not apply to everybody, but we found many commonalities that were too important to ignore.

One truth we found about father loss is that the emotional fallout usually goes underground for a number of years. When a daughter loses her father, she is thrown off-balance, but in all of the unsteadiness, she is expected to remain strong. The negative emotions and their costs often do not start to come into clear focus until a girl becomes a woman and hits a huge bump in the road, stopping her dead in her tracks. The bump is usually triggered by a loss or abandonment that resembles the pain she experienced in losing her father. It is then that she realizes the coping skills she acquired from whoever raised her may no longer work now that she is an adult. She comes to a crossroads where she recognizes that after years of taking care of everyone else, she has been left with little time or knowledge of how to take care of *herself.* This is where the real life-changing work begins. It is time to acknowledge that she did her best as a young girl, and it served her well because she survived and helped others survive. Now it is *her* time to work on herself and develop the new tools that will help her become who she was meant to be.

The second truth about fatherless daughters is that we typically harbor a deep-rooted fear of being abandoned . . . again. The trauma of being deserted tends to echo inside of us as an ever-present reminder that we were left behind. We guard our hearts, hypervigilant to signs of being left and reexperiencing the pain of abandonment. Our reactions can appear overly dramatic and, dare we say, crazy to those who are not familiar with our emotions. Often when we're faced with the threat of being deserted again, we become lost and directionless. For the grown fatherless daughter, the fear of abandonment often overrides her mature senses and sensibilities. Even the strongest among us can become subconsciously guided by anxiety, determined to protect herself physically, financially, and emotionally.

Coco, twenty-eight, confessed to lying to her boyfriend out of panic that he was leaving her for the weekend. "I literally lost control because I started to sense that he was pulling away. He was leaving for a guys' trip to Vegas that weekend, and I was sure he would realize that we were better off apart. So, that Thursday, I called him up in hysterics and told him that a strange man had just tried to carjack me. I was crying and yelling into the phone like it really happened! I am so ashamed, but I completely panicked. I wanted him to choose me. While I got him to stick around for that weekend to console me out of guilt, we ended up breaking up a few months later. I was devastated. I can't even believe some of the things that I pulled to try to keep him."

We are unaware of the trickle-down dynamics that play out in our relationships and so many other areas of our lives. One emotion leads to the next reaction, leading to the next emotion, and we aren't even aware of the dysfunction that we are bringing into our lives. The truth is we are scared of being left. But being scared without an awareness of the source of our fear can lead to irrational patterns in relationships. Our lives can be led by extremes. Like Coco, we tend to take off impulsively or hold on too tightly to significant others, not fully understanding our feelings and being incapable of seeing the big picture of the relationship. We get blinded by our fears and have difficulty realizing when to stay and work things out, or when to leave and work on ourselves.

The third truth for fatherless daughters might seem quite obvious, but it is something that a lot of us do not get to voice often enough. Most of us miss our fathers—or who we wanted our fathers to be. We miss being a daughter to our daddy. We miss his hugs, the sound of his voice, and the feeling of safety when we knew he was just around the corner. If we never knew him well, we miss who we imagine he would be. We become used to that pit in our stomachs we feel each time we hear about a friend going to her dad for advice.

If you were abandoned, you might wonder, "How can I miss someone who doesn't seem to miss *me*?" If your father was flawed in his lifestyle or his parenting, it may seem unacceptable to others that you miss your father. If your father passed away, people may put a time frame on grief and express eagerness for you to move on. But there is no time limit on how long losing someone you love affects your life, because it will *always* affect your life. Those who do not fully understand the longing you have for your father may have mistakenly told you to get over it or to try to let it go.

People are not generally comfortable with another person's grief. There is a tendency to want to lessen it, fix it, or push the person past it, because sitting *in* it can be highly uncomfortable. But they have not been where you have been. While their suggestions are well-intentioned and often rooted in not wanting you to hurt anymore, they are not realistic. Having emotions invalidated or being scolded for feeling a certain way only makes a person want to retreat inward or fight outward. It's OK to miss him whether he was Father of the Year or a Disaster of a Daddy.

A fourth truth about fatherless daughters is that many are compelled to grow up too quickly. We miss out on a lot of things that girls who are allowed to mature at a typical rate experience, and there are consequences. It is painful for a young girl to have to tend to family matters while her friends are engaging in activities and building memories with each other and their fathers. While this is yet another loss for fatherless daughters, we have found that maturing ahead of our time can also have a positive outcome: It puts us ahead of the game as we age. We become resilient much earlier than peers who have not experienced loss and, despite its cost, that is a powerful advantage for life's future challenges because we learn how to be strong and resourceful on our own.

Living without Your Father

There are things you cannot change. Whether your dad died, was sent away, or left on his own accord, he is gone. He will not be there for all of those big and small moments in your life. Depending on when you lost him, you may carry his encouragement and support with you, but there is no substitute for his presence in your life. Being different from most of your friends can feel isolating and frustrating. For whatever reason, you did not get the father–daughter relationship that you should have. You are and will be deprived of experiences that those around you collect with each passing season, often without realizing how blessed they are to receive them. You may have what we call "wonder conversations" with yourself when you are at the ballpark, hardware store, or your in-laws' for the weekend: I wonder what it would be like if he were here. What would he say if he saw me now? What kind of grandfather would he be? You continue to march through the moments, but life's milestones can be the places that stop you still with emotion.

Fatherlessness brings with it so many questions, some that do not have answers and some you'd rather not have to ask in the first place.

Who will walk me down the aisle? Who will tell me when my college boyfriend is a jerk and just not good enough for me? How will I spend Father's Day when everyone else is at their family barbeque? On how many birthdays will I cry because the phone doesn't ring with him calling to say "I love you"? Who will show up in the rain when I get a flat tire? How will my husband feel about not having a real father-in-law? Who will go to my child's school for Grandparents' Day?

Your mom, grandfather, or older brother might do their best to fill in the gaps in your life. There can be surrogate fathers (if you are lucky), other male role models, or even a wonderful husband who might try to father you in some way, but they will never be *your dad*.

Sometimes it's important to mourn what is no longer or maybe what never was. When you yearn to be taken care of, you can try to take care of yourself. But, without the right coping mechanisms, you may be at risk of falling apart. Lacking a strong support network might mean you pull away from loved ones or stay in bed for days. Without the help of a counselor, pastor, or mentor, you might not know how to take care of your mental and spiritual self and run the risk of slipping into depression. If you catch yourself isolating from others for more than a couple of weeks, or experience an ongoing drastic change in your sleep or eating habits you may be suffering from depression. If a month goes by, and you don't find yourself seeing a window of hope, it is time to reach out for support. You can also help yourself by creating ways to be productive in your life, returning to those things that bring you joy and investing in your own self-care. (We discuss depression in depth in the next chapter.)

You may consciously, or subconsciously, look for a father figure in your mate and choose someone who is incapable of being who you need him to be. Or you might avoid attachments and choose to forgo companionship all together, maybe becoming a workaholic who gets ahead in every area except her own emotional growth. Behind a lot of your adult decisions is an emotion of pure and simple missing. You miss your dad, and that has a profound effect on you.

The Emotional Cost

Is it any surprise that, after suppressing our stories, our health, especially our mental health, can become greatly compromised? Women are already at a much higher risk than men to suffer from anxiety, depression, and eating disorders. All of these disorders can be precipitated by significant loss, prolonged grief, and lack of sufficient development of self-worth. When we do not experience having a father in our lives, we can react on psychological, spiritual, and physical levels. Eating issues, drugs, alcohol, and other addictive habits may have become a distraction or a problem if you are not being accountable to yourself or those you love.

Our survey revealed that 90 percent of women felt they were affected emotionally by losing their dads. In addition, 65 percent of women suffered mentally, 35 percent felt their spiritual selves were compromised, and over 30 percent of women felt that they were impacted physically. As you continue to read, it is important to keep in mind that you may not be aware of the comprehensive impact that fatherlessness has had on the many dimensions of your life. Pay close attention to how any topic hits you in your gut. If you feel like rereading a specific paragraph, or a story resonates with you, that is your history speaking, and your spirit is feeling a connection. Allow yourself to stop along the way and process your emotions. This is your time to honor, feel, and release those things that have been hidden from view. Because of the sensitivity of their loss, fatherless daughters might seek to not feel their abandonment, attempting to mask their symptoms by focusing on external details or choosing to ignore the feelings of abandonment and fear as they bubble up. They often do not feel worthy enough to seek change.

As with most survivors of trauma, the body, soul, and mind of a fatherless woman go through a period of self-preservation. The emotions can be too intense, and so in order not to feel, the daughter might engage in addictive behaviors, choosing whatever feels good or numbing in that moment, to avoid feeling the pain. Fatherless daughters are at risk of engaging in these behaviors because they are often required to deal with mature issues at a young age; the family is immersed with tending to its own survival and can't impart skills to the daughter. Without the proper support and modeling about how to make her own wellness a priority, a fatherless daughter may develop a lower self-esteem than fathered daughters, and her coping mechanisms will most likely be formed around what she witnessed at home.

In addition to the psychological confusion she faces at a young age, a fatherless daughter might suffer life-altering losses in her family due to financial problems and a host of changes within the extended family and community. Who steps in and who steps out? If the father is alive but not present, there can also be a lack of accountability and involvement by the father, leaving the daughter in need of additional support in her life.

According to Carol Gilligan's landmark research out of Harvard University, girls establish their identities in the world by the way they see themselves in their relationships. When the connection with her father is taken away, a girl's psychosocial development can be affected in a variety of ways, including challenges formulating her new identity. She may experience sadness, anxiety, and extreme self-doubt. Fatherless daughters are left to face myriad challenges as they try to navigate the world with all of the emotional consequences of losing part of their identity.

Fatherless daughters tend not to know when to trust (others *and* ourselves) and are overly wary of others' promises. In adulthood, their lack of understanding of male–female relationships can become a handicap at home, at school, in the community, and in the workplace. When they find themselves considering a commitment with someone, they might feel a great deal of anxiety about how much of themselves to give away. They struggle because commitment means they are vulnerable to loss, yet they yearn to feel loved, protected, and valued. Relationships are a catch-22. Fatherless daughters can feel like victims because their fathers left too soon or for unfair reasons. This can lead to living in a victim frame of mind, with the propensity to live out that role, primarily in relationships. They try to convince themselves and others that they are suffering by no fault of their own, and thus remain snugly wrapped up in their role as victim. They believe it and continue to draw themselves toward it. It is familiar, and while painful and lonely, they feel safer than if they fully let go, because that requires risk.

They can also self-sabotage. If they choose not to let anyone into their lives intimately—and no one can meet their list of qualifications—they are deprived of being part of a couple, miss out on love, and reject the support of a partner.

On the other hand, if they give too much of themselves in a relationship and don't receive all that they need, they usually start blaming again. By attributing the failure of the relationship to someone else's shortcomings, they play the victim. Without fathers, they might not have fully learned how to be loved, and many of them subconsciously want to punish the men in their lives out of unresolved anger. So they might expect the unachievable in a mate and set them up for failure from the beginning. If their partner fails to be everything—partner, protector, father, and counselor—these women can lash out again and again, re-creating the victim role and dooming their relationships to fail. By becoming aware of your role in this cycle, you can begin to understand your issues, work on where your emotions are coming from, and start attracting something different into your life.

Working It Out in the Workplace

A fatherless daughter's struggles and patterns can also infiltrate her professional relationships. Some may choose a career path based on the amount of time they will spend working alongside or taking direction from men. Some women report subconsciously choosing female-dominated careers to avoid being peers with the opposite sex. Others have realized that they chose careers that were highly competitive so they could show the world that they were worthwhile, despite their fathers making them feel the opposite. Some women look for father figures in the workplace who can provide the validation they crave.

Fatherless daughters can be challenging to work with because their need to be in control can be detrimental. They might have trouble taking direction because they have directed themselves for so long. To superiors and co-workers, they can come across as uncoachable or know-it-alls. But people cannot see their deep-rooted insecurity and need to feel valued for their achievements. They typically desperately seek approval and praise and have a hard time if they don't get it right the first time. Rejection at work can trigger the pain of old emotions and cause them to take things more personally than they should. They can have difficulty enjoying work, love, and play because of the unresolved issues of the past. On the flip side they are natural-born leaders, effective problem solvers, and are loyal to a fault. Once a fatherless daughter understands how to channel her learned abilities, the sky is the limit. Her appetite to excel and win only grows stronger when she finds someone who believes in her.

Our Hope and Our Sisterhood

The journey to heal from the loss of a father is not simple, and the stages of grief can be unpredictable. Grief is actually a cyclical process, not a linear one. Emotions need to be addressed and revisited, because how you relate to your father's loss will change as you grow. We strongly encourage you to draw on your internal resources to handle this journey, and we are confident that you will be rewarded by building up resilience, wisdom, and compassion for yourself as well as for others who come into your life along the way. The future can surprise you.

The possibility for healing and recovery is real, wonderful, and life-changing. When the time is right, facing the truth will be exactly what fatherless daughters need. We have to be willing to do the work of humanizing not only who our fathers were but also who our fathers were *to us* in order to put the loss into perspective. And we need to accept our own frailties and strengths as lessons and gifts that can help us become more fully and boldly alive.

CHAPTER 2

Death, Divorce, Desertion, and Other Ways Fathers Leave

The father's job is to teach his children how to be warriors,
to give them the confidence to get on the horse to ride
into battle when it's necessary to do so. If you don't get that
from your father, you have to teach yourself.

~Cheryl Strayed, *Wild: From Lost to Found on the Pacific Crest Trail*

For a son, his father is his first hero; for a daughter, her father is also her first love. Unfortunately your father may have also been your first heartbreak. Becoming fatherless comes in various forms, so each woman's story has unique time lines and circumstances. You may have even lost your dad in more than one way.

According to the U.S. Census Bureau, one out of every three children lives in a home without his or her biological father, and the statistics are getting attention. New research has shown the wide-ranging impact that the loss of a father has on young girls' lives and underscores the fact that resources and support need to be available to them. Children and adolescents who have suffered loss often isolate or feel lost, and because of their experience, the trajectory of their lives can change dramatically through adulthood—especially when compared to daughters who have strong relationships with their fathers. From the many in-depth interviews we have conducted, we noticed a strong chain of consequences play out in women's lives linked to the circumstances under which their father left the home. Each story is different and has its own fallout. Your story affects how you relate to men, your dad, and yourself.

Your Dad and Mom Divorced

One in two marriages will end in divorce, according to the most recent statistics. In our own study, divorce was the most common cause of father loss.

Statistics also tell us that daughters of divorce usually suffer more psychologically than daughters who lose their fathers due to death. Surprising as that may seem, it seems the feelings of abandonment in the case of divorce are far more overreaching and can linger well into adulthood. Tendencies for daughters of divorce, as compared to those whose fathers died, include:

- They seek more attention from boys their age.
- They are the most critical of their fathers.
- They have more defiant behavior toward authority.
- They constantly seek attention from adults, especially men.
- They are more physically aggressive to both their male and female peers.

We know being a child of divorce stings (the sting lasts into adulthood). It is not a child's fault that her parents' marriage did not work out and that she is left with the baggage to sort through. Unfortunately, many parents who go through a divorce tend to get wrapped up in a blame game over their own relationship and forget to acknowledge what their child is experiencing. Although the parent in the home may be relieved to be divorcing, the child will inevitably be filled with anxiety and confusion over her own sense of security. She may wonder, If my father could leave that easily, will my mom be next?

Divorce is painful for everyone involved, and unfortunately, in many instances, the child is used as leverage to continue to hurt the other parent. Frequently the father is pushed out of a daughter's life due to the unfinished business between her parents.

As research has begun to uncover, the divorce causes emotional stress in a child's life, by introducing instability, creating a high-conflict atmosphere, and distressing the child, especially if she is forced to choose sides. Over time, the daughter can build up a great deal of resentment because of what she has been through, especially when she realizes that she should never have been placed in the middle of two adults when she was young.

Resenting your father can come in many different forms. Maybe your dad left for another woman, another man, or another life, and you were left behind. You may do what most kids do; in that big empty confusing space, you may create your own explanation for what happened. You may feel as if you had something to do with it, as if you had done something wrong. You may even believe you were not worthy of love or deserving of your dad's hanging in there—because he didn't.

The message he is sending you with his actions is that this other person or thing in his life is much more important than *you*. They win; you lose. You hear that message echo deep down and start to believe it in your soul. If you are faced with the uncomfortable truth of your father remarrying or even dating, it brings on a whole new set of emotions. Do you befriend his new girlfriend? Would that be disrespectful to your mother? Will it last? If they break up, will he come back to your family or choose someone else . . . again? The statistics are not pretty. One out of ten children of divorce experiences three or more additional parental marriage breakups in their family. Abandonment tends to repeat itself in broken families. Eventually, it threatens to play a part in your own relationships. Girls of divorce are bound and determined not to repeat the same mistakes as their parents. They will do just about anything not to reexperience the pain of abandonment.

What if you found out your father left your family for another man or is gay? This experience can initially feel isolating or confusing because who your dad was and is has shifted. You have to give yourself time to assimilate that into your reality. Perhaps you have had suspicions about his sexual orientation and are relieved that the truth is finally out. Or maybe you had no idea and are shocked. Either way, the root cause of your emotions is your underlying relationship with your dad and how his choices affect you. Yes, he should be allowed to live the life that is most authentic to him, but you should not be left behind in the process. When you feel ready, ask for answers. Express how you are feeling to him or to someone who cares about you and ask for help sorting this out. Be patient with yourself and allow your own acceptance to have its own process.

Ask your father for time alone together and see where you can find common ground and understanding. In studies on children with parents who come out as gay, children did better when they felt trusted to handle the truth from an early stage. The breakup of your parents' marriage is likely to be more painful for you than your father's new identity, and your age at the time your father comes out is a significant factor. According to experts, a young daughter will tend to be matter-of-fact about the situation; accepting things, yet expressing the need for both parents to still help care for her. A school-age daughter is likely to experience some fear about what this might mean to her stability and friendships. She is apt to worry about being teased at school and will need support from counselors and teachers as she finds her way through this new reality. Teenage girls have an especially difficult time accepting news about their father's sexual identity. Their emotional experience could go from being hyperexpressive and wanting to know more about the situation to being withdrawn, angry, or isolating. Her reaction to the change in the family dynamics will largely depend on the stability of the family unit before the transition as well as on her own self-confidence. Daughters tend to report that the experience of father loss far outweighs the pain of confusion of finding out their fathers were gay, although the consequences of feeling misled about their fathers in childhood can be quite difficult to maneuver.

Author Jill Di Donato talks in a 2014 *HuffPost Live* interview about her struggles with finding out at age twenty-two that her father is gay. "Finding out at that point left me a little bit angry at my parents for sort of hiding this and deceiving me. As a result, I sort of felt like I was continually—in my relationships with men—always trying to figure them out." She remembers picking up on clues about her father when she was young. "I do think that children . . . pick up on things, and we pick up on things being hidden. My dad was really living a double life, and I picked up on it, and I just didn't have a name for it." Di Donato notes that there were very difficult times after her father came out, but she gives hope to daughters by saying that she was able to ultimately have a "fresh start" with her father and get to know him in a more authentic way than ever before.

If you are a daughter who has found out that your father is gay, do not be surprised if you have questioned your own identity or that of others. If the truth was hidden from you, you could have residual challenges with trust. Pay attention to any ways that your belief system has been affected and know that there are others out there who can relate to you. Children of Lesbians and Gays Everywhere (COLAGE), is a great place to turn for a support network (colage.org).

If you were abandoned after the divorce and did not maintain a relationship with your father, you may constantly wonder where he is, and if you are going to run into him somewhere, somehow. You wonder if the next call is going to be from him. You're not sure what you are going to say if that happens. Confusion can keep your mind churning if you allow it. You constantly shift between two emotions. You miss him dearly, and you are mad as hell that he left.

Rebecca is twenty-eight, but she was eleven when her father left her mother for another woman. "My dad is the flashy type. He drives a Mercedes and wears a Rolex. Soon after my parents' divorce, we went from a manicured estate to a two-bedroom apartment. Our family was the only family who had furniture picked out by a designer sitting in a dinky apartment. My brother and I lived between two different lifestyles. When we were with my father, we ate at nice restaurants; when we were at home, it was Hamburger Helper. I relished the good food, but honestly, I needed new clothes more than a medium-rare steak. I remember asking my best friend, before my father came to pick us up, if I should wear my new dress that I got for Christmas, or my old jeans, so he would know just how much we need money. Looking back on that moment breaks my heart. How could he have been so selfish?"

Although the pain and missteps of your father were inflicted on your young life, they *do not have to define your adult life.* And they do not have to define you. Yes, your father's departure is a part of your life's story and, in some ways, makes you the resilient woman that you are. However, it is up to you to start seeing his decision as only one aspect of your life. You are an adult now and in charge of your own well-being. You don't have to be bulletproof or sniffle-proof, but you have to learn to be victim-proof.

Your Dad Passed Away

Marie Lyn Bernard, aka Reise, editor in chief of *Autostraddle*, wrote one of the most poignant articles we have ever read on losing a father. In "Before You Know It Something's Over," she talks about how losing her father at the age of fourteen was the worst thing that ever happened to her. She also says that it is something she will have to tell people forever. She declares, "I am what I have lost." The article speaks to exactly how many of us feel about losing our father—it is part of us. She goes on to say, "I want to talk to you about how it feels to spend your whole life grieving, to have your ghosts precede your actuality, to feel that nobody you know will ever truly know you because they never knew him." Reise compares the stories she shares with people about her father to a song that never gets old. She, like many daughters who lost their fathers too early, has felt frustration that there will never be a new album to talk about. She worries, as you may have, that people don't want to hear the same stories over and over. Yet, in stories our loved ones can come alive. It is a gift we can open and listen to over and over again.

Daughters who lost their fathers to death rarely tire of learning or knowing more about their fathers. They feel like they will never really get to know an important part of themselves and their history. There is no way to go back and speak to your father once he is gone. You can't ask him about how he fell in love with your mother or what his best child-hood memory was. You are left with whatever information you had before his death, so you recycle the stories and memories in your head and retell them to your friends.

Daughters who lose their fathers to death tend to feel cheated, for they will never have that chance to be fathered again by their real father. If he was not a great father while he was alive, he will never have the opportunity to become one. The difference between losing your father to death compared to other fatherless daughters is this: You don't get another chance face-to-face.

Lane, forty-eight, tells us of a time in her childhood when she could not grasp that her father was really gone. Her father died in a car accident when she was six years old. There was no open casket at the funeral, so she never saw his body. "It was so hard for me to believe my dad was really dead because I never saw him dead and wasn't even sure what that meant. So I held out hope for years that maybe it was not true. How could it be?

"I remember when I was, like, eleven, I started looking through phone books for his name. You know back then, there was no Internet, so finding someone was not as easy. Because his name was not common, when I ran my finger down the page and saw his name there, in black, bold type, I thought, *I found him!* I really believed I had solved the mystery. I had convinced myself that he might be in the witness protection program—that is what they said about Elvis after he died.

"I went to the kitchen phone and dialed the number. When a woman answered, I burst into tears, talking a mile a minute. 'Your husband is my dad. There must be some kind of mistake. Please tell him I miss him and want him to come home. Pleeease!' I begged. Somehow we hung up the phone. I don't really remember how it ended, but I anticipated seeing him again. Later that night, my mom explained that the man in the phonebook was not my dad. My dad had died, and the man in the phonebook and my dad merely shared a name. I was devastated. All over again."

Death can be extremely hard to fathom during childhood. For most daughters, it takes a lifetime to come to terms with the permanence of the loss. Research suggests that compared to girls whose fathers left the home for other reasons, girls whose fathers passed away tend to do the following:

- Avoid contact with males
- Have a more idealized concept of their father
- Feel deeper sadness about his loss
- Experience intensified separation anxiety
- Deny and avoid feelings associated with losing their dad

Isabel, fifty-four, whose father died when she was twenty-two said, "Watching your father become ill and eventually die is, as you might expect, pretty awful. A part of you wants to spend as much time as possible with him; another part of you wants to escape and not be a witness to his suffering. It's painful to see someone you love in pain. It's confusing to see the source of strength in your life weak and debilitated. The cancer took its toll and left an active, energetic, funny man bedridden, tired, and quiet. He was my dad and not my dad at the same time. In a sense, I lost him from the moment he got the cancer, but it took him four years to die of it. Four years is a long time to have death lurking in your life. Guilt, anger, sorrow are all there. You're losing your dad (and you feel sorry for yourself because of it) but he is losing his *life*. And, even if you have been expecting it, the day he dies is a shock and the world feels less safe, less stable, and less secure. It's so final. He's free of his pain but yours continues. You need to go on with your life without him. For years I wondered if there was something more I could have done for him. I can't remember if I told him that last day that I loved him."

Helping take care of a sick and dying father can be meaningful yet debilitating. It can also feel like a burden that can trigger feelings of guilt.

Few people understand this experience (unless they have traveled the same road). It is too depleting to try to explain the experience to anyone who says, "At least he did not die suddenly—at least you got to say good-bye." In fact, you may not have said good-bye because it might have felt like giving up on him surviving his illness. So you learn that it's easier to take a deep breath, just say yes, and move on, too exhausted to recount the agony of the loss.

To compound his death, some women have lost their dads once before to divorce or emotional absence and have to live with the fact that there are many unresolved issues between the two of them. When there are layers of loss, the body must deal with processing each piece mentally, emotionally, and physically, and this can be something that is often overlooked.

For example, an issue that comes up for women who have lost their fathers to diseases like cancer, amyotrophic lateral sclerosis (ALS), or heart problems is the concern that they too are likely to suffer from these diseases someday. Ironically, when they seek a doctor's care or engage in preventative measures it serves to remind them of their loss once again. The mind can cycle through catastrophic thinking and fear leading up to medical visits, which further stresses the body and compromises immunity.

Lifestyle changes go a long way to give you strength and help you develop trust in your ability to stay healthy and free of disease. It is important to prepare yourself emotionally before doctors' appointments or medical testing through self-quieting techniques (like yoga or meditation), positive affirmations, and reality checking.

Some daughters lose fathers who hurt them during their lives, others lose fathers who were their best friends. Kourtney, forty-five, talks about her father with tears streaming down her cheeks. "I will always remember the very last words my dad spoke to me. 'Are you happy?' he said softly, lying weakly in his bed. I looked at him and smiled. 'Yes, Daddy, I am happy.' I told him I was happy, even though I was the saddest I had ever been. He was dying, and I felt like I was dying inside too. After those words, he closed his eyes and lost consciousness, and I stayed right by his side until he took his last breath. It was the saddest feeling I had ever experienced, but in a way, the most peaceful thing I had ever witnessed. What I miss most are our daily talks and his encouragement. He was a great dad. I really strive to be that person to my son because I get it. I see how much his love molded me into the woman I am today, and I want to pass that same kind of love to my child." Kourtney was lucky. She had an amazing father who showed her everything a dad is supposed to be. He was her confidant, her protector, her provider, her hero, and her first love.

Sudden Loss

If a dad dies suddenly, the loss comes out of nowhere, and the world is turned upside down. In an instant, life is changed.

Fauzia, now forty-six, and her family moved to New York City from Pakistan when she was twelve, in search of a better opportunity. She took to the city easily and soon made many friends. A well-known journalist back home, her father struggled a bit to find his place in America. By the time Fauzia was eighteen, her father had decided to take a political role back in Pakistan, but she spent the rest of her high school and college years in the States. Subconsciously, she said she felt abandoned but stuffed those feelings down deep knowing how much her father adored her. "He was just doing his job," she told herself.

Fauzia met the love of her life in her late twenties and began to plan a grand wedding. In the midst of all of the planning her father unexpectedly passed away. She was devastated. Because of her grief, she canceled the big wedding and had a very small ceremony. The loss of her father was always with her. She admits,

> In the back of my mind I was always waiting for the other shoe to drop in my marriage. I felt my husband would also leave me. I would say things like, "When we break up . . ." to which my husband always shook his head and said, "I am not going anywhere."
>
> Then one day close to ten years into our marriage we attended a friend's wedding. My father was really on my mind that day, and I felt uneasy. After the ceremony, I needed to go to the ladies' room, which was downstairs in the dark church basement. I really did not want to go alone, so I asked my husband to come with me. When we got there, I felt silly and told him he could go back to the reception. I would be fine.
>
> I walked into the restroom. When I came out, he was waiting for me. Time seemed to stand still. I said, "What are you doing here?" He looked me in my eyes and said, "I wouldn't leave you." It was at that moment, almost fifteen years after the loss of my father that I realized I had been waiting all of this time to lose him just like I lost my father. With those four words—"I wouldn't leave you"—I let go. I let go of the pain of losing my father, and I knew I had a second chance for real love.

Like so many fatherless daughters, Fauzia's loss intensified anytime she felt love from a man. Her gut told her not to trust in forever, because men leave. Although she thought she had long since dealt with the loss of her father, it continued to play a vital role in her relationships. What a beautifully unexpected moment of healing she got to experience with her husband. You never know when your moment might show up.

Your Father Died Violently

Some deaths are more complicated than others, and the loss is not the only crisis you will have to bear. If your father was killed or you suspect someone caused his death, you have multifaceted grief. You not only grieve his death but also worry about what happened and the details of who did it. Will the perpetrator hurt you or your family? You can become scared and tortured by the brutality of someone being able to take your father's life. Didn't he or she know your dad had a family?

This is where the story of your father's loss may need to be worked and reworked in order to deal with it in public. It is OK to keep the specifics to yourself to protect yourself from upsetting questions that may force you to relive the trauma. For some women, everyday life changes in unimaginable ways: Scary movies are unwatchable and a program on murder can send her spiraling down into the horror of that time in her life.

After losing her dad, Denna carried around the fear of something bad happening to her mom. "For a long time, I would freak out if my mother did not call me back immediately after I called her. To this day, I am petrified that something horrible is going to happen to her or someone in my family. I have learned to talk myself out of the fear and to remind myself that it is over and most likely will never happen again. The little girl in me, however, is still scared. It takes time."

If a father dies a violent death, a girl's happy childhood is taken away and replaced with pain, along with the realization, at a young age, that the world is a scary place. People hurt other people. These fatherless daughters probably have a heightened awareness of the people around them and react to their gut feelings quicker than most. If they sense something is off or someone is in danger, they will be hypervigilant about getting out of the situation. They also often react with anger when they are truly afraid. They can feel abandoned and cursed because of what happened to their family and their dad. Someone out there changed the trajectory of *their* lives.

Society seems to give victims a bad rap. If someone was murdered, people don't look only at the murderer; they want to know what the victim did to deserve the fatal blow. We are curious creatures and often hunger to know the details without considering how painful they might be to the survivors. We are driven by the need to protect ourselves: If there was a reason or discernible cause for the person losing his life then we want to be sure that the same thing isn't going to happen to us. No daughter should ever have to defend her father for who he was or why he was killed. What he did or did not do does not matter. How he loved and was a father are the most important issues. One of the things Denna said she would want to say to her father's killer is, "Not only did you take my father's life, you essentially took mine for many years. You took away my innocence and toughened my heart, but because of my strength, I rose to the challenge and started something beautiful out of something so painful." For many years Denna questioned her faith and wondered what kind of God would have allowed this to happen. Coming to terms with death is not easy for anyone, no matter the circumstances. What helped Denna was working through the pain and continuing to grieve the loss of her father through every stage of her life. Writing this book and fighting for fatherless daughters are ways she turned the most unimaginable pain in her life into something meaningful.

Your Father Committed Suicide

Another complex and heartbreaking way of becoming fatherless is through suicide. Unfortunately, suicide is on the rise. According to the

Centers for Disease Control and Prevention (CDC), more people die today of suicide than in car accidents. The biggest question is always why: Why couldn't I have prevented it? Why didn't he love me enough to stay here with me? Why did I not see that he was in so much pain? Why did it happen on that day?

Suicide has been called a selfish act, but the reasons for it are far more complex and painful. Sometimes the father is trying to relieve the family of the financial or legal trouble he has caused. He has convinced himself his family would be better off without him. Maybe he has battled depression or illness for decades and just wants the pain to go away. The truth is, the suicide is not about wanting to leave you; it is about him seeing a solution to something that seems too difficult for him to carry any longer, that seems as if it had no possible resolution or relief. That person usually suffered much more pain than anyone really knew or truly understood. It is no one's fault.

Far more men than women take their own lives. The National Strategy for Suicide Prevention reports that almost half of all suicides in the United States occur in men between the ages of twenty-five and sixty-five. According to Mental Health America, men over forty-five who are depressed or alcoholic are the most likely to have committed suicide. In a longitudinal study, suicide was discovered to be twice as prevalent among divorced men as among married men and eight times as common among divorced men compared to divorced women.

Some would argue that suicide rates increase with financial stress and a failing economy; while others may blame it on the increase of prescription drug usage or on firearm laws. In any case, it is clear that people who die by suicide usually have an emotional or mental disorder, primarily depression or bipolar disorder.

Whatever the cause, the pain for the ones left behind is incomprehensible. The reverberations feel as if they were the waves of an atomic explosion. First there is shock. Shock leads to guilt and helplessness. You want to obsessively review your last conversation or email exchange and look for clues. Could you have prevented it? You want to blame yourself. You wanted to help. The grief is torture. If your father committed suicide, it is normal to feel everything from shock to guilt to anger to helplessness. Shame and embarrassment may have prevented your father from reaching out because of the stigma around mental illness in our country. The CDC estimates that "about 25 percent of all U.S. adults have mental illness and that nearly 50 percent of U.S. adults will develop at least one mental illness in their lifetime." It is an epidemic that needs attention. If mental health issues were a part of your dad's life, please talk to someone you can trust about how you are feeling and lean on your support network. For myriad reasons, this is a time when you should seriously consider seeking professional help.

If your father committed suicide or struggled with mental illness, you may have wondered, Am I doomed to suffer? or Do I have the suicide gene? If you are left alone to deal with this fear over the years, it can even feel like a ticking time bomb. As you age, you might wonder how to gauge your feelings of sadness and your own capacity for depression and suicidality. Reaching out to a mental health professional can help you sort through what you are feeling. The process of grieving in the wake of a suicide is complex, as you are not only dealing with complicated emotions about your father but you are suddenly grappling with your own fears and questions. If suicide is even a fleeting thought for you, you should reach out today for support, whether that be to your best friend, the National Suicide Prevention Lifeline, or a therapist who can see you immediately.

You can find information and resources online regarding suicide and the risk factors and warning signs. For example, if you have narrowed in on a plan for taking your life, made arrangements for your belongings, have the means to follow through on the plan, are feeling hopeless, and believe that the world would be better off without you,

you are at high risk. Help is available. Start by calling the National Suicide Prevention Lifeline at 1-800-273-8255, which is available twenty-four
hours a day, seven days a week.

The goal is to try to accept your father's choice, release your own
feelings of guilt, and try to understand what was really going on at the
time of his death—and most of all, that his choice was not about you.
It is important to know that you could not relieve his pain, nor were you
responsible for doing so. It was overwhelming for him, and he decided
to make a choice all on his own. He would never have wanted you to
blame yourself, experience the pain you are in, or become so depressed
that you stop living the beautiful life that you are in.

Depression can come in many forms, from periods of deep sadness,
lasting a day or a week until you start feeling better, to major depression,
which can be recurring and debilitating. Of course, there is a continuum
of depressive manifestations that can be a significant part of an individual's life, such as that associated with bipolar disorder, in which the person cycles from highs to lows. If you experience at least five of the
following symptoms, including the first two, most of the day, every day,
for a period of at least two weeks, you would be considered by a clinician
to have clinical depression.

Common Symptoms of Depression
- Feelings of sadness and helplessness
- Loss of pleasure in things and activities that used to be
  enjoyable
- Irritability and angry outbursts
- Sleep disturbances from insomnia or sleeping too much
- Lack of energy so that even the smallest tasks take too much
  effort
- Changes in appetite, from overeating to no appetite at all
- Slower thinking and/or body movements

- Trouble concentrating, remembering things, and making decisions
- Physical pain (e.g., headaches and backaches)
- Frequent thoughts of death or suicide

Be your own advocate and build up your support team. Ask for help—medically, emotionally, and financially. Let people know what you are going through. Those who love you will appreciate the chance to help. Take it one day at a time. You have the ability to change lives, starting with your own. Force yourself to do something that you normally enjoy, even if you do not feel like it—doing so will help your body effectively release the feel-good neurotransmitters it needs to feel better. Play a musical instrument that you used to love, go for a walk in the woods. Create a feel-good file that includes emails, letters, and pictures that make you feel proud of yourself. Review things that have meaning to you and lift you up—even if you do not want to get out of bed. Decide that you can help yourself and ask others to hold you up when you cannot. See Resources on page 262 for organizations that can give you the help you need.

Your Dad Was Incarcerated

"When a parent goes to prison, they never go alone. . . . Their children go with them." This was the compelling introduction to a video produced by the Children's Justice Alliance, which spoke of the reality of what happens to a child's needs once their parent is incarcerated. There are more than 1.7 million children in the United States with an incarcerated parent. If your dad is absent from the home because of bad choices, he may have left you feelings of shame, adding to the burden of your living without him.

Maybe you never met your dad or have no memory of him because you were very young when he was incarcerated. Perhaps you have lived your whole life knowing that he walked into a jail cell and out of your world. Or your dad might have gotten into trouble with the law when you were in school, and the rumor mill ran like wildfire. While you have friends who love you, you might silently feel like you wear a stamp of shame on your forehead reading, "My Dad's a Convict." You may live in fear that the subject is going to come up at a party, because you never know what to say. You pray you did not get criminal DNA.

Now that you are an adult, if your father is still in prison, you have had to figure out if and when to visit him, and it is never easy. You may feel confused, angry, and betrayed. You may have asked yourself, How am I supposed to be good when my role model broke the law? You may have decided to rebel and have gotten in with the wrong crowd in order to be someone different or more like who you think he is. Many fatherless daughters go through a rebellious phase. They may shoplift or bully others to hide their own pain. If you were smart enough to stay out of trouble and not inflict pain on others, we commend you—you were strong beyond your years. If you stumbled down the wrong road for a while, it is OK. You were coping the best way you knew how, and you are here now.

Maybe your dad got out of prison, made amends, and decided to change his life. There can be a lot of work to do emotionally with family members, but we believe in second chances. However, if your dad got out of prison and decided he was not going to come back and resume a life with you, the pain can deepen. You have now lost him twice. You can no longer blame the system for taking him from you, but you likely blame him for not having the courage to come back and make things right.

It's almost impossible for you to explain to people how deep that void is as you wonder every day if he will come back into your life. You wait for the phone call, and you half expect him to be on your doorstop when the doorbell rings. You can't figure out if you'll hug him or punch him, and you are deeply afraid of both.

Shannon, thirty-four, lost her father to prison when she was ten; he did not get out for ten years.

We had a fairly normal life, from what I remember. My dad was a big deal in our community and served as a local politician. At some point while I was in grammar school, things started to change. His standing in the community began to fall from grace. Everyone was using the word *embezzlement*. Before I could truly grasp the enormity of the situation, my parents sat my brother and me down to tell us that our dad would be standing trial.

The rumors started, and everywhere we went people began to stare and speak in hushed voices. My dad was sentenced to ten to twenty years behind bars. I only went to see him one or two times and eventually summoned the courage to tell my mom that I did not want to visit him anymore. I was ashamed. By this point, I was in middle school and distance was the best medicine for me.

As time passed, I realized my dad was not the hero I had once considered him to be. He was flawed. I was becoming flawed, too. I threw myself into dance and school activities. I developed an eating disorder from all of the turmoil around me. I wanted to be in control. I could control my food. I got down to about eighty-eight pounds before I realized that I needed some help. Determined, I rallied on. I grew stronger. I was going to excel despite my circumstances.

I was in college a few states away by the time he got out. He came to see me; we were practically strangers. He took me out for pizza and asked me to sign what I thought was insurance paperwork. It turns out he stole my identity. Needless to say, I suffered not only financially for years, but also emotionally; it still lingers. Now, as an adult, we have gotten past a lot of that history. Well, not actually past it; we just don't speak of it. I guess it is for the best. I have my dad back in my life. He calls me; I can see him if I want to—that's what I tell myself. The truth is, I'm still experiencing a lot of pain from my childhood. I have body issues and major insecurities from my years of competitive dance. But I have been able to be successful. Last year, I signed a contract to be the interior designer for a major chain. Yes, I have been married and divorced, but I still have not found The One. I am a work in progress.

Your Dad Was Emotionally Absent

Our research results revealed an interesting finding about women—almost 80 percent of them acknowledged that during their youth, their father was either totally absent or emotionally absent.

Maybe he was traveling, never home, or tuned into sports twenty-four hours a day. Maybe he refused to emotionally connect with you, or anyone in his life, and preferred to stick to whatever made him happy. Some men can find themselves wooed by the power and prestige of success, leaving their family behind. Oftentimes the stress of work can be so overwhelming that men mentally disengage from their responsibilities and relationships. Years later, they often feel like it is too late to change things when they realize what has happened between themselves and their daughters. They become too afraid to try. So the absentee father continues to be a phantom. He is not really with you, even when he is with you.

This can be an incredibly tough weight to carry because your childhood could be very misconstrued by others. Perhaps they see your dad in the family pictures; maybe he was very successful and maybe he is fun to be around. But he never sat you down for a real father–daughter talk, never watched you practice ballet, and never rocked you to sleep when you were sick. You aren't going to go into these details with people who assume your dad was awesome, so you walk around feeling like no one has any idea of what your life is like. You feel misunderstood. You are lonely and feeling a huge emptiness you can't explain. And no expensive gift on your birthday is going to change that. While you have learned to smile and pretend, what you really want to say is, "Thanks, Dad, but what I really need from you is your time, your arms, and your wisdom." When fathers are emotionally absent, they are unknowingly giving carte blanche to their daughters to look for someone or anyone to show them attention. Good or bad.

Anna, forty-one, remembers her aha moment when she realized she felt fatherless. "I was at a workshop a few months ago. About an hour into it, two women piped in about how their lives have been forever altered by bullying. My brain started spinning. Not only was I bullied but my emotionally unavailable father's response was to tell me to 'just toughen up.' My mother's response was denial or breaking down. I seriously had zero emotional protection in that respect.

"What I realize now, at forty-one, is not only did I have a father who was not emotionally present but my mother was gone too. Essentially, at thirteen, when everyone else was developing self-esteem and who they are, I lost my chance of a normal childhood by being bullied and sent away to boarding school to be raised by my peers. In my twenties, I found myself in an abusive marriage. It isn't until now, twenty years later, with the unconditional love and support of my new husband, that I feel like I can exhale a bit and be the person I'm supposed to be."

Perhaps Anna's father wanted to bond with her, but had no idea how to do so. Maybe because she seemed OK, he believed she was. We have heard from many men who did not know how to bond with their daughters. Paul, seventy-two, said he felt inadequate and afraid to talk about the past with his daughter, Patti. They have had casual contact most of Patti's adult life, but now that she was forty, he could feel her wanting more answers. The last time he saw her, she got upset with him for not wanting to go into the details of his history with her mother. He could not understand why she needed to know so many details now. Paul said, "I think the past should just stay in the past. I don't see how dredging up all of the old issues can help our relationship today." Paul and Patti still need to find common ground on those things that need airing out. While it might be very uncomfortable, it could be incredibly healing to break down the walls of silence in a gentle way that opens the door to a more authentic connection. The key is finding a way to have open, safe communication that focuses on deeper understanding between father and daughter, without the threat of conflict.

What most daughters will find out is that their fathers deep down are just afraid—afraid of being judged, rejected, or shamed. Fathers, likewise, would be surprised to know how deeply the daughters truly wish to feel close to and loved by them, but that there are some truths standing in the way of that trust. Once the truths are faced with love, the two can reach new levels of closeness.

While having conversations, confronting the past, and facing our fathers are things we might yearn for, the process can be very complicated. Even if his choices were solely his, there can be lingering feelings of resentment, confusion, and sorrow. A fatherless daughter can understand that she is not at fault for her father's behavior but at the same time be angry that he did not make more of an effort toward her. Being able to express these feelings either in person or in a letter can be cathartic, releasing a great deal of toxins that a daughter may have stored up for decades. This is the time for your healing, and part of that is deciding what you are going to hang on to and what you are going to release.

We encourage you to release any guilt over *his* decisions. He was the dad; you were the daughter. It was *his* responsibility to figure out how to connect (or reconnect) with you. Let go of the self-blame, and know that things can be different now that you are an adult. You may need to focus on building self-esteem, erasing old negative messages of worth-lessness, and reminding yourself that you are a priceless creation. Whether or not he is willing or able to listen to you, you can manage the reconstruction of you.

Your Dad Had an Addiction

Be it drugs, alcohol, or gambling, addictions take our loved ones away from us, even though they may still be physically present. They may pass through the room, but their minds are otherwise occupied by their cravings. Watching your father become consumed by his addiction is painful not only because of what he is going through but because your relationship with him gets stunted.

The range of addictions is broad, and the family's cost is wide and deep. If things that you saw in your home because of the addiction trau-matized you, we encourage you to get specialized support to help you work through that trauma. It is real and can affect your life in ways that are psychologically disrupting. We learn our coping mechanisms from our parents, so if you have gone down the same path as your dad, please use this book as your springboard to make a change. Your life is worth more than repeating what your dad did or remaining a victim. You can turn things around with the right help.

If your father was an addict, the silent message that you received from him might have felt something like this: "Even though what I am doing is not only ruining my life but also our family's harmony, I don't care. I might say I am going to stop, but unless I really want to, it's not going to happen. So what matters to me is drinking/drugs/gambling/women. It is more important than you."

An addicted mind thinks in a different way from a nonaddicted mind, and trying to reason with an addict or get through to him on an emotionally sensible level can feel impossible. Rational thinking is virtually unachievable. He needs help, and you are not his savior.

A father who pursues an addiction can be absent in the same way as a father who is emotionally absent, but there is another layer to dealing with a dad who is struggling with drugs, alcohol, or gambling. Dads who aren't home because they are working at the office are socially acceptable; a dad who is constantly at the bar is a different story. You have had to learn a pattern of coping, which probably involves covering up, lying, feeling ashamed, and maybe even witnessing violence in the home. You may be in a pattern involving co-dependent behavior, which means you could have been supporting or enabling your dad's behavior by allowing him to be reliant on you without consequence. You may have protected him from pain or punishment for years because you felt it was the loving thing to do. A book that can help you better understand your particular situation is *Adult Children of Alcoholics* by Janet Geringer Woititz. Find a network of support and a place to feel safe enough to work through your story. Support groups can be extremely helpful in assisting people in dealing with these issues because they provide a feeling of belonging, being understood, and not feeling alone.

Teresa, twenty-five, told us that her friend recommended she check out the group Co-Dependents Anonymous (CoDA.org). This came from countless conversations in which Teresa was feeling overwhelmed by her boyfriend's addiction (a repetition of her father's behavior), leaving her feeling as if she needed to fix him. After being initially embarrassed to say "Hi, I'm Teresa, and I'm co-dependent," she sat back and listened to the strangers around her. It wasn't ten minutes before she heard elements of her own story being told by someone else—the cycle of guilt, the feelings of betrayal, and the underlying confusion of love—and her soul relaxed. She felt she could engage and be understood without telling her whole story. The people in that room already knew it because they had lived it. It was one of the best decisions of her life to join the CoDA family. Her friend was right. If CoDA does not sound right for you, look into Al-Anon, Nar-Anon, or a similar group in your community.

You will need the extra support to discover what healthy looks like. It will be wonderfully healing for you to see how your father's addiction has affected your life, your coping mechanisms, and your relationships. Likewise, we encourage you to become keenly aware of your relationship choices. It's common to be attracted to a partner who has the same addiction as your father because you know how to deal with that particular dynamic. But you can make the choice not to.

If, as a young girl, you witnessed the effects of addiction in your father's life, this might have been a very scary experience for you. Seeing someone in an altered state is more than confusing, it creates a feeling that life is not stable as well as the belief that you cannot trust people or be confident in your expectations. It can be unsettling to not be sure which father was going to walk through the door: the sober one, the drunk/high one, or the one who is highly agitated because he needs his drug of choice. If you grew up witnessing an array of personality traits that seemed to blur each other out, you learned to function on a watchful, hypervigilant level, always looking for cues.

Denise, thirty-four, told us multiple stories about the fear of the unknown she felt every night after her father started using drugs.

He would begin to talk slowly and eventually start stumbling through our house. It scared me because he became someone totally different, and I didn't know what would happen next. My parents finally got divorced, and while it was the right thing for my mom, I knew my dad would struggle.

One time Daddy picked us up, obviously buzzed. My stomach dropped, and I put myself on high alert. My sister pretended like nothing was wrong, so I got into his car with her, hoping she was right. Driving us to his house, he hit multiple curbs in the neighbor-hood, never stopping but continuing to drive extremely slowly. When we finally got to his house, he walked straight in and started rolling a joint. I grabbed my sister and took her outside so she did not have to see what he was doing. When we turned around to go back in, the door was locked. He locked us out of the house and passed out. I banged on the door in tears. "Daddy, let me in!" We sat there on the front steps feeling like orphans. We finally knocked on the neighbor's door and asked for help. She let us sleep on her sofa that night. Dad did not remember any of it.

Children of addicts often live in a world between knowing and not knowing their dads when the addiction takes over. To say the least, the ongoing instability and fear can take its toll.

However, as she matures, a daughter of an addicted father can turn her fears into strength. After getting support and healing for her mind, body, and spirit, she can find a path to overcoming her fears and turning them into strengths. She can see that while she was forced to grow up quickly, missing precious years of her childhood, she was also taught how to read people at a young age. She can embrace her ability to be addiction-free, a quick decision maker, an alert observer, and a self-protector, transforming those traits into something good. Perhaps you can help lead a support group for kids going through the same thing and pass along the strengths that can come from the lessons they learned.

Your Dad Abused You

Being abused by the one man who you trusted to protect you is nothing short of a tragedy. We are not going to cover this topic in detail because we believe that it deserves special care that goes beyond the scope of this book. There are many forms of abuse, and each takes on its own set of physical, emotional, and mental consequences in a woman's life. We strongly recommend that you seek additional, specialized support for your healing. A highly acclaimed book by one of the leading experts on trauma and abuse is Judith Herman's *Trauma and Recovery*. Herman writes, "Many abused children cling to the hope that growing up will bring escape and freedom. She is still a prisoner of her childhood; attempting to create a new life, she reencounters the trauma."

But the personality formed in the environment of coercive control is not well adapted to adult life. The survivor is left with fundamental problems in basic trust, autonomy, and initiative. She approaches the task of early adulthood—establishing independence and intimacy—burdened by major impairments in self-care, cognition, memory, identity, and the capacity to form stable relationships.

If you are a child abuse survivor, special attention should be paid to your history, building coping mechanisms, and finding freedom in the future. Your experience needs validating, your spirit needs healing, and your body needs to build its power back. Your experience of father loss is surely multilayered, and turning to those who truly understand what it is like to walk in your shoes is critical. An organization that specializes in the support of adult survivors of child abuse is the National Association of Adult Survivors of Child Abuse (NAASCA).

The Gift of the Stand-In Father

Sometimes the void left by a father's death or departure is filled by someone else who becomes a stand-in dad. While no one can ever really replace your dad, we have heard many wonderful stories where a stand-in adopted father, uncle, older brother, or family friend serves as the main role model in a girl's life. This man can make all the difference, teaching a girl about healthy, bonded male–female relationships. The hard part for an abandoned daughter is accepting the stand-in and allowing him to love her. Many girls feel too hurt or rejected to let another man into their lives. They don't want to risk loss happening again. It takes a special person to embrace all of the broken pieces and love her through the pain and to the other side.

Denna recounts her own stand-in story with pride.

My parents divorced so early in my life that I have zero recollection of them ever being a couple. I saw my dad on some weekends and Christmas, when we went to his parents' house and played family for the day. It was always just enough time to remind me how much I wanted him in my life. I always thought there would be more time for us, but it was just not meant to be. I have a vivid memory of standing beside my uncle at my dad's funeral when he leaned down and took my face into his hands. He said, choking back tears, "I will be here for you at any moment you ever need me, Sugar. I love you so very much." I stood strong. He loved me; I was sure of that, but I knew he had his own family to take care of too. I would need too much. Plus, he lived in Minnesota, and we were still living in Charleston.

As I grew older and time passed, our contact slowed down to cards and the occasional phone call. After years of bottled-up pain, I put myself into therapy. Once I was strong enough, I went to visit him. As we sat on his brown leather couch, he put his hand on top of mine. I felt like I was a thirteen-year-old girl again. Anxiety, fueled by the emotion of being loved, ran up my body and settled right into the hole left by my daddy. My mind raced. I had no idea how to react. I had never sat still hand in hand with a man before. I wondered, "How long should I hold his hand before it becomes weird? Do I count to ten or twenty?" I look back on that day and feel sorry for how sad I was, lost in my own hunger for my father. The one thing that I now know is this: I wasted a lot of time. I should have contacted my uncle earlier. I should have spoken up. He was always there. My uncle Bill always tells me just how beautiful and smart I am. He is my constant cheerleader and tells me weekly how proud he is of me and how loved I am. He gave me away at my wedding, mended my fragile heart, and is, by all intents and purposes . . . my dad. He was and is my perfect stand-in. Looking back, I had a few stand-ins. My uncle Albert was there to encourage my schoolwork and reward me when I got good grades. My brother let me follow him around and showed me how to do everything a boy could do, sometimes even better. My paternal grandfather taught me to expect the best and ask for nothing less. I am grateful for each and every one of them.

Not every girl will have an uncle or brother that stands in, but we all can have mentors if we open the door for them. There are people who love us enough to stay in our lives. Perhaps your support does not come from a man but from the strong women in your life. Maybe it is a professor, basketball coach, or boss who can also become your teacher and encourager. Don't be afraid of asking for someone's time or support—if they are meant to be part of your life, they will be. Be your own advocate and find strength from believing in yourself as you grow.

Another tremendously powerful way of turning your loss into something meaningful is becoming a mentor yourself. Be available. By helping others who can benefit from your strength, you are giving each other a valuable gift. Make a change by being the change: Volunteer as a mentor to teen girls in your church, a community organization, or the high school in your neighborhood. We formed a mentoring program within our nonprofit to encourage fatherless daughters to help those younger than them. Find where there is a need and plug yourself in.

The Gifts of Building Your Support System

We know this chapter covered some difficult ground, but we hope you better understand that how your dad left changes how you reacted to the loss. Each fatherless daughter's story is different, but there is a commonality of experience, which shows that you are not alone. We encourage you to find your home in this sisterhood and let go of guilt, shame, or self-doubt about why you reacted the way that you did to your dad's leaving you. You did your best then, and you are doing your best now. Take a deep breath. With knowledge comes power, and with power comes confidence, strength, and the ability to do things that you never before thought possible.

We cannot stress enough how maintaining your own support system is key. Do yourself a favor and get encouragement from a therapist or life coach who can help guide you to a much stronger place. A good counselor is one of the best investments that you can make in your life.

Some daughters we talked to were unsure of which type of professional to turn to for support. Here are some pointers to guide you along the way.

If you truly want to examine your mental and emotional self and understand your life patterns and stuck places, a licensed therapist or counselor with a specialty in the area that challenges you is a great person to reach out to for guidance. He or she can help you sort through issues that might be too daunting to handle on your own. Perhaps you believe that there is something that needs identifying and reworking in your life, and you want to figure out what that is and how to fix it. A psychologist (PhD, PsyD) is trained specifically in testing and diagnosis and can be your best confidant in the journey toward healing. If you have issues that are longstanding and perhaps need medication or monitoring to bring balance to your emotional state, a psychiatrist (MD) is someone to add to your support network, as he or she can do testing, diagnoses, and prescribing of medications to help you feel more stable and alive.

Maybe you really want to focus on your goals and what is getting in the way of your living the life you desire. Denna has found great reward in mentoring as a friend and life coach over the years. "It never ceases to amaze me how many people get 'stuck' in their own way when it comes to getting what they want out of life. I get it, and can recognize it, because I lived that way for a period of time." It often takes another person to give you new perspective and push you out of your comfort zone to see your true potential. Any of these specialists can be just what we need to get the motors running and launch our lives in a more positive and productive direction. If you have found yourself in a place of deep introspection, spiritual unrest, or awakening, reaching out to a faith-based therapist, intuitive, spiritual counselor, or energy healer can also help you to reach a new level of health, awareness, and oneness. Karin has found that helping people as a spiritual counselor opens beautiful doors of growth in their lives, facilitating feelings of deeper purpose and teaching them how to live with greater authenticity. Finding the person whose work resonates with you the most is a significant factor in your journey to healing.

While building a foundation of support from experts, friends, and family is instrumental in your process, spending time alone is equally as important. Starting the day with a prayer, ritual, or self-affirmation can be the grounding that makes all of the difference. As you practice centering yourself, be intentional about how all parts of you participate in those moments. Pay special attention to where you hold your tension. Relax your mouth and forehead. Notice your breathing and be deliberate while inhaling and exhaling. Getting in sync with your body and its fluidity can slow down your heart rate and ease your mind no matter what your surroundings may be. When you are stuck in traffic, try turning off the radio, and sit in a relaxed state doing deep breathing and speaking gratitude for what is good in your life. Each moment, each person, and each decision has the potential to build you up to the place where your life is stronger, lighter, and healthier.

CHAPTER 3

Timing of the Loss

Old as she was, she still missed her daddy sometimes.
~Gloria Naylor

There are clear differences in the emotional, physical, and psychological challenges for women who lost their fathers at different ages and stages of their lives. While all fatherless daughters experience sadness, fear, and lack of stability, their reactions are further affected by how old they were when their father left and how his departure was handled by their family.

A father's guidance helps his daughter in ways that she internalizes over time. With both parents' support, a daughter is much better equipped to handle what comes down the road because she is receiving insight from two perspectives, which helps her create a more balanced viewpoint in her life. According to studies, a girl's self-esteem and sociability are significantly higher when her father is involved and engaged in her life than when he's not.

When a father's guidance disappears and he himself is absent, the daughter may initially feel that this critical piece of her foundation has been yanked out from under her feet. As the years pass, this loss can interfere with her personal development. A daughter can become emotionally stuck at the age of her loss and not know how to move past it on her own. It's important to know that you were not in control of the impact your dad's loss had on you, no matter how old you were when it happened. How you reacted at the time and how the event created a lasting impact on your behavior and your physical and emotional state are not your fault.

You might wonder where you fall in the mix of fatherless daughters and how common it is to lose a father at the age at which you lost your dad. When we asked fatherless daughters how old they were when they became fatherless, here is what we found:

- 9 percent fatherless at birth
- 33 percent lost their father between 0 and 5 years old
- 18 percent between 6 and 10 years old
- 15 percent between 11 and 15 years old
- 8 percent between 16 and 20 years old
- 8 percent between 21 and 30 years old
- 9 percent lost their father after the age of 30

The experience of loss for each of us is unique, but your age at the time of the loss makes a difference and is important for understanding exactly what brought you to the place that you are in today.

A fatherless daughter may relish going to friends' houses who seem to have perfect families because of the safety and warmth she feels there. She may be eager to know her friends' fathers; however, she might feel awkward because she might not have learned how to connect with her own.

Children develop their belief systems about the world based on their own home experiences, especially through their adolescent years. Normal is what they know and encounter on a daily basis. Even if a child is exposed to other families, she may not fully recognize what she is missing in her own home until she is much older and able to look back with a new perspective. This is what we refer to as father loss "going underground." You may have truly believed that you had dealt with your pain years ago, only to have it resurface in the form of anxiety, mistrust, fear, anger, or dysfunctional patterns later.

The past has an influence on the present. For example, Latricia talks about realizing the impact of fatherlessness on herself, her sisters, and her mother. "My dad was an alcoholic and my parents divorced when I was eight years old. He died when I was eighteen from cirrhosis of the liver, although he was dead to me long before that. When he died it was kind of the closure that I needed. It was embarrassing to tell people, like new people I met in college, my dad was a bum. My mom did a great job of raising my sister and me. She also was a fatherless daughter. Her dad died when she was four. I have a wonderful husband who is also an alcoholic but has been sober for twenty-one years. My mom and sister also married alcoholics. My mom is still married and my sister is divorced."

The influence of the past on the present is similar for many fatherless daughters. What you learned to live with is how you learned to live. Typically, fathers are an instrumental part of your learning years. Girls are supposed to receive the gift of self-esteem from their fathers as well as the understanding of safe, protective male attention. Research has shown over and over again that girls who had little to no contact with their fathers, especially during adolescence, later had greater difficulties forming long-term relationships with men than girls who had close connections with their fathers.

The Ages and Stages of Father Loss

The age and life stage at which you lost your father can affect you developmentally, socially, emotionally, spiritually, and physically. Understanding where you were developmentally when you lost your father will allow you to gain insight into your past and current behaviors as well as to see more clearly where you need to focus your energy for the future.

Infancy: Birth to Two Years

Do you know much about your mother's pregnancy? How was her emotional state? How was her physical and mental well-being? Has she avoided discussing the topic altogether? An unborn child is not only fed physically in the womb, but her systems are also being impacted by the mother's stress levels. Daughters whose mothers were overly stressed while pregnant due to fatherless-related factors—such as a sudden death, an abusive relationship, financial strains, or lack of support—likely experienced being dosed regularly with stress hormones from the mother in utero. In his book *Magical Beginnings, Enchanted Lives*, renowned metaphysical expert Dr. Deepak Chopra speaks about anxiety being passed from the mother to the baby in utero. Stress and fear can be transmitted into the bloodstream of the mother and cross the placenta into the unborn child.

After birth and into infancy, stress levels can become further heightened if the home is not a secure place. If the father dies or is absent, abusive, addicted, or incarcerated, a daughter's sensitive body and well-being are affected by what is happening in her environment and the level of care that her mother is able to give. The primary need for babies, beyond air, food, and shelter, is a sense of security. A little girl needs to feel safe, taken care of, and loved in order to have healthy physical, cognitive, and emotional development.

If the parent is present and gives affection easily and consistently, the infant will most likely view the world as trustworthy, safe, and pleasing. If the parent fails to provide love and security, the child can develop feelings of mistrust, insecurity, and fear. As she continues to grow, these feelings can manifest into emotional instability, suspicion of others, withdrawal, and lack of self-confidence.

If you were lucky, despite the absence of your father, your mother provided you with a stable, predictable environment and filled you up with love. You were blessed if other family members stepped in and cared for you, provided for you, and guided your early development. However, although your mom may have done a terrific job meeting your needs, you still lost your dad, and there are simply some spaces that a mother cannot fill.

Loss is confusing, especially for a child. You might ask, How could I be so affected by fatherlessness if I don't remember my dad? Even without knowing your father, you suffered a primary loss, and emotions around that loss are valid. Find time to honor your loss and ask questions about him. Find out about who he was and build a clearer picture of him. Are you like him? Do you have any of his physical characteristics? Ask your mom how he felt about having a daughter. Give yourself the gift of knowing your dad *now*. Getting to know who your dad was can help you to know yourself better as well. Ask questions, do research, open the boxes of photos, and open yourself up to understanding who he was. If he was gone before your mom or your family got to know him, and it feels like an important missing piece in your life, do your own exploration like Denna did. There are experts and websites that can do incredible ancestral research and can give you some sense of what he did and where he came from.

Toddler: Ages Two to Four

During the toddler years, girls are learning a sense of self-control and autonomy as unique little people. Their days are filled with exploring their environments and learning how to do small tasks on their own. Developmental studies have shown that little girls tend to observe, listen, interpret, and imitate what they see in a keener way than do little boys. They watch for cues from their parents on what is good or bad behavior and are learning if it is OK to be their curious selves. They learn when to be proud or ashamed by the feedback they receive. The absence of a father's approving voice can become an echoing void in her life. A mother can indeed step in to encourage her daughter in phenomenal ways; however, there is a special meaning to a father's support and encouragement that cannot be duplicated by anyone else.

During the toddler years, little girls are finding their *own* voices. They are usually ahead of boys in language development, and if given adequate guidance, their communication skills become the main ingredient to self-expression, problem solving, and relationships. At this stage, the foundation of male–female communication is likely not formed for a fatherless daughter at the same rate as a fathered daughter. And if the mother is emotionally overwhelmed or living in a conflicted situation, she may be incapable of providing her daughter with important mother–daughter interaction. It is no surprise that with all of this relation with the world around them, toddler girls also tend to form emotional and social connections differently from little boys. They are more attuned to eye contact, voices, faces, and reading emotional expressions. Even at this young age, they are starting to make sense of the world and relationships around them. If she senses conflict, a toddler may say to her father, "Be nice to my mommy." If her developing connection to others and to the world is interrupted by the heartbreaking loss of her father, she is seeing, hearing, and feeling more than parents might think and is encoding the loss into her memory. The interplay of all that is around her is contributing to the emotional and social person she will become.

A daughter is born trusting her parents to take care of her and teach her to learn, laugh, and play. When she experiences something different, her body responds in a way that reflects the environment she is in. The stress of father loss can have a significant impact on her body's health.

Research has begun to reveal the significance of the toddler years and the measurable effect that chronic stress can have on the life of a child. According to the Center on the Developing Child at Harvard University, "[H]ealthy development can be derailed by excessive or prolonged activation of stress response systems in the body (especially the brain), with damaging effects on learning, behavior, and health across the lifespan." If the fatherless home is filled with such stressors as instability, dysfunction, financial suffering, and lack of support for the daughter, there can be long-term repercussions.

Harvard researchers found that when a child is exposed to extended, intense periods of stress and adversity, such as chronic neglect, economic hardship, emotional or physical abuse, subjection to violence and/or caregiver mental illness or substance abuse, her system can develop a toxic stress response. Experiencing toxic stress response for prolonged periods of time can interfere with the healthy development of her body's organs and systems, ultimately increasing the daughter's risk for stress-related diseases and cognitive impairment as she ages.

Your loss at this young age may be the reason you developed a nervous stomach or a weak immune system. Taylor, eighteen, remembers getting nauseous every time her mother dropped her off at daycare. "I was afraid she would never come back just like my dad didn't."

Little girls need to interact to make sense of their world. If you did not have someone serve this role when you were young, you can begin talking about things now with someone who you trust to give voice and clarity to your story.

Early School Years: Ages Five to Seven

In the early school years, a girl is tasked with learning direction and initiative. She is no longer a little girl but is learning how to take control of her environment and feel independent—largely based on the approval of others. If she feels like she's not adequate the way she is, her self-confidence will suffer and she will likely feel guilty for not living up to the standards around her, especially those set by her parents.

A father plays a large role in the emotional and cognitive experience of a daughter at this age. If the father disengages from her or leaves the home, she may wonder, Is it my fault that my parents are getting a divorce? or What is wrong with me that my dad isn't coming to see me? These internalized feelings can cause regressive behaviors, such as bed wetting, crying, fingernail biting, twirling or pulling out hair, or becoming uncooperative due to anger and sadness. If you lapsed into any of these stress reactions as a child, you may not have been equipped with the coping mechanisms to handle the situation yourself, and your behavior was an attempt at self-soothing.

Losing a father at this age has a different impact from losing a dad when you are a toddler. You were old enough to know what was missing from your life—positive and negative. Perhaps there was conflict between your parents during their split and you recall feeling scared or obligated to take sides. If he passed away, you might have had many questions that you did not dare ask, and so you remained confused, hoping that you would make sense of things by watching those around you. Maybe taking care of your mother made you feel needed, special, and close to her, but it was too much for you at that age. If you had siblings, things changed in those relationships as well. Whatever was happening, you were a little girl trying to become a big girl, and your roles in the family and with your father altered permanently. Most children want their parents to be happy, healthy, and together, and when that is not the case, the loss can feel destabilizing.

Loss of a father at these young ages can affect reproductive maturity and sexual activity in later years. Research shows that girls who lost their father in the early school years and who were exposed to a stressful environment were much more likely to have "an early onset of puberty, precocious sexuality, and unstable relationships as adults." Young daughters who watched their newly single or widowed mothers dating, perhaps introducing unfamiliar men into the home, not only likely experienced instability but were at risk for seeking out boys' attention and affection just as they witnessed Mom doing. Daughters who felt that their mothers were dependent on a man may have rebelled and subconsciously told themselves that they would not need a man to be happy in life.

Young girls are not only watching and developing but are beginning to find their passions and are building the courage to try new things. During their daughters' early school years, fathers begin to take an active role in their lives, engaging in vigorous play and encouraging them to be strong and brave. If a father is not there to foster exploration and discovery in his daughter's life, her innately courageous spirit could suffer. She will likely feel left out when she sees other fathers and daughters interacting around her. She may not be able to name those feelings, which, as a result, are often expressed in the form of tears, bad dreams, or upset tummies, but she knows that she feels an absence in her life without a daddy.

At this stage, girls usually become abstract thinkers. Their imaginations and thoughts are always buzzing. Unfortunately, they have also determined that the world can be scary and people aren't necessarily permanent. Because of this, as a fatherless daughter matures, she might imagine situations in which she is also abandoned by her mother or her siblings, and so she perpetually carries this fear inside her. The support of Mom, grandparents, or other caretakers is critical and creates the safe space she needs for healthy development. The girl needs to be heard, reassured, and have her own feelings assuaged—no matter what the mother is going through. Was your grief honored and given the time that it deserved? Were you allowed to share your true feelings, or did you feel like you had to hide them? Your experiences through your loss informed your future coping skills—this is where you learned how to handle adversity.

When a child is five, six, and seven, she realizes that life exists past her front door. She begins to be influenced by experiences at school and in the community. Her interactions with teachers, neighbors, and peers are part of what is shaping her. She is starting grade school, and father absence might have a negative impact on her focus and academic performance.

Kids whose fathers leave the home at these ages often get behind in verbal, social, and perceptual skills, especially if their dads left by choice. When self-confidence and stability drop, girls' grades usually do too. If you fell behind at school at this point, we hope it heals some old wounds to know that what you were going through at home made you struggle at school more than your peers—it was not about how smart you were, it was about how much you were hurting. You may have also found yourself in situations in which you had to tell others that your dad was not around. It can be awkward and embarrassing to explain why you are not participating in making Father's Day cards in class.

Reflecting on your childhood experiences and needs and remembering if you were supported or neglected are important pieces of your healing process. Now that you are an adult, you can reexamine old wounds and do some work to help them heal. Group therapy, journaling, letter writing, and private counseling are all wonderful ways to help you make sense of those memories. Remember, the most important thing that you needed was a sense of security and a feeling that you mattered in the world, but if you lacked that in your early school years, it is not too late to achieve it now that you are the decision maker in your life. You can go back and hug that little girl and tell her that she is safe and that you are going to make things right. She did nothing wrong and is now being taken care of the way she deserved back then.

Childhood: Ages Eight to Twelve

During the middle childhood years, a daughter begins to see herself more as an individual. She typically establishes a stronger sense of independence and wishes to spend more time with her friends. Developing healthy self-confidence is critical at this stage so that she can thrive during these transitional years. A middle grade girl craves feeling smart, productive, and worthwhile and is sensitive to feeling inferior or different. Peers and popularity are driving forces as she searches for her social life and a place to fit in while at the same time depending on her family for stability.

Spending more time in friends' homes, she starts to compare her family to others. Maybe she realizes that her father is an alcoholic or is always traveling while other dads are home. Perhaps her father moves out while she is away at camp or on a trip, and she soon learns that she will have a new stepmother. Maybe her dad dies unexpectedly, and—unlike her peers—in an instant, her world changes. All of a sudden, she is different. Who does she turn to? What is going to happen next? Where does she belong? She can make sense of only so much on her own.

If things at home are conflicted during the loss, the stability she relies on from her family can evaporate. She might face a move, spending extended time with relatives, or changing schools, all of which means being uprooted from her social circle—a core part of her identity. Her role in the family will likely shift to taking on new responsibilities. With these new expectations, the time she once was able to spend with friends, on schoolwork, or playing sports might now be needed to help clean the house, pack, unpack, handle funeral details, make meals, or care for siblings or Mom. Many of the things she valued in her growing world now take a backseat as the family tries to find its way without Dad in the picture. Middle grade children, especially, can be very self-focused and resent anything that takes attention away from them. They can become angry for what they have to give up. Because their bodies are undergoing the dramatic shifts that come with puberty, these girls are flooded with hormone-induced emotions that require an outlet.

Because her thought processes are maturing, a fatherless daughter at this stage will have a fair understanding of the interactions and energy in the home. However, she is still a child and isn't equipped to handle or identify all the emotions she is experiencing, so she may act out in ways that seem uncooperative, disengaged, or attention seeking. On the inside, she is trying to yell, "I am hurting! I am scared! I don't know what is going to happen next!" while on the outside she might try to assert herself by rebelling, lashing out, or retreating from the family altogether. This age is already so complicated, and a girl's support network is critical to helping her through her grief. She deserves to grow into adolescence with predictable routines, the permission to feel, and peers to lean on.

A preteen's identity is typically highly connected to her social world, so if she doesn't have a trusted friend to talk to, she may suffer in silence. If you did not have adequate support at that age as you returned to school after a death or family crisis, you may have experienced isolation or bullying. Other kids just do not understand the emotionality of father loss at this age. You were trying to figure out the world right in the middle of a drastic loss. At the same time, because there were social standards that you were adapting to, learning who to trust and how to behave publicly regarding your loss may have been quite challenging.

Attachment to your parents during a loss caused by divorce is a critical factor for preteen daughters. According to psychologist Carl Pickhardt, "Children (up to about 9) tend to respond differently to divorce . . . because the child is still so dependent on and attached to the parents. [She] tends to be more prone to grief and anxiety at the loss of family unity and security. For a while the child may cling, lose confidence, and act sad." For the daughter who has tried to loosen her attachment to her parents, feelings of guilt or responsibility may set in.

Grief is a unique experience for each daughter who has lost her father through death. The Harvard's Child Bereavement Study at Massachusetts General Hospital confirmed what so many fatherless daughters have felt: Grief does not end at a specific time. It is not something that you get over, even when the rest of the world moves on. It is OK and totally normal if you lost your dad at this age and then struggled for a long time. According to a study by William Worden and Phyllis Silverman, kids can show signs of social problems, withdrawal, anxiety, low self-esteem, behavior issues, and emotional struggles for years after a father's death.

Margo, twenty-five, realized the impact of her withdrawal after her father's death almost twelve years later when she started her writing career. "My writing coach suggested that I take a grammar class, which totally embarrassed me. There were basic rules of grammar that I was unable to absorb in middle school due to my preoccupation with what was happening in my home life. I passed the class, but I was too withdrawn to learn the essential skills I would need later as an aspiring writer. It was yet another task I would need to accomplish as an adult."

"You did the best you could to get through something that was out of your control. Find a place of grace and love for yourself by releasing any judgment about what you did wrong or could have done better." As *Eat, Pray, Love* author Elizabeth Gilbert said in a 2014 interview on Oprah's *Super Soul Sunday*, "[My] grace says, I am magnificent and did things just the way that I should have."

Teen: Ages Thirteen to Nineteen

The teen years are some of the most complex years of a girl's life. She faces so many new struggles and needs the support of her father more than ever. She needs a protector, a guide, and a catcher for all of the curve balls that are going to be thrown her way as she goes from little leagues to teenager. With so many physical, emotional, and social challenges, facing a major loss can blow a huge hole in her world. She is just starting to figure out who she is, and now that her father is gone, who is she? What are the kids at school going to say? How is she going to figure this out without him?

A teen daughter's body is changing. No matter if she is first or last among her friends to physically mature, it is a difficult transition. She needs reassurance from her dad that she is perfect just the way she is. If his feedback is not present, supportive, or encouraging, her self-image can be deeply affected.

Moving from adolescence to becoming a young woman is meaningful, yet complicated. A teenager's body and emotions are changing faster than she has time to fully comprehend. She will begin having sexual thoughts and experiences, and she is meant to receive help and openness from those who are taking care of her. During these years, she is trying to understand exactly who she is and may move through a few identities, ranging from sports lover to political activist. She wants to fit in and be herself at the same time, and this can often be like balancing on a tightrope. She needs support and guidance from her parents to help her believe in herself, even if she is pushing them away. She needs to know that they are there.

As a teen, a daughter is also learning about her own personal space. Once she starts spending more time away from her parents, she typically learns how to establish boundaries with others and interpret the intentions of those around her. These are critical life lessons for parents to teach and model. A father should be the first example of appropriate boundaries with the opposite sex through the way he interacts with the mother as well as the daughter. If he is absent and his daughter's self-confidence has not been firmly grounded, she can find herself lost about how to physically set limits with males.

A teen girl is not only learning to see herself differently but she is watching and wondering about her parents from a new perspective. If her dad leaves her life by choice, she is left with no father to watch and understand. She might ask herself, "Is my dad a good guy?" or "Did my mom cause him to leave?" or "Why doesn't he love me enough to stay?" In a healthy, supportive environment, a teen girl will receive the reassurance that she needs to get through these years. If given the time to explore and understand her emotions, she will be more likely to develop a firm sense of identity. If abandonment or loss interrupts this process and she is not given the safe space to work through her grief, a litany of problems can occur, including sexual promiscuity, drinking, the need to belong to someone regardless of the costs, eating disorders, cutting, drug experimentation, and maybe even suicidal thoughts. By losing her father, she has lost a part of herself, and trying to heal that wound on her own can be overwhelming.

Gretchen, thirty-one, lost her dad at age thirteen due to a divorce caused by his abusiveness and chronic infidelity. "Being sad was all I knew. I thought every teen girl cried at night. The tears would just start flowing as soon as I shut my door and curled up on my bed. I did not understand why he did not love me enough to stay. It made me hate myself and hate him. I was so confused about what I was hearing about my dad, and I did not understand why he loved these women more than us. I learned how to be treated by the way Dad treated Mom all those years. I remember sitting in my room with my little brother and a tape recorder, recording the screaming so we would have evidence, but for whom? We never let anyone listen to it.

"He would yell at us constantly and whip us, but I still just wanted so badly to be Daddy's little girl. I really never was, and that still makes me cry. Looking back, I did not know I was depressed all of adolescence. No one asked me how I was doing or came to knock on my door. I had no one to talk to. I felt so lost, and I was angry at my mom for letting it happen, so I just hid from everyone. I had never heard of cutting, but I would take these long scissors and run them down the inside of my arms over and over again. I did not do it deep enough to raise suspicion, but I know feeling the cuts made me feel a release from the torment. I thought about killing myself a lot, but I was too scared to. Honestly, what saved me was being a Christian and worrying if I would go to heaven or not. I know now that I was a depressed, self-loathing teen, which I have had to grieve as an adult. I lost about five years of my life without anyone noticing. I just wish someone had come and helped me through it."

Often, a fatherless teen daughter will isolate from her family or lash out at them. She might do a great deal of door slamming, object throwing, and screaming to get out her anger. She might turn inward and punish her mom for the divorce by saying to herself, "They didn't consult me about this decision, so I am not going to consult them about mine." She might desperately need someone to listen to her. She can become vulnerable to falling into the wrong crowd or being susceptible to an inappropriate relationship with a much older male. She can change her behavior and involvement in after-school activities and fall behind in her grades as a result of the feelings that are swirling around in her mind.

What did you do with your emotions back then? Can you see now that you truly did not understand why you were acting the way you were? If you made some decisions that you now regret, compassion for yourself is key to moving forward. You were not an adult—you were a teen who just wanted her heart to feel better, and so you looked in many places to find relief. You were trying to survive. See yourself differently today. You are resilient, you have changed, and you have done your best. Forgive that young girl—go back and talk to her and walk her safely into today. Ask for help with your healing, and find the freedom to move forward.

Young Adulthood: Ages Twenty Plus

The quintessential question for women in adulthood might be, Can I create a secure life in which I love and am loved? The adult daughter who has a connection with her father sees him as an important part of her past as well as a significant person in her future. He is supposed to be there for all her future milestones: graduation, career, marriage, motherhood, and major decisions. If he disappears from her life, where does that leave her?

A daughter's relationship with her parents has likely deepened in her twenties, as she gets to know them with a new awareness. In fact, all of her relationships start to deepen as she decides which friends she can trust, lean on, and learn more about as a young woman. This transition into independence is one of the most challenging in her life cycle, as she is not just physically moving out of the house but also relationally, emotionally, mentally, spiritually, and physically coming into her own. She learns more about who she is and how to care for herself. Her growing independence may take her farther from home, but she still relies on her parents for support. Knowing that dad is only a text away helps her feel protected.

The daughter who loses her dad as a resource as she finds her way in the world educationally and professionally can doubt her own ability to do things on her own. In a six-year study on adults who experienced the death of a parent by the National Institutes of Health, women who lost their fathers after the age of nineteen experienced feeling a lower level of personal mastery and a compromised level of psychological awareness.

If the newly fatherless daughter has also had a change in her relationship status or has recently become a mother, the loss of her dad can feel all the more complicated. While grieving, she may also have to take care of children or a spouse, and if she has not had children yet, she must mourn the loss of a possible future milestone: Her father holding her child for the first time. If she is still single and hopes to marry, she must mourn the loss of the father of the bride. Who is going to walk her down the aisle? What about the father–daughter dance? Whatever the circumstance of her family or love life, suddenly she has to face the loss of the days that she dreamed about with Dad, with her kids' grandpa, and with her family—however she hoped it would look.

In her thirties, a woman's biological clock is ticking, and the pressures of family, career, and community can become overwhelming with demands on her to do it all and be everything to everyone. She needs her father for moral, spiritual, and perhaps financial support. Without him, she may feel like she has no backup or shoulder to cry on when other men in her life disappoint her. If he passed away, she must not only face the reality of his life ending, but she now sees her own mortality in a new way. Nothing is permanent. The world is telling her to handle things like a grown-up, but she often feels like a young girl again, looking for a daddy whom she cannot find.

The loss of her father can derail her career or relationship goals. She is struggling with finding balance in her own life but is thrown off-kilter by the loss of her father. In Daniel Levinson's landmark study of thirteen hundred women, major transitions in this life stage became clear, "Either she is going to become an independent person with an identity of her own, or involved in love, marriage, and family." Levinson continued, "The sense of one or the other is very strong."

If she is in her twenties and not married yet, she might tend to avoid intimacy so she is not vulnerable to losing a man again. A fatherless daughter in her thirties may have already gotten divorced, decided to live in a partnership, with or without a long-term promise, depending on where she is emotionally. If she is divorced, perhaps she repeated a pattern or married for the wrong reasons and can now see things more clearly. Perhaps she has decided to take some time on her own to work out what has become tangled up inside her.

Maybe she wants to walk in her treasured father's footsteps and focus on her independence and career. If her relationship with her father was not healthy, she might opt to pursue professional success to show the world that she is strong and valuable, something he did not validate. She may isolate herself from intimate relationships if she has experienced loss, rejection, or pain. She focuses on the attainable: a career that she can do all by herself. Over time, if her values begin to shift, she might ask herself, Have I been too focused on career and not on the relationships that I want in my life?

Self-preservation may work for a time, but it does not keep you warm at night. If you want an intimate partnership in your life, something must change. It might be time to go back and do your emotional and spiritual work to identify where your pain is the heaviest, what you really want in life, and how to make the changes to grow into your life's purpose.

Life is very complicated at this stage because a fatherless woman has many conflicting roles: worker, spouse, parent, and self among others. She is pulled by so many areas that need taking care of that when the heaviness of her loss hits, those around her might not fully understand the depth of her grief. On the other hand, she might have been committed to building a strong and healthy support network around herself, which can act as a buffer when things feel overwhelming. If she has found the right partner and has been in a stable marriage or partnership, she can have the wonderful resource of someone who understands, encourages, and loves her. Her relationship choices truly make all the difference.

Fatherless daughters who have excelled in their work lives often use the leadership tools they learned in business to get them through trying times in their personal lives. Molly, thirty-six, told us that when she is depressed she gives herself an hour each day to "sit in her pain" and feel sorry for herself. She said what keeps her moving is giving herself time to grieve and talk about her issues with friends or loved ones. Then, she makes sure she sets a goal for the day no matter how small (like organizing one drawer) so she ends her day feeling accomplished.

Many studies have demonstrated the feeling of isolation when an adult daughter loses her father because of the tendency for others to dismiss the intensity of the loss. The twenties and thirties have been considered the years when the loss of a father feels the most intense. A daughter is expected to bounce back quickly and handle things like an adult, but inside, the loss might be the most significant change she has experienced in her life. She can be faced with insensitive comments from friends, such as "Death is a normal part of life" or "At least you weren't a child." No one knows what you know: You will never really get over this, but you are taking things a day at a time and figuring out how to get through it.

While each form of father loss bears its own pain, we are never really prepared for it to happen to us. Even if the road was long, the end still feels sudden.

Most people are not able to understand the grief that is wrapped around an adult fatherless daughter. Marriages can suffer, family relationships can become strained, and a daughter's well-being can become significantly compromised if she does not receive the support that she needs. Medical research has demonstrated how unresolved pain and grief can manifest as physical sickness or disease. A daughter who has just lost her father needs someone to listen to her, sit alongside her while she cries, and validate (without judgment) the enormity of her loss. She needs this for a long time, as her grief never truly disappears. When she has the support and space to adequately grieve, she will begin to shed the layers of pain and reclaim her future. It happens one day at a time.

There are other situations that can further complicate father loss. Quite often, as a daughter ages, she becomes the caretaker of her aging or sick parents. If you were helping to care for your father before he passed away, you may bear a host of other emotions. You might feel an overwhelming amalgam of guilt, relief, responsibility, regret, sadness, and despair. This is a very difficult road to travel because, depending on the extent of your father's illness, he counted on you, and that has had a substantial impact on your life. While your relationship with him might have deepened and transformed, you also likely had a highly emotional and exhausting journey as his caretaker. There can be many complex issues with prolonged death, including dementia (which means you already lost him once), family discord, taking time away from your own family, and feeling obligated to support your mother or siblings through all of it.

Perhaps there were some unresolved issues between you and your father. Maybe you had not been connected to him for years before his death or lost him a time or two before to divorce or emotional absence. Maybe he never faced his own demons or made things right with you, and you were left behind with unsettled pain. You might have been planning on contacting him, but put it off, and now you feel regret or confusion about your inaction. Perhaps his addiction or lifestyle was the reason that he passed away, and you are angry that he did not change his life to be more present in yours. Weren't you worth it? The psychological truth in these situations is that you will deal with the same issues in his death that you did in his life. But now you know you will never be able to have that conversation and tell him how you truly feel. This is a perfect time for you to seek counseling to help you resolve these issues and find peace and clarity. You need someone to hear and validate what you have carried and offer you empathy for the lack of resolution in your life. Once you feel understood, you can move beyond your questions and create a life of acceptance and growth.

Your experience through this grief is multidimensional, no matter the status of your relationship with your father or the way he left your world. You are not only experiencing reactions on an emotional, physical, and mental level but also on a spiritual level. What is the meaning of it all? How could God let this happen to you? Where can you find answers and strength? How can you find hope for the future? By working on mental and emotional clarification, building up your personal and spiritual connections, and taking care of your physical self with healthy movement and nourishment, you are creating a masterpiece from the inside out . . . and the outside in.

Ask for what you need and accept it when it shows up. Share your story with those who have earned your trust, and lean on them. Tell the truth, feel what you are feeling, and let healing begin. Over time, you will learn that you—not your history—are in charge of your life. In the meantime, protect your family, don't make any other big changes, and shield yourself from those who will invalidate you. Give yourself permission to join friends, laugh, and celebrate life. Release the guilt of enjoying moments and teach yourself to be present to blessings. Let people know if you would like to talk about your dad or if you need a quiet day. Journal, write him a letter, or paint a picture that symbolizes where you are on your journey. Anything that provides a release of emotion will bring you a moment closer to restoration. You are right where you are supposed to be. Feel, honor, and reclaim what is yours.

We hope you are beginning to see how the loss of your father has played an important role in many aspects of your life. By understanding who you were then and who you are now, you can begin to connect past and present and learn to heal. As you discover new strength by learning to live purposefully through your loss, you will find the freedom to reclaim your life.

CHAPTER 4

Family Dynamics

There is no doubt that it is around the family and the home
that all the greatest virtues, the most dominating virtues of
human society, are created, strengthened, and maintained.

~Winston Churchill

In early 2012, as Denna was researching fatherless daughters, she traveled to Chicago for a girls' weekend with a dear friend. That weekend she met Seren, a beautiful and exceptionally smart Jordanian woman who grew up in the States and who was a fatherless daughter. On Valentine's Day in 1981, as a second grader coming home from school, Seren sensed that something was wrong. When she got home, she was told that her beloved father had died from a heart attack.

"At eight, I didn't understand death, mourning, tragedy, loss, pain. I was smart enough to know that Baba wasn't coming back, ever. I remember feeling embarrassed at school, not having a dad. Anytime someone would talk about their father, or mention parent–teacher day, I would turn away or act busy. Later, of course, I couldn't help remembering that of all days it had happened on Valentine's Day."

That wasn't the only death she faced in her young life. When she was thirteen, her brother died from leukemia.

For several years after Baba's (my dad's) death, we would visit his grave, which was next to my brother's. I would wait in the car, once again avoiding, ignoring. I didn't want to show my emotions, or even worse, break down and cry in front of my family. I didn't want to draw that kind of attention. Although I was young, I remember his sense of humor, a jokester. He loved to tease me—laughing all the time. That is something he gave me, his gift of humor. I bet he didn't know that his gift would save me. Laughter and finding humor in difficult times can heal.

I slept in Mom's bed until I was eleven. Looking back, I suffered from separation anxiety. This prevented me from having a "normal" childhood. The true mourning process for me began during my teenage years. Mama became the focus. I often felt bad going out with friends on the weekends and leaving her home alone.

To this day, I mourn Baba's death. Every time I leave my mom, it makes me sad. In my late twenties to early thirties, I would have anxiety and panic attacks, always in the mornings, just as I would be waking up, thinking, "Oh my God, I only have this one life. I'm not spending enough time with my family. I miss my mom. I'm scared, I need to do all the things I want to do before I die."

I believe the experience has defined me on some level. The first word that comes to my mind is *strong*. When I pray to God, the first thing I thank Him for is just that. "Thank you, God, for I am very grateful for all that You have given me. Please continue to give me the strength and guidance that I need to live a fulfilled and content life. Protect my family and friends, for they bring so much comfort and joy into my world."

Despite the tragedy that has struck my family, we all seem to have found an optimistic view of now, and for what is yet to come. Some people, even friends, don't understand my "Let's do it!" perspective on life. I wake up every morning with the goal of doing the things I enjoy the most: dining, working out, seeing movies, traveling, and being in the company of friends and family. I try not to waste a moment.

Experiencing the death of a loved one forces you to dig deeper; it compels you to find truth and meaning in life. Because you know how very precious life can be and how very quickly life can be taken from you. Sometimes I feel at peace, and other times I don't, naturally. I've learned to accept this. The times I don't, I simply remember the first sentence in the book *The Road Less Traveled*. "Life is difficult." I find solace in this. Indeed, life is difficult.

In the Wake of Loss

When the father leaves the family or passes away, those left behind are now missing something critical in their lives. There is an empty space at the family table. The dynamics in the family can take a dramatic shift, roles change (for a few years or permanently) as each family rewrites the way the family script is played without Dad.

Sometimes an individual makes a dramatic shift in his or her life. Perhaps Mom goes back to work or school and becomes the breadwinner and an older sibling takes on the role of caretaker to younger siblings, or another family member moves in. Your mother's reaction to the loss can have a great impact on your life, as you look to her as your guide. If you have siblings, the road can be easier or more challenging with traveling companions. These relationships can deepen or become fraught with conflict as each sibling deals with the loss in his or her own way. Generally, how your family behaved with one another before the loss will be a great predictor of what will happen after it. People can move apart, come together, or continue the sibling rivalry until they are eighty. Yes, at eighty, it still matters who was the favorite.

Nora, forty-four, shares the story about her complicated family dynamics after her father passed away: "It was my worst nightmare. When my dad died, even though he had been sick for a long time, it was a total and complete shock. Between my mom, my brother, my sister, and my half-siblings, it was like a bomb exploded in the living room. All of the things that were wrong before got worse.

"My family has always felt like Dad favored our half-siblings, and while it caused a lot of pain when he was alive, it felt worse now that he was gone. All of us are so grief-stricken over his death, but it seems like our sadness keeps turning into anger.

"I was taking care of him when he passed, and I cannot seem to get past that. I feel like I could have done something else to keep him alive. It's overwhelming. No one understands how I feel. Everyone is too busy with their own stuff. I feel like I need to take care of everyone else but on the inside I feel like I am tortured. We all keep competing over who gets what and who has the last word on family decisions. I am so tired of all of the stress. It's taking its toll on all of us."

What Nora describes is not uncommon because of the huge role that a father is supposed to fulfill in his family. When that is yanked from the home, the family as a whole, and each of its members, gets thrown off-kilter.

The Bowen Center for the Study of the Family has developed a theory about family dynamics: "It is the nature of the family that its members are intensely connected emotionally. Often people feel distant or disconnected from their families, but this is more feeling than fact. Family members so profoundly affect each other's thoughts, feelings, and actions that it often seems as if people are living under the same 'emotional skin.' People solicit one another's attention, approval, and support and react to one another's needs, expectations, and distress. The connectedness and reactivity make the functioning of family members interdependent. A change in one person's functioning is predictably followed by reciprocal changes in the functioning of others."

Looking at the family this way explains the monumental task of reorganization required when a father dies or leaves the family unit. The family has to tend to one another and themselves, finding new places of relating. Family members will deal with the loss differently, based on the relationships that were present beforehand. Keep in mind, your ages at the time of your father's departure will influence how you each think about and react to the loss. So family members can come together, bump up against each other, and drift apart, as they search for a way to find personal stability and family connection. It is not an easy task. Even people with the greatest of intentions can get misunderstood, hurt, and bruised along the way.

Each family member's bond with the father was unique—some were close, some were fractured, some had seasons of both. Likewise, the family members' existing relationships with one another will be affected as the stages of grief play themselves out. From the arrangements of the funeral, to working out any unresolved issues, to the mom (or a child) adapting to the new role of head of the family, families can experience very emotional, complicated journeys. Some family members find that they share similar emotions and can bond in new, more intimate ways, while others might open old wounds and engage in the blame game instead of dealing with their own anger about what happened, or did not happen, when Dad was around. The way families react to the loss is generally the way they react to any crisis, collectively and as individuals.

If your father is still alive, the family dynamics play out in similar ways. One sibling may forgive more easily, while the other holds on to the hurt. There can be confusion and, often times, blame between siblings when their own agendas differ. We all heal differently and grow along our own timelines. Some of us pray for forgiveness and unity, while others get stuck in grief and victimization.

Your Mother

For many fatherless daughters, Mom took on the roles of both mother and father. It probably was not what she dreamed of when she had children with your father, yet it is where life's path took her. Have you thought about those days? What was it like when Dad left or passed away? How did your mother change? How has it been between the two of you? Have you taken the time to reflect on your journey together?

We, Karin and Denna, have both also had meaningful journeys with our mothers. Despite all of the pushing and pulling, we are closer to them than ever because we are joint survivors. We draw strength today from what they did in the past and how they taught us to stand up for ourselves and discover our own paths. It is because of them that we are able to write this book. Denna's mother taught her to have strength and confidence in who she was and what she had to offer the world. She also encouraged Denna and Denna's brother to use laughter as a coping mechanism to get through much of the pain. "Of course, looking back, things were not always easy. The three of us were all finding our own way. We were all in so much pain over my father's absence, but when we could, we laughed."

Karin's mother gave her spiritual strength and encouraged her to work hard on her own healing. "My mom is extraordinary—despite the losses and challenges of her own life. Her ability to survive the storm and speak her truth makes her my hero. I would not be as healthy, courageous, and spiritually grounded as I am today had it not been for her."

Your dad was gone and you were left with your mother. How your mom handled the loss has had a tremendous bearing on your connection with her and how you see the world. Although we strive for independence from our mothers, a mother's affection, treatment, and responses to us are extremely powerful and lay part of the foundation for our lives. When a father dies or leaves, a daughter looks to her mother for support and guidance for how to respond. Where did that leave you and your mom? Was she preoccupied with her loss and not attentive to yours? Was she a source of love and support?

In our interviews, we came across some daughters who had very strained relationships with their mothers both before and after their fathers left. In some instances, daughters said they felt that their mothers blamed them for their fathers leaving. Others reported that addictions and lack of good coping skills led to their mothers being both mentally and physically absent.

Alice, twenty-one, said she felt her mother was always in competition with her.

> After my dad left, my mom seemed to go backward and started dating her high school sweetheart. It was a volatile relationship from the beginning. They would fight and make up on a monthly basis. My mom's boyfriend would routinely remark that I had a good body. It made me feel uncomfortable, and even more so when my mom was around. Looking back, I think she started becoming jealous because it was like I was "the other woman" living in the house with this man who was not my real dad. To top things off, we just stopped talking about my dad. Her boyfriend made her take all of the pictures down of our family and get rid of everything of my dad's. I felt so helpless watching Dad's things disappear one by one. Mom became so consumed with her new relationship. She started borrowing my clothes, trying to lose weight and dress much

younger than her age. It was beyond embarrassing for me—it was like she was competing with me. There were so many times I wanted to tell her that she deserved better, that I did not feel right about him, but I knew it would fall on deaf ears. I couldn't get out of there fast enough when I turned eighteen. Luckily I knew what I *didn't* want in a husband or in my own home, and I ended up marrying a wonderful man despite my childhood. I think my mom still harbors resentment toward me; she is still ultra-competitive, but I have learned to pull myself out of it. The difference is that she sees herself as a victim. I do not.

Another daughter we spoke to, Serena, thirty-four, who lost her father to prison when she was in elementary school and is still estranged from him, talked to us about the co-dependent relationship she has had with her mother her entire life.

"My mom goes from relationship to relationship looking for love and money; the money is always the most important thing to her. Her relationships never last. I feel sorry for her, or at least I did for a very long time. She always calls me after a breakup asking me to pay her car insurance or property taxes. Keep in mind that she does not work and lives in a half-a-million-dollar home that is totally paid off. I finally started seeing a therapist because I was having anxiety attacks last summer. When I told my therapist that I felt guilty that my mom was alone and always seemed to be struggling, she told me to replace the word *guilty* with *empathy* when speaking of my mom. I have to tell you, it completely changed my outlook. Now I can have feelings because she is my mom, yet I don't have to feel guilty anymore."

While we think it is important to talk about what happened in the past so you can better understand the circumstances and aftermath of your loss, your mother may not be as open to speaking about it as you might wish. Our generation is one of self-help and self-reflection, whereas many of our parents may have been taught to push aside the pain and try to leave it behind them. Unsealing deep-rooted hurt can be painful and will no doubt be emotional. Ask for what you need from your mom, keep a check on your expectations, and work on understanding her experience from your adult perspective. But remember that you are still the daughter. You can give each other support, but each of you must deal with your own issues. By doing so, you can give each other the gifts of honesty, compassion, and patience, reforming your relationship into one of growth for both of you.

Father Loss Is Different from Mother Loss

Hope Edelman affirms the findings of the 1996 Harvard Child Bereavement Study in her book *Motherless Daughters*: "In general, mother loss is harder on children than father loss, mainly because it results in more daily life changes for a child. In most families, the death of a mother means the loss of the emotional caretaker, and a child has to adapt to all that this means and implies." This explains the fundamental reason why father loss is not understood to be such a traumatic loss in a child's life. It is commonly believed that Dad might leave, but it is understood that Mom will stay.

Because of its prevalence in our society, father loss can be minimized, which may leave the daughter with little understanding of what it all means. Mother loss is more openly mourned as people tend to gather around the daughter, validating the enormity of her loss, stepping in to help care for her and her family. Father loss is usually not dealt with at the same level of urgency. As a result, a daughter's needs, emotions, and life changes might go unnoticed, pushing the internal struggle underground as the world around her continues to travel forward.

Who Is the Parent?

Depending on the age that you were when your father left or passed away, you may have gone into caretaking mode to help your mother through the challenges of facing life alone, although you were hurting deeply yourself. If your mom wasn't able to comfort you, you may have resented her for not acting as your parent. On the other hand, you may have felt guilty about not having helped her in her time of need. A "temporary" dependent or co-dependent relationship can last into adulthood. Eliza, thirty-nine, looks back on when this role reversal happened in her life:

> I have felt protective over my mom my entire life. I was two when my father died. Mom married my stepfather two years later. We never really talked about my birth father in our new family. We just kind of moved on, which left me feeling lost about the other half of me as I started to try to make sense of things over the years. Eventually, my stepfather ended up being caught in numerous affairs and was being sued for sexual harassment at work. I was eighteen and had just started college when everything erupted and Mom finally left. Guess where she came? My college dorm room.
>
> She just showed up one day, pretending to be on a surprise visit. That night, she broke down sitting on my bed, telling me everything—about the abuse, the affairs, and the pain she was in. She cried like a little girl in my arms. I just held her. It totally turned my life upside down and made me hit a place of tremendous confusion about who I was. But I had to help my mom get through her pain, so I held it together around her and did not let her know how much I was also falling apart. She needed me, and I felt so blessed that she trusted me.

For that week, it was just us. Life permanently changed for everyone, and so I felt so very sad for her and the end of our family. But the timing had my heart and needs in conflict. I was in college, and I wanted to sprout my wings, not fly back to the nest—but I was so torn. She needed me, but I needed to grow. It took a long time and counseling to work through all of our stuff, but we did and now love each other from a much more honest place of knowing and understanding.

Eliza's story expresses the common conflicting feelings toward the mother that many fatherless daughters feel: guilt, worry, and the need to care take along with the frustration of putting off her own healing. Guilt can become a driving force in her life for good reason: She loves her mother. She hates to see her mom hurting, and her mother has probably made remarks about needing her daughter along the way. If the daughter took care of her mother before taking care of herself, their relationship could be tense.

To be fair, Mom deserves a break; she truly needs support, and her daughter is likely her closest ally. For many fatherless daughters, Mom sits right up there close to all the saints for valid reasons. It was our mothers who had to forge ahead after our dads were gone. They had to go it alone. They may have had to not only take on the majority of the parenting and domestic duties but also shoulder the financial stressors of living with a single income. Doing that and washing every towel and sock in the house between work shifts and carpool was not easy.

The way a fatherless daughter's mother coped with her family's situation not only affected the mother's journey but the daughter's as well. If she found a way to figure it out quickly, her daughter did too. If Mom floundered, coped poorly, and engaged in failed relationships, her daughter learned by watching. If the mother gathered support and took care of herself, her daughter was taught to do the same. In fact, the Washington State Parenting Act Study concluded, "Children of divorce do better when the well-being of the primary residential parent, [the mother], is high. Primary residential parents who are experiencing psychological, emotional, social, economic, or health difficulties may transfer these difficulties to their children and are often less able to parent effectively. Primary parents tend to function best when they have strong support networks, such as kin, friends, and support groups, and when they have residential and financial security."

Without your mom knowing it, she might project her own thoughts, judgments, and coping mechanisms onto you. This can cause inconsistencies in the emotional connection between the two of you *and* between you and your father and siblings. She might forget for a while that your loss is also overwhelming, and as a result your needs may get put on a shelf. She might forget that you are half of him and by putting him down she is hurting you. It is unfair to expect a daughter to be a confidante when it comes to the unresolved matters between her parents. The mother might lean on her daughter like she would a best friend, which is a tremendous burden for a daughter to carry around, eclipsing her needs to unburden her own pain. The fatherless daughter then becomes the listener, the nurturer, and the holder of secrets. Often being too young to navigate through the new open field of adult expression, she feels obligated to do what she can to side with her mother and protect her, even through her own confusion.

How do you cope with all of this, take care of yourself, and move forward as your own woman, while also having the responsibility of taking care of your mother? With increased self-awareness, honesty, and reflection on what happened over the years.

Clara, forty-six, told us about her situation with her mom. Her father died in a car accident when she was twenty-three, and things were tough. She says:

When everything happened, Mom fell apart and my three sisters and I had to take care of her. Today things are better, but she still really does not have her own life, so she is overly involved in mine. The most difficult thing was learning to tell her no or back off. . . . When I stayed with her, she got very involved in my dating life and always had something to say. There was a lot of clashing between us because of her need to control me. For instance, she was terrified that I would die in a car accident. Every time I left the house, whether I was driving or not, it was a big deal. I had to keep her posted constantly on my whereabouts, and I just wanted room to grow.

I talked to my friends a lot and finally met my husband, which made things even more difficult because I got more independent. Mom was so used to having me around. I was the caretaker in the family. But after I got married, I had to draw the line. It was one of the hardest things I've ever done, but one of the best, too. I had to learn how to stop telling her everything and instead encourage her to have her own life. In a sense, I was still the caretaker, but it helped. She still tries to butt in and manage my life, but I have learned how to say, "I understand your opinion, thank you," and move on with my own choices. I had to do that work for both of us.

As Clara's story demonstrates, fatherless daughters can experience years of choices to enmesh, distance, or find a healthy balance with their mothers. There is no simple formula and the best-case scenario creates a connection between mother and daughter while respecting the independence of each. When you reflect on your own relationship with your mother, you can start realizing which of your needs were met and be grateful for that. As you reflect, you can also uncover the needs that were not met and find a way to reconcile any old wounds so you can heal.

As you mature and step into the world on your own—perhaps becoming a professional, a wife, or a mother—you may realize you are walking in similar shoes that your own mother once did. You may start to see and understand her in a different way. You may now be the age she was when she experienced her loss, and you may wonder how in the world she got through it. You might find yourself amazed that she was able to handle it, or perhaps you begin to feel resentful that she made some bad choices. As you begin to understand all that occurred in your family, you will likely more fully understand why things played out the way they did as well as have new questions that you'd like answered.

You may see your mom in a new way. She was doing the best she could with what she had. Have compassion. Ask for more details if you are ready for them. Maybe you can begin to understand more fully the home she grew up in, her own relationship with her father, and what her mother taught her about womanhood and handling stress. Just like you, she coped in ways that she thought were best. As an adult, you are wiser and perhaps see that things might not have turned out as you would wish. Seeing your relationship with your mother in a new light can leave you feeling a mixed bag of gratitude, guilt, and disappointment. This is a significant stage for a fatherless daughter and can help cultivate healing.

Seek a counselor to help you figure out your authentic feelings and decide what you want to work on in your mother–daughter relationship. If you feel like it might bring you closer, let your mom know that you want to move forward and heal by working through some things on your own. The ideal situation would be for her to do the same and then meet you in the middle to find a space for growth as well as increased trust and restoration between you. We have heard many wonderful stories of mothers and daughters going to family therapy together, opening up to each other, or taking a trip together to be completely open and willing to bring healing to each other. You never know when those moments will come, and they are gifts when they do.

Gabby, twenty-two, whose father died of suicide, had a surprise moment with her mom, with a little help.

My first real job after nursing school was at a Catholic hospital on the critical care floor. My mom worked in the building attached to the hospital. My job was both overwhelming and liberating. I was finally making my own money. After my father died money was tight, and I vowed then that I would focus on my education, graduate, and get a good job so I could take care of myself. I would not be like my mother and be dependent on a man.

One day, I went in to see Sister Mary Jenks, a therapist, to talk about a patient. I was the last person to visit her that day. She told me she had had a slow day and would love to spend some time with me. My shift was over so I took the plunge. Within five minutes, I was sobbing uncontrollably about how this family was about to lose their father. Before I realized it, we were talking about my own father loss. She soon became my confidante about everything. I saw her every week like clockwork, and I loved it.

I ended up confiding in her about everything. I told her how I really wanted to travel the world and that working as a travel nurse seemed to be my ticket out, yet the thought of me leaving my mother gave me anxiety. She was my best friend. Sister Jenks mentioned nonchalantly that I should ask my mother to come to our next session. The next week my mom and I walked in hand in hand. Sister Jenks quickly got down to business. "Gabby tells me she wants to travel the world. How do you feel about that?" *Gulp!* Was she crazy? I had not told my mom that. I panicked.

With that, my mom smiled. "I know Gabby is a dreamer. I doubt she would ever leave her hometown, though," she said, winking at me. Sister Jenks turned her attention to me. "Does your mom know that you have been saving money to start traveling?" I quietly said, "Umm. I don't think I have mentioned it." Then I turned to my mom and started to cry because I cried about everything. "I have a money jar. One day I would like to move away and see the world. I would wait until you were remarried and happy, though. I mean, I am not ready to go yet," I said as tears rolled down my cheeks. I felt like a fifteen-year-old again. My mom started to cry because she cries all the time too. Sister Jenks looked at my mom and placed her hand on her knee. "Your daughter is ready to spread her wings. It is you who is holding her back. She is ready. Gabby just needs to know that you do not need her to stay for you." Our joint therapy session changed the course of my life. It was the first realization I had ever had that I was OK. I could walk away. It was my mom I was staying for.

If you and your mother have unresolved issues, and those dynamics are hurting your life, it's OK to make a change. Your mom is a big girl and will be fine. She may simply be continuing in a comfortable pattern and has no idea how it may be constricting you. It is hoped that by opening the door to conversations, you can both release shame and allow love and empathy in. There can be some beautiful moments for you to share because you survived things together. Find those golden nuggets and realize that your mother was a woman (just like you) trying to make it the best she could with what she knew. She deserves credit for getting you all through the years. But you also need to live your own life, and with support, you can balance gratitude with honesty and make the changes that you need to create a healthier dynamic between the two of you.

Your Father

Your father is gone, whether by choice or not, and he is not filling the paternal space in your life. You might be shouldering a backpack of jumbled emotions including remorse, anger, and sadness. These feelings may pop up at unsuspecting moments, leaving you feeling raw and riddled with anxiety. It is very likely you are confused about what to do with these emotions because your dad is not there to help you. How in the world are you supposed to resolve things without him in the picture?

First, every single emotion you are carrying is valid. No apologies. No shame. No self-judgment. The beginning of self-growth is acknowledging and accepting what is present. What we know for sure is that fatherless daughters tend to stuff their own feelings deeply. If they have learned to cope with life's challenges by stuffing, it can take an enormous amount of strength and vulnerability to pull themselves up and begin to deal with all that they have suppressed. Years of refusing to acknowledge one's feelings can result in the manifesting of certain coping mechanisms, such as not sharing your opinions with others for fear of rejection, putting other people's needs in front of your own so much that people simply expect that from you, and never letting people see you cry even when you want to. By routinely pushing the mute button on your own feelings, you can fulfill your belief that your feelings are not valuable. But this can change. Speaking up and revealing the emotions you have so fiercely guarded for so long can begin to free your mind and lighten your heart.

Identify your feelings in a letter, a counseling session, or by telling your absent dad out loud how you feel as you sit with his picture. Name the feelings and let them out. Ask the questions that keep stirring in your heart. Did he regret his choices? How could he leave you behind?

Why did he do what he did? Why are you left holding all of this all by yourself? Take some time to release what has been festering inside of you. Shame and pain love nothing more than staying locked up inside of you where they can have more power to keep you feeling like a victim. They hate truth, and they hate to be acknowledged, because those are the two things that disarm them.

As a counselor, Karin has helped fatherless daughters find their voices through whatever channel of expression feels most authentic to them. Some find release through journaling, others express themselves through artwork, and some simply take a long walk in the park and talk through their feelings in the outdoors. One particular client, Dani, had a great deal of unfinished business with her father, who had left the family when she was fifteen. This became increasingly apparent during the sessions as Dani often said things like, "I just wish I could tell him how much his leaving affected my life" and "I just wonder how he could explain what he did." So Karin and she agreed to use a Gestalt-based role-play called the Empty Chair Technique. This method can be extremely useful. The fatherless daughter expresses her feelings to an empty chair, which represents her father. After she speaks her piece, she sits in the chair and talks back to herself as if she were her dad. This form of role-play creates a safe space for self-reflection and allows for thoughtful processing about what the other person would say.

Although the sessions became very emotional, it was a huge turning point for Dani. She got to spill all of the feelings that she had bottled up and pour them onto the chair that represented her dad. She also got to sit in her dad's place and attempt to make sense of what he might say or what was going on in his life. Dani was able to tell herself, as she role-played her father, that he was just not capable of being the father she needed. He could not handle the demands and did not get along with her mother. Dani basically looked herself in the eyes and said, "It's not about you, it's about him." For the first time, she was able to see this clearly, and as the sessions continued, Dani's awareness about her own feelings and her father began to come together. By committing to doing this type of work when she wanted to deal with something about her dad, Dani also learned how to express herself and became more assertive and confident.

Moving from acknowledgment to understanding to healing is a journey, and you are already on your way. Now that you are an adult, clarify your story and get a more informed grasp on what happened. Call trusted relatives, ask to see documents, and look through family albums. Talk to someone who is safe, write out your feelings, and go through any form of expression that feels releasing to you. If you have some things to work out with your father, *you* are the one who has to do it, but not without support. You can start right now by not taking on the blame or the guilt of causing his departure or of not doing enough. You did the best you could do. Although you are an adult now, you were not back then.

There is one thing that will never change, no matter where you are on your journey: You are his daughter, and he is your dad. He was supposed to be there throughout your life. Because he was absent from it, you have known there was a void next to you through important milestones and events. Although he is not here, part of him is here because you are thinking about him. And, some believe, if he has passed on, there is a great chance that he actually *is* here watching over you. It is said that relationships never actually die; they just change forms. What you two had has not disappeared, it has just transformed. And that form, emotions and all, travels with you wherever you go, whether anyone else knows it or not. Violet, thirty-one, found solace after her father's death in spiritual counseling. She explained how she has had many sessions over the years where she has had spiritual communication with her father. "I have found peace knowing that my father is still around me in some form. It has helped me to work through my feelings in a beautiful way that is all about love and acceptance. The gift is that I actually feel closer to him now than I ever did before."

If Your Dad Left by Choice and Is Still Living

Selena, nineteen, is a child of divorce and her father is an addict. She told us:

> My dad is around. I mean, I can get him on the phone or to exchange a text message or two, if he is not busy. He tells me he loves me if I say it first, but I just don't know. He is not there for me like other dads. He forgets to acknowledge most birthdays or give me a gift. I struggle with guilt because he is not gone, per se; he is still out there. My parents divorced when I was three, but the first time he left was when I was six weeks old. Recently, I have started to get mad and confrontational.
>
> I contacted him and went to see him and my stepmom over spring break. He only spent one night out of four in the house. I am sure he is cheating on her just like he did to us. On my last day there I got up the nerve to ask him a question I wish I had never asked. "Dad, why don't you ever want to spend time with me on the rare occasion that I get to see you?" I wanted him to apologize and tell me things would be different. But he just looked over at me and said, matter-of-factly, "We really just don't have much in common." I will just never understand what I am to him.

Having a father who is alive yet choosing to live his life without you can be the ultimate emotional abandonment. It is confusing and disheartening to a daughter who deeply craves her dad's love. The pain and disillusionment is understandable, but if you have reached a point where it's clear that you can do nothing to change things, you should spend your time focusing on other things in your life that bring you validation and strength. His walking away from you was not your choice—you were the child, he was the adult. Reclaim the value of *you*.

If you are the child of a bitter divorce or the daughter of a man who is emotionally detached, major milestones can bring on feelings of intense anger and isolation. You grow, you live your life, and there is an empty chair next to you, even if no one else sees it. Maybe his invitation to your high school graduation was returned in the mail or he simply never returns your phone calls. One day you will probably have to explain to your soon-to-be mother-in-law that your father will not be walking you down the aisle or paying for the wedding or attending your child's baptism or bat mitzvah. Or that he may show up, uninvited. All of these realizations can leave you feeling embarrassed, abandoned again, and emotionally vulnerable.

You cannot make excuses for your father or the circumstances that he created nor do you need to forever cling to the story of why he is not in your life. This is your life now and you can decide the direction of your conversations. You may use your go-to story until you feel comfortable enough to share what is really in your heart, or you may decide that you don't need to explain anything at all. Although you might secretly wait for him to run in late to your graduation ceremony or show up at your daughter's sixteenth birthday, you can come to terms with what is possible and what isn't, even if it hurts for that moment. It can be quite liberating to release shame or blame and accept what is. Decide to reclaim your life by letting go of what is not yours and embracing what is.

Julia, thirty-one, did just that. After receiving counseling for her father's abandonment, she felt clearer and more excited about her own life. She hired Denna as her life coach, to help her define her goals and set a plan in place. She quit her job at a law firm to explore her love of photography. Today she is an in-demand photographer who credits coaching and therapy as her two best friends. She says, "My life now is so much better than I could have ever imagined. Letting go of the resentment that trapped me for so many years gave me the freedom to find my true calling."

In our documentary, beloved and retired Atlanta news anchor Monica Pearson talks about the insight she has gained through the years, after becoming fatherless as a baby and ultimately reconciling her loss in later adulthood: "What [a fatherless daughter] really needs from her father if he's not there is to understand that he's not there because of *you*. He's not there because of what's going on with *him*. That you did nothing wrong. . . . You wonder, 'What could I have done that made you give me life but then not want to see me grow into that life?' And I think when you realize that is their problem, not yours, that you can't take on that guilt—that's theirs—only then can you grow into the woman that you are supposed to be."

Monica's words remind us that grief is a process and that age brings more than wrinkles—it delivers wise rewards.

A Stand-In Father

If you did not have anyone notice that you needed a stand-in father figure in your life, you had a tougher journey than those who did. The road toward learning how to be comfortable in a male–female relationship might be more challenging for you—you never got to peek at a road map. Coming to terms with the absence of male support in your life is also a part of your healing process. This can feel like another rejection, as you truly were worth being protected and guided. A caring person should have stepped in safely and strongly for you and held on when your dad left. Someone should have been checking on you, cheering for you, and loving you through your life's milestones and rough spots. You deserved that.

You might decide that it would be meaningful to cultivate a nonintimate, safe male friendship in your life to experience trust and closeness with. If you want to fill in the gaps of things you might have missed, talk to your girlfriends about the lessons that they learned from their fathers and read articles written by loving fathers. Pray for a feeling of safety and love, especially on days when you feel alone. Ask a mentor to help you develop standards in your life and build your self-confidence. Deepen your connection with a higher power so that you might feel a spiritual blessing of the ultimate fatherly love. Forging these connections will help you to learn what you need to know about yourself, seeing your value, and building your own self-confidence. Your role in your own restoration can serve as powerful evidence to the resilience and strength that have always been inside of you.

If Your Dad Passed Away

If your father passed away, he is still very much with you. After all, he is half of your DNA. Your relationship with him since he died has likely been confusing, painful, and overwhelming. If he was a good father, you know what you are missing, and you feel a deep emotional void where he once stood.

If you had a close relationship with your father and you feel that your connection is going out of focus, don't let it. Keep his memory alive with every milestone. Decorate your home with pictures of him and talk to your kids and loved ones about your bond with your father. When you are ready, peruse any old letters or watch old movies. He was and will always be your father. Countless daughters revealed that they still talk to their fathers and can feel his presence. Some pray for signs of guidance from him when making a decision, while others talk out loud to him in their car or as they go about their day.

If you were estranged from your father or hardly knew him before his death, you may have to depend on other family members to help fill in the blanks. Initially, it may be emotionally difficult for you to be vulnerable enough to ask for what you need. Also, what you need may not be available or possible. Sometimes, after time has passed, people can't remember intricate details of events, the people you most need to speak to may have passed on or you have long since lost contact with them. Most people have no idea how much a single story can bring comfort to a fatherless daughter. Ask for it.

For Denna, "Hearing stories about my father can bring him back to life for a moment. It is kind of like finding a four-leaf clover when you have been looking in the grass for years. I encourage anyone who has lost a father to ask people who knew him to share their stories. When Karin and I got the green light to write this book my mother sent me some yellow roses with beautiful pink tips on them. When I called her to thank her and tell her how uniquely gorgeous they were she said, 'Your dad used to send me the same flowers.' A huge smile came over my face. The gesture now took on an even more personal meaning."

It is also a great idea to speak to your siblings to better understand their relationship with your father. After all, you shared him. Ask them to tell you about their memories of specific moments or stories and you try and do the same. Share with each other how you saw him and related to him. You may surprise each other with new insight. Putting the pieces back together is not an easy undertaking, but it is deeply meaningful. Let those close to you know what you are attempting to do. Ask for help. Going back in order to move forward can have huge emotional rewards and liberate you to embrace the present with a deeper understanding of the truth.

Siblings

Without a doubt, your relationship with your siblings will be affected by your father's absence. Your siblings are the only ones who share your story. While this can deepen your relationship, it can also put a strain on it because each of your relationships with your father was unique, and that made it special, difficult, or both.

One child may have been closer to him, one punished more, or one had more years with him. Perhaps there are adopted, stepsiblings, or half-siblings that further complicate the puzzle. Each of you has a grief that is your own, and you should. You knew him at different times in his life, and you experienced him in your own way. You played off each other differently, and you saw his relationships with others through your own lenses. You might not see things the same way as your siblings, and that can cause friction into adulthood. You each are going to face your own struggles with the pain of his absence. If you were the favorite, your siblings might resent you. If you recover more easily, your siblings might punish you. If one of you has taken on the role of the black sheep, that sibling may feel like he or she is the primary victim of the family loss. Each of you will react out of your established roles with your father, wherein you will find endearing commonalities as well as wide differences.

Angie, thirty-three, has faced challenges with her brother since their dad left the family:

> We were both still in middle school when Dad and Mom divorced. It was really hard—we handled things so differently. I ended up struggling for a few years, but after getting my degree, I decided that I was going to prove to the world that my life would mean something, so I opened up a shelter for abused dogs. Meanwhile,

my brother struggled with alcoholism for years and has gotten multiple DUIs, which meant he could not keep a job. He has been diagnosed with depression but refuses to get help. It breaks my heart because I love him so much. He could have done anything he wanted, but the pain seemed to hold him back in every way. He sees himself as the victim of a life that should have been. It makes me so sad. All of these years, I have tried to support him and fix things but I can't. I can't make up for how much Dad hurt us. [My brother] wants to remain the victim, and I do not. We just see things so differently now.

Research has shown that fatherless sons, like Angie's brother, tend to go through a much more complicated psychological battle due to the loss of the father, often leading to delinquency, depression, and questions about their identity. They feel like their loss is bigger and harder. Many times they are angry if their mother remarries, for they feel they need to be the top priority and at the same time protect her or the memory of their fathers. Other sons feel burdened that they are expected to be the man of the house and can get lost in adjusting to the new expectations put on them. It is a role they never asked for. How do they win? It is the same story; their childhoods were also cut short.

Your age, gender, and place in the birth order at the time that your dad went absent greatly influenced the way you and your siblings experience the loss. It is usually understood (although not always the case) that the oldest child tends to gravitate toward positions of leadership, the youngest child tends to feel more comfortable in a role behind the scenes, and the middle kid can be caught somewhere in between.

Often, in sibling groups, each chooses his or her place as either the hero, the mediator, the black sheep, or the jokester. Of course, this theory is not binding, as we have seen many families where the siblings turn out totally opposite, but it is interesting to consider. Think back to your childhood and what you felt was expected of you during good moments and trying moments. Because of where your sibling position lined up, you had a relationship with your father based on how he perceived you. Can you see how that influences your feelings and actions today? Knowing your role and place in the sibling dynamic could be very helpful for you in understanding why you processed the loss the way you did and why your feelings might be so different from your siblings'.

Your time with your dad also has had a tremendous impact on how you have related to your siblings since he has been gone. If you were born first, you had more years with him, therefore, you likely have more memories. The youngest child might not feel the same attachment if the father was taken away when he or she was very young, and that can cause frustration and resentment. The older sibling might resent that the younger one is not feeling the depth of emotions he or she is feeling, and the younger sibling might feel guilt that he or she is not feeling the same intensity, or vice versa. These discrepancies in sibling order also lay the groundwork for jealousy or sibling rivalry, just as it did when Dad was in the home. These feelings do not disappear when he leaves— in some families, they may become more intense because of the complex layering of emotions that occurs when Dad is gone. On the other hand, these differences can also be what brings siblings closer together if they choose to embark on a road of openness and reconciliation together to honor the bond of their shared experiences.

There can be a dramatic shift in family roles when Dad is taken away. If he was the head of the household, who is left to carry the torch? Who is closer to Mom now? Are you taking sides? Who is the truth teller? Who is the black sheep? Who is the caretaker? Who gets the heck out of Dodge and builds a life far away? If estrangement, mental illness, addiction, or any other serious challenges enter the picture, the family can experience another emotional loss. Making your family a priority by listening to one another, avoiding judgment, and trying to understand that you have your own journeys can release tension when honesty is honored. You have been through so much together, and your relationships are worth fighting for. Take a step back and ask for a family meeting, leaving accusations, negativity, or blame at the door.

Have a heart-to-heart talk together as siblings and give every person his or her own time to have the floor. If you can, agree that you are all different, all have authentic feelings, and no one is wrong or right. You can agree that you will do your best to show respect (despite what you are thinking). Even if you disagree, you all desire the same thing: to be heard and understood for your own feelings and not be judged.

Angela, fifty-two, said that she found that she and her sister did better when they did not include their respective spouses in conversations over disagreements. She said, "We have our own dynamic that our husbands just don't seem to get. For us, it is best to use the truce words *time out* when things get too heated between us. It allows us to take a step back and cool off before things are said that we cannot take back."

Truce words are just one example of something that may work when you and your siblings get together. It can also be healing to take time to laugh—tell those silly family stories about who seemed to accidentally injure every family pet or liked to collect ceramic pigs for a spell. Knowing that fun will be part of your get-togethers will help you all look forward to releasing some steam with the few people in the world who really know the whole story.

You Are an Only Child

Although siblings have differing relationships with their father, as an only child there is no one who also knew him as a father. An only child can feel as if there is no one in the world who will ever truly comprehend what she feels—she is a lone wolf. An only child may have isolated herself, been in disbelief, or suffered pain and anger about being alone to cope with the loss of her father. Because only children tend to develop an independent personality, those around her might not have been able to interpret her isolation as a cry for help. People may have thought she was stronger than she felt on the inside.

If you are an only child and your mother was in your life, your relationship with her most likely transformed and you probably sought out others for comfort and connection, very likely those who were also lone travelers. Let friends and family know you need support and let down the tough-girl exterior if you are feeling weak on the inside. It is OK to be mad that you had to go it alone and you did not have a sibling to share the burden of loss. Talk about it, write it down, and express what you have carried on your own. You will find that others can relate to you more than you think.

Stepfathers, Stepfamilies

Half of divorced women get remarried within five years after the divorce. The likelihood that a fatherless daughter has had a stepfather or stepsiblings is pretty high. This adds an entirely new dynamic to the story. These new families can prove far more challenging than the original family, and research shows that stepfamilies are likely to have up to three times the amount of stress of those in first marriages during the first few years.

It seems that the majority of people think that they are going to do it better the next time around, only to have the second or third marriage turn out like the first. If the work has been done to face the issues that were malfunctioning in the first family, there is a much better chance that better choices will be made and healthier family dynamics will be put in place when starting a new family unit. However, if there is hastiness, or they do not face and work through the emotional fall-out from the first loss of the father, the family is likely to repeat the same patterns in the future.

A lot of questions can go through a fatherless daughter's mind when a new family is formed. How valuable is she going to feel now that there are other people in the family? Will her mom change? Whom can she trust? Just how much authority will her new dad have over her and the family? What about her biological dad? If there are stepsiblings, there can be complex sibling rivalry, as everyone wants to maintain or establish special spots in the family hierarchy.

A primary challenge in stepfamilies is adjusting roles for the individual members. It can be unclear where you are going to fall in the mix, and accepting your new stepfather can be an uncomfortable adjustment, especially if you are still grieving your birth father. Maybe you got a new last name or were told to act in a different way. Perhaps you noticed preferential treatment toward certain children. Maybe you thought your new stepfather was terrific, but you struggled with how to accept him in your life since you still missed your dad.

Anna, forty-two, reflects on how she felt as a child getting a new dad and how confusing it was for her.

My parents divorced when I was four, and Mom got custody of me and my sister. Dad moved to another state, and I remember Mom working and dating. We visited my dad twice a year, with little communication in between. Mom finally remarried just after I turned six, and we got a little brother in the deal. Our stepdad, Jack, made it pretty clear that he preferred his son over us—it was just how it was. We knew we were not *really* his daughters, and although

I deeply wanted to be Daddy's little girl, it never happened. There was always this distance between us. It was just understood that he was Jack's real dad and we were not blood family. Mom kept trying to make it all look pretty from the outside, but on the inside we felt rejected. We did a lot with Jack's family growing up, and I loved them because I finally felt like I belonged somewhere. But the truth was, I really didn't. I always knew that I wasn't really related to all of my cousins, and so I carried around this emptiness. I never saw my birth dad's family, and my mom's lived in another state, so they were all I had.

Jack punished my sister and me more severely than our brother, blaming it on the fact that we were girls. I remember growing to hate him. We both did. We tried to run away a few times, and he would whip us when he found us. Jack was not fully willing to be our father, and when they eventually divorced, we were left picking up the pieces that were never really connected.

While some stepfamilies can go awry and leave fatherless daughters reforming their lives yet again, there can be wonderful situations when the timing and love is right. If your mom did some personal work, she might have made a conscious effort to wait for her own healing before trying marriage again. If she recovered well, taught you resilience, and picked the right person for her and for you, you were given a beautiful gift. We have heard from many fatherless daughters about stepfathers who filled in the gaps with love, safety, and acceptance and who changed their lives for the better. Often, stepsiblings or half-siblings can become just as close as biological siblings, which is an amazing blessing. Healing and closeness can be the center of blended families if members decide to have gratitude for the gifts of bonus family. Sometimes gaining a stepfather becomes one of the best things that can happen in a fatherless daughter's life. Tess, eighteen, reflects:

I remember when my mom started dating my stepfather, and I felt like the third wheel. It had been my mom and me for most of my life since my dad took off right after I was born. Fast-forward almost twelve years later, and my stepdad is like my best friend. He was there for my first broken heart and he taught me to drive. The biggest lesson he taught me was that I am worthy. I know he is in it for the long haul. After all of this time, I know that I would not be who I am without him—he is a true blessing in my life.

Grandparents, Uncles, and Aunts

Many fatherless daughters are raised by extended family members who decide to step in out of altruistic love. If that was your situation, you were given an angel on Earth.

Tameka, twenty-four, says,

My grandmother raised me. My mother loved me but had a hard time staying clean. Dad knew that Grandmom was raising me, yet he never stopped by or even sent me a birthday card. I had a lot of trouble in my youth with promiscuity and staying out late partying. My grandmother used to say, "Meka, you're not a fool, so quit acting like one." She was right. I eventually got it together enough to get into nursing school. I had to pay my own way and work a full-time job all four years. One semester, I just couldn't come up with all of the money for my books. I had taken on as much overtime as I could but was still about $500 short. My grandmother was frail, so I did not want to ask her. She barely survived on Social Security as it was. With no other choice, I reached out to my dad. It took him about a week to finally answer the phone. "I just don't have it," he said, never asking me how I was or even how school was going. As usual, he let me down. It was like I was just an acquaintance and not his own flesh and blood.

I graduated with honors and bags under my eyes. My grandmother was dying but wanted to attend my graduation. I drove to Georgia that morning and picked her and my aunt up. We drove back to Clemson in time for my ceremony. We had a wonderful time together that day. Grandmom was so proud of me. She died about a month later. At the funeral I saw my dad. He was walking around telling everyone how proud he was of me for graduating. Like he played any part in raising me or helping me through college! I told my aunt what he was saying and that I had once asked him to help me financially and he said he was broke. I had always imagined that he barely had any money and probably lived in a lot worse conditions than us. My aunt said, "Look, baby, your daddy is not destitute. He is just not a good man. He is and has always been selfish. He is a foreman at the plant. He makes like sixty thousand a year."

I got so mad. I marched over to him and his friends. Interrupting them, I said, "You should be ashamed of yourself carrying on like you were a good father to me. You did nothing to make me into the woman I am today! My grand did it all. She worked past retirement to help me while you were making plenty of money and never so much as bought me a pair of shoes!" I am not proud of making a scene at my grand's house. She did not raise me like that. However, I do not regret a single word I said to him.

Tameka is like many fatherless daughters who were raised by their grandmothers, aunts, uncles, or other family member who put their lives on hold to make these girls' lives better. We applaud all of the family members out there who raised strong fatherless daughters. What an act of incredible love.

For some fatherless daughters, extended family play different roles (or none at all) in their lives. In some cases, the maternal relatives strongly disapprove of the father. They have witnessed the dysfunctional relationship between the daughter's parents and want better for their girls. If this is the case, there can be ongoing tension as family members speak critically about the father in front of his daughter. It can be uncomfortable for everyone. The one who gets stuck in the sticky middle of the name calling is the daughter. Even if the father has done things in his personal life that are inappropriate, it is not healthy for a family to wedge the child between their unkind words and her love for her father. What is important to her is his love, protection, and presence.

Eva, twenty-nine, agrees. "My aunt has had no qualms telling my mother that my dad is a 'no-good asshole' for my entire life. I know she does not like him, and I see why, but he is still my dad. Recently, I told her I was sick of it."

The truth is that you can love your family while sometimes not liking the things they do. Maintain your healthy role in the dynamics through authenticity, respect, and gratitude. On the other hand, if you were estranged from family you might feel like a part of you has been missing. Do you want them in your life? Do you have questions? Or have you made peace with who your real family is? It is up to you if you want to reconnect and fill in the blanks. Only you know what you need. Trust your gut. Powerful things can happen if they are meant to be.

CHAPTER 5

Relationships

We are not held back by the love we didn't receive in the past,
but by the love we're not extending in the present.

~Marianne Williamson

We all want to love and be loved. Most fatherless daughters feel like they have had to suffer more than others in the love department because . . . well . . . they may have. Love might not be easy, but you can have your happily ever after. It just may take a little introspection, understanding, and time. First, it is important to take a step back and realize that just as you have changed over the years, your idea of what love really is has too. In fact, at different stages of your life, you are likely to desire a love that is rooted in something different as your needs change. Reflect on what is most important to you now, compared to five or ten years ago. Is it friendship? Security? Intimacy? Fatherly love? Romantic love? How have your values shifted over time?

Daughters need the love of their fathers as the primary example of masculine closeness and acceptance. As we mature, we crave his unconditional support, protection, and guidance so that we gain self-confidence to explore the world. As we become women, we start to wish for the love of a partner, someone like our dads were supposed to be, someone we can love through thick and thin and who will love *us* right back.

Finding that special someone makes us feel validated and worthy of love. Love can be healing and beautiful in its best moment but also elusive and dismantling in its worst. Love is the one thing we all strive for, but as fatherless daughters, it is also the one thing that can rock us to our cores when it slips through our fingers. For us, real, honest, stick-through-it-all love might remain somewhat of a mystery. We want unconditional love from our father *and* we want unconditional love from our partner. Is it the same? What does healthy love from a partner even look like? It might just be that we prevent ourselves from finding out what love is because men make us nervous—and that stress holds us back.

Looking for Love

Think about your dating life through the years. Look back to the time that you felt heartbroken for the very first time and try to recall what emotions you felt and why. Did you feel alone or supported? How did you bounce back? Did you feel as if you took things harder than other girls around you—as if you weren't able to bounce back as well? Becoming emotional when brokenhearted is part of a teen's life. However, for a fatherless daughter, the heartbreak that comes with a breakup can be devastating. If she has already lost her dad, she knows how rejection or loss feels in a way most girls do not. Instead of moving on, she can get stuck and interpret the breakup as further proof that she is not valuable and that loss is inevitable. She can have help getting through these tough times by leaning on her family or friends, and if you learned to do that, you were headed in a healthy direction. However, if you isolated, felt strong feelings of negative self-worth, or even began having thoughts of hurting yourself, you likely did not have the caretakers in your life that you should have had. So what did you do to bring yourself back around? Did you ever really come back around? Knowing these patterns in your life is key to seeing the lessons you have or have not learned along the way. Spend time getting to know who you have been and how you have become who you are right now.

Fear of abandonment is the main hallmark of a fatherless daughter. Love is not guaranteed. People leave. Fatherless daughters witness this in monumental ways, and fear can be triggered the minute they get close to someone. Just because someone claims to love you, that does not mean he or she will stay in your life. A fatherless daughter differs from most of her friends in this regard because her emotional defense mechanisms and fears kick in to prevent her from getting hurt again.

Girls with a healthy father–daughter relationship can find solace in the arms of their fathers when their hearts get broken. He is there to reassure and encourage her. Her father may help her to understand that not every guy's love is meant to be The One. He can show her by his own actions what real love looks like. A fatherless daughter doesn't have her dad to model what is appropriate. So, rejection feels like abandonment and can quickly make her feel devastated. Love is gone, and she has no idea if it will come again—or last.

Take some time to seriously consider what you learned around the time you lost your father and consider how it might still be playing out in your life. It can be helpful for you to use the box on the next page to list your current coping skills. How do you react to fear? A breakup? An argument? Next to each coping skill, write down how you learned to react that way. What or who taught you that this was a healthy way to cope? Begin to think about which skills are working for you now and which are not. Be honest with yourself.

EXPERIENCE	YOUR REACTION	ROOT OF THE BEHAVIOR	IS IT WORKING?
Fear			
Breakup			
Affection			
Argument			
Threat			
Rejection			
Love			

It might be helpful to share your list with your best friend and ask if this is what he or she sees, too. Your friend's observations might be very enlightening. Ask your friend to help you be accountable for unhealthy coping patterns and educate yourself on learning new ones, like openly communicating, listening to the other side of the story, journaling about your feelings, meditating, working off stress through exercise, or connecting with friends. These are ways to expand your life, and we will discuss them further in the next chapter.

Sex

One way we may try to avoid being hurt is to exercise control of our bodies. In an important 1994 study documented in her book *Where's Daddy: How Divorced, Single, and Widowed Mothers Can Provide What's*

Missing When Dad's Missing, Claudette Wassil-Grimm found that girls who have little contact with their fathers, especially during adolescence, experience difficulties forming lasting, intimate relationships with men. They either become sexually aggressive or shy away from men altogether. They often feel a desperate need for male attention because they did not learn how to interact with the opposite sex. Within their need for male attention also exists a feeling of mistrust and uneasiness around men, creating feelings of dissatisfaction and self-criticism. These fatherless daughters are apt to form relationships in which they are very eager for approval, yet not so eager to return it. This can create obvious negative cycles in an intimate relationship.

One of the most telling consequences that can play out in a fatherless daughter's life is using her sexuality to cope with her loss. Since this can manifest in many ways, it can have long-lasting effects on her development.

According to Franklin B. Krohn and Zoe Bogan, girls who lost their fathers to abandonment or divorce have more physical contact with males than girls who did not. This could be considered a coping mechanism to fill in the void of father absence. On the other hand, girls who lost their fathers as a result of death tended to be more scared of men and less inclined to seek their sexual attention. Neither encourages healthy sexual development. Jen, twenty-eight, whose father died when she was three, contends that she really does not understand how to articulate her sexual needs. She thinks that she can be much more aggressive sexually if she does not feel an emotional attachment.

She says, "I can be seductive in the beginning, but the minute I connect with a guy emotionally, I turn into a prude." She not only had no direction as to how to form healthy male–female bonds but has learned how to use sexual avoidance to protect herself emotionally. The need for closeness is there, yet, like so many other women, Jen believes it makes her too vulnerable, and she backs away.

Star, thirty-six, whose father was a workaholic, uses sex in the opposite way. The minute she meets a guy, she pursues and sleeps with him. She has no boundaries about where and how she has sex. She craves attention to create a temporary feeling of self-worth. As a child, Star learned that feeling worthy was short-lived, and that she had to work very hard to get it before it was gone. So she did. Although she felt a rush of conquest and value from physical contact, the feeling quickly faded, leaving her emptier than before. It took her many years and many mistakes to realize what she was doing to herself. After years of working on herself, Star changed the way she was attracting men and ended up finding a love that was right under her nose all along.

The reason a fatherless daughter's appetite for sex exists on two ends of the spectrum goes back to the mystery of how to attract and gain love. It is also connected to the way your dad made you feel when he was there as well as when he left. You might be carrying some needs that are begging to be satisfied or protected and so you try to fill the void or isolate yourself. In some ways, you remain a little girl at heart and use avoidance and fear to navigate the decision making in your intimate relationships. When you are honest with yourself, you need to know at all times where you stand in a relationship and what is going on. If the pain of your father loss was traumatic, you will want to protect yourself from ever feeling that again.

Many fatherless daughters wonder what a "normal" father–daughter relationship is supposed to look like. You know you have suffered a loss, yet you have no idea to what magnitude—the loss was all you knew. The good news is that you can begin to recognize what may have been happening in your intimate relationships. Empowerment comes from awareness.

The Father–Daughter Relationship

Research shows that women with absent fathers usually carry around a confusing discomfort about how to handle male–female relationships. They are likely to idealize what they did not have and fantasize about the perfect father. As they interact with the opposite sex, they tend to be unsure about what men are all about, but in the middle of their uncertainty, they deeply crave connections with them. They can wonder things like, What are adult men really like? What are we supposed to give each other? What makes men tick? What are my boundaries supposed to be? Not knowing how to find the answers, they assume that what they have experienced regarding love and loss will occur again. By repeating the pattern of attracting relationships that are not healthy, they often end up fulfilling their own negative beliefs over and over again.

This confusion about relationships is all too common for girls who lost their fathers as children or adolescents. Following is a compiled list of what researchers have found to be the significant components of a healthy father–daughter relationship. Grimm-Wassil suggests that fathers are most influential in these specific areas of child development:

1. Fathers encourage a daughter's independence. They are generally not as protective as mothers, encouraging exploration and risk taking.
2. Fathers are primary role models for assertive and competitive behaviors.
3. Fathers expand their daughters' horizons. They can be the link to the outside world because of their resources, jobs, and activities.
4. Fathers serve as the alternative parent. They can enhance the quality of mothers' parenting by reducing their stress and

stepping in during hectic times. They can help bring solutions to crises.

5. Fathers are usually stricter disciplinarians. They tend to accept fewer excuses and have higher expectations for their daughters as they grow.

6. Fathers are men—the masculine role models. They teach their children about respect and boundaries and help put daughters at ease with other men throughout their lives.

Studies assert that daughters need the example of what a man really is, how he is supposed to act, what he truly needs, and how he generally thinks. From our own research talking to both fathered and fatherless daughters, we compiled the following list of what girls need from a good father.

- Security: emotional, financial, and physical
- Understanding how to be treated and loved by watching him with Mom
- Lessons in career, future aspirations, and financial management
- Help finding the balance between the feminine and the masculine sides of themselves—when to speak up, when to take care, and when to hold strong
- An ideal model of the man they want to marry
- Knowledge of the physical and intimate boundaries they need to set with men
- Self-worth, developed through the time he spends with them
- Protection, knowing that there is a real hero in their life who will fight for them
- Confidence and self-esteem, developed through affection, approval, and words of encouragement

- Perseverance: learning how to keep going, even when things get tough, and building the self-assurance to never give up

If you had the time with your dad to learn some of these valuable lessons, you received a gift. If not, you may be quietly angry that he would not or could not give you what you needed. Hidden anger is part of the process, and by facing it and validating it, you can move on and accept the love you deserve.

Fear, Anger, and Resentment

If you have not been successful in love, you may feel frustrated or lost. One of the most common emotions we heard women talk about in our research is the pain they feel in relationships. The more they shared, the more they realized the most common roots of their pain: anger and fear. Fatherless daughters usually try to avoid or deny these difficult emotions because dealing with them can feel impossible. Fatherless daughters may become masters of acting confident and bold; they might also have moments of acting irrationally when their fears get the best of them and their fortress temporarily topples over.

It is possible that anger and/or fear are at the roots of your actions. Experiences that stir up anger or make you feel scared can trigger a spiral of emotions. You might get lost in the cycle and not be aware of your irrational, repeating pattern: feel → think → believe → react → feel, and so on. Thus you might do crazy things. You may feel unprepared for what is happening and your irrational mind can take the wheel. Sloan, twenty-five, admits to doing hourly drive-bys to see if her boyfriend was really home when he claimed to be. Most of us have our own embarrassing stories. Our friends shake their heads because, yep, we did it again.

In honest moments, friends may confront us about it or a boyfriend may have been the one to say, "You need therapy!"

Has someone said this to you? Did it piss you off? Who wants to have to do the hard work in therapy about something that happened *to* them? You may think that it's not your responsibility to sit on some couch for hours on end working on something that you did not bring on yourself. You may also be unaware that your unresolved daddy issues are causing your current problems. This goes back to your rusty, old relationship coping skills. You have learned how to take care of yourself, right? You can work it out on your own. Maybe you can. But maybe you need some support and insight.

What may be going on every time someone throws the therapy suggestion at you is that you're angry at someone; you're afraid of something (and it isn't the soon-to-be-ex-boyfriend who is telling you to get help). It is not his fault. You're angry at your dad, maybe your mom, and maybe even your stepdad, too. You are just sick and tired of being mad, fearful, and so wound up with anxiety that sometimes you don't even recognize yourself.

Anger and fear are often rooted in loss. You lost a confidant. You lost a protector. You may have lost part of your childhood. *You* were traumatized. Losing him was *huge*. And with his loss came grief, which can often be expressed through anger.

During the grief process, anger tends to be the piece that we hang on to the longest. Although it is not satisfying, anger empowers us and feels more secure than the emotion of sadness. We can blame somebody. We can stay the victim and feel entitled to act out. We can feel some sort of control over the situation. In relationships, usually dysfunctional ones, we can act out our grief in irrational ways, and sometimes let our reactions get the best of us by doing something, yes, crazy.

While sometimes these stories of cuckoo moments can make us spit out our cocktails laughing with our girlfriends, the truth is, under each moment is a deep-rooted emotion that is being triggered.

I Had a Miscarriage!

Mara, thirty-three, told us:

> I met the man of my dreams in Miami. He was the opposite of my soon-to-be ex-husband. He was surrounded by a group of his golf friends, full of charisma, and breathtakingly handsome. I was in trouble and drawn to him like a moth to a flame. We spent the entire week attached at the hip.
>
> After my divorce was final, I moved to the city where he was living. Our courtship was not easy. He was a player and a womanizer, but I just knew I could tame him. Although we dated off and on for about six years, and I know he loved me, he cheated on me. The signs were all there, and I could feel the tide shifting. He wanted out. Although I could not have articulated this at the time, I did not want to be abandoned, again, by a man I loved.
>
> Here is my cuckoo moment: To try to stop him from going on a golf trip with a dozen friends, I lied and told him I thought that I may have had a miscarriage. I called him—at work, mind you— and told him he had to cancel his trip because I was too scared to be alone.
>
> Our breakup is what ultimately got me into therapy to face my daddy issues. I am now the woman I was always supposed to be. My fears are put away in a small little box. The man that I later married knows the contents and helped me put them away.

From California to Vegas in the Middle of the Night!

Jasmin, thirty-six, told us:

I started dating Mike right after breaking off my engagement to a guy who cheated on me. In the beginning, Mike and I were just in it for a good time. As time wore on, I fell hopelessly in love with him—or perhaps it was the fact that I could not keep his focus. My dad had been a womanizer and a professional gambler. I saw a lot of the same qualities in Mr. Immature. Right when we were getting serious and talking about a future, he up and took a job in Vegas. We decided to try long distance for the first few months. Within a month he had quit answering his phone when I called him on weekends, claiming he had fallen asleep or his phone was dead.

My cuckoo moment: One night I got super freaked out, so I decided to drive from my home in California to his house in Vegas, at midnight. I got angrier with each mile that passed. I finally arrived in the wee hours of the morning and banged on his door. It was clear he was not home. He had lied, telling me he was going to sleep early. I let myself in and started snooping around. I found a girl's curling iron and toiletries in the bathroom; I broke down sobbing uncontrollably. Why had he lied? Why did all the men in my life cheat?

I fell asleep waiting to confront him. He never came home. I left a letter behind telling him to never contact me again. The betrayal left me feeling helpless and deeply depressed. All of the pain led right back to my father's abandonment. I took a sabbatical from dating and finally took my friend's advice. Therapy was the best money that I ever spent.

In sharing some of these stories, we hope you can see that anger is simply fear in disguise. What you have really wanted all along is *love*. You are not cuckoo. You were afraid of feeling abandoned again. You love deeply, and because of your experience, you are a strong, resilient woman. You will make a superb partner one day because of your loyalty and wisdom.

You are not a lost little girl anymore. You can have a healthy, loving relationship, *but* there is work to do. You can start by researching what you truly want. Begin looking for healthy role models who live the way you'd like to live. Do you know someone who seems to remain confident and intact through relationships? Are you curious about how a specific woman seems to be OK on her own? Take her out for coffee and ask her how she handles the tough spots and what she tells herself. Whose relationship do you admire? Have you seen a couple that has a healthy, loving bond? If so, talk to them. Ask for some thoughts from both of them. How did they fall in love? How do they stay together? What does respect mean to them? What happens when they disagree? Start taking inventory. Let your mind imagine your own happily ever after. It is coming. Tuck all of this knowledge into your toolbox. By gaining wisdom, you are gaining power day by day.

Your Relationship GPS Has Failed

Achieving a healthy relationship is not as easy as doing what your parents did right or wrong. There is more to it than that. You have to look not only at your parents' track record but also at your own. What do your patterns seem to be? What has not been working? What do you want and are not receiving?

By now, you are probably tired of being too picky or consistently attracting the wrong guy. You might feel like you have to always look your best, stay in shape, smile when smiled at, and accept blind dates even when all you want to do is throw on sweats and order a pizza. We are here to tell you to get off of the treadmill. Take some time. Give yourself a break and relax for a while. Your body, mind, and spirit need a bubble bath. Take a deep breath, sink in, and know that your reboot is on its way. Here's what we believe short-wired your directional system: You didn't learn how to be in a supportive, committed relationship with a man because your dad wasn't able to teach you how. Your Relationship GPS is tuned to a few types of partners who cannot give you what you need. Knowing where you tend to make the wrong turn can help make corrections in the future.

The Average Guy, the Good Guy, and the Bad Guy

How many of you have taken a long winter's nap with Mr. Average just to avoid trimming the tree alone? Fatherless daughters love to love—they are just not sure how. When you receive love, you will give love, even if it is just for a short time. You crave that connection and approval. Many of us feel that if we choose the Good Guy on paper, we are getting it right. The Good Guy can be, well, pretty *good*, but for it to last you have to love who he is on the inside, and not just *like* who he is on paper. Average is as average does. Is that what you think you deserve? No fireworks, just cookouts; no passion, just conversation? What you accept into your life is your decision.

Many fatherless daughters say they chose the Good Guy when they needed to lick their wounds after the Bad Guy. They are heartbroken and vow never to let the Bad Guy into their lives again, so they look for the opposite. Fatherless daughters tend to live in extremes when making choices. When your childhood is filled with so many ups and downs, extremes can feel normal.

Pam, thirty-one, said, "I refer to my first marriage as my freshman twenty. I was barely twenty-two years old. He was my first real love, a Christian and convenient. When we got engaged, I knew I was too young; I was scared. Scared to let go. Scared to stay. Scared to leave. I married him because I could not go home. My dad was long gone. My mother had moved in yet another boyfriend; I just did not feel comfortable at home anymore. Jason's small apartment was a safe haven. He took care of me while I finished law school. He would rub my neck when I came home after late nights of reading in the library or bring me chicken soup when I was sick in bed with the flu. The problem was the spark had long blown out before the honeymoon was over. I ended up having an affair with my law professor. I have always felt horrible for how I treated my first husband. The fact was I had no idea who I was back then."

Maybe you have found yourself staying in a bad relationship (or four or five) simply because you can't handle being alone. You have no idea how to pick Mr. Right, but you have mastered picking Mr. Wrong, and your biggest fear is being Ms. Alone. Don't get stuck in a relationship where you are not being respected, treasured, and protected. Mr. Good may be great on paper yet still not right for you.

Greta, twenty-seven, was cheated on by her ex-husband more times than she could count. They went from being madly in love to marriage in their early twenties. At first, they could not get enough of each other, but after six years, she learned he could not get enough of other women either. Even after a terrible divorce, she had a hard time letting go. Because she was reliving her daddy loss all over again, she felt all of her old emotions of betrayal and abandonment rush back in, and yes, she went cuckoo. She eventually found herself in bed with her ex again and again, but the kicker was that he had remarried. She had a wakeup call when she finally told her friends the truth, and they made her promise to cut her ex loose. She listened and took charge. "I changed his name in my phone to 'Lying, Cheating Ass—Don't Pick Up' in order to humiliate myself into not answering his late-night calls. It worked and made me laugh every time he called when he was out prowling the town. It was time for me to get some help, get stronger, and stop letting him dictate how I felt about myself. So I did."

Until you know who your authentic self is, you probably are not in a place to pick Mr. Right. It might be the perfect time to do your own growing and become Ms. Right for yourself first. You might even realize that you are actually just fine traveling solo for a while. If your time alone is about your personal choice to work on and get to know yourself, then you might be in the healthiest place so far! If you have made the decision that marriage is not right for you, it may not be. Trust your instincts. Not every woman longs to be in a committed partnership. Know that some of your issues are bound to be reenacted in other close relationships in your life, so keep your eyes open for reemerging patterns in your social world even if you only set the table for one at home.

In the following sections we talk about a few typical relationship behaviors in which fatherless daughters engage that keep them from truly connecting with the right partner.

The Push and Pull

The minute you feel uncomfortable with your boyfriend, you break up with him before he can abandon you. The irony is that you really just want him to stand up, chase you, and fight for the relationship. You want to be chosen. You missed that from your dad if he left, and you crave it deeply. You must be careful not to let yourself get comfy in the victim role.

If a partner loves you, your story will help him understand your pain and appreciate your resilience. If you are not feeling that respect and admiration from your significant other, something is off. Are you playing games, pushing and pulling between jealousy and fear? Are these situations warranted? Do you truly deserve this? Are you testing him because of what your father did? If you are in something good, search your heart and be honest. Love him for his integrity and let him know you are grateful he was brought into your life. Ask him to give you room to work on yourself and know that this is not about him. Tell him that he needs to reassure you that he is committed to you. Own your fears and ask for his love as you work through them.

The Clinger

Are you clingy? Are you holding on for no other reason than you don't want to be alone? Likely you have broken up with the same person countless times. Everyone from your best friend to your spiritual adviser has suggested that you cut bait, but you won't.

Cynthia, forty-two, says:

I knew Doug wasn't right for me after our third date. He had all of these quirks that were driving me crazy, but on paper he was so great, so I kept trying to make it work. Then the unthinkable happened, and I lost it. I found a stream of emails with another girl on his computer talking about how much he loved sleeping with her the previous weekend! I came completely undone, leaving him hateful messages, telling our friends what a #&@^ I thought he was, and even sending the girl my *own* email. Then, all of a sudden, I wanted him *more*.

We got back together, and I became obsessed. I wanted to make him love me. The worst part was that our relationship totally shifted, and he started being a total jerk to me. But I couldn't let go. I turned up the love and started doing everything I could to make him happy. He became less and less interested, but that just made me chase him harder. We broke up every other week for the next year. It was a mess. Now, I am well aware that this was really all about my fear of being betrayed because of my dad, but at the time, I was just mad at *him*.

Every one of my friends was, like, "Girl, you have got to get him out of your life!" But I couldn't. It's like this old fear of being chosen over just came flaring up like a monster, even though I knew he wasn't Mr. Right. It took me a long time to stop the craziness. He eventually stopped it by getting married to another girl. Is it any surprise that we were texting during his rehearsal dinner? Talk about a lesson long learned.

Clingers are usually the ones who hang on through years of dating when the man has yet to promise a commitment. Why? The answer is simple. The little girl in her still has her hand up quietly saying, "Pick me. Pick me." If your dad did not pick you, you are bound and determined to prove to yourself, and to your dad, that someone will. Dating should be the fun part. The hard part comes later with kids, age, and life's roller coasters. But you can ride it out only with someone who is fully committed to you.

Attracted to Daddy Imposters

It seems that our fear of abandonment and need to feel valuable drives whom we pick to be the next guy in our life. If you walk into a room of a hundred men, you are likely going to pick the one who most resembles your dad. You may not realize it, and physically he may not look like your dad, but his actions, interests, or lifestyle might be too similar to be a coincidence.

Was your dad a workaholic, so you set your sights on marrying a surgeon because you subconsciously know he will never be home? Perhaps dad was very affectionate and filled your car with gas every week, so you look for someone who gives you gifts and attention. Or maybe your dad was absent because he was out chasing other women, so you marry an athlete or a musician who is constantly on the road and runs around on you from day one. Perhaps he is as old as your father and takes care of you, unlike, or like, Daddy did. Relationships with daddy imposters who have similar characteristics as your father can be one of your most painful self-fulfilling prophecies if you don't become aware and decide to do things differently. On the other hand, if you pick a partner based on the positive qualities that your dad possessed, you are headed in the right direction. Take a look at whom your radar draws you toward and be honest about your role in choosing relationships that benefit you and the other person.

The Relationship Hoarder

There is a strong chance that you have a long line of exes that you have not been able to let go of for one reason or another. You would rather dunk your new designer bag in tar than delete their contact information from your phone (or wherever you are hiding them). You are doing only what makes you feel safe. It's not really about *that guy or guys*—it's about your fears. Hoarders are afraid of losing their worth, and of letting empty spaces come into their lives so they will be forced to deal with their pain. As a result, they seek, they gather, they try to save . . . everything to fill the vacuum.

There are many reasons why it can be difficult to let go of failed relationships. You went through a lot of emotions losing your dad. Remember, your relationship GPS is faulty, and you might not have a full understanding of what the boundaries and standards in relationships are supposed to be. Second, one of your deepest fears is being left, so you will do anything to hold on to a relationship that makes you feel connected. If he is not willing to make a commitment, you will do what you can to convince him to do it because you (and the little girl in you) *need* that. It's the security blanket that you have refused to let go.

Third, being alone might make you feel like you are unworthy. Again. Having a man by your side tricks you into feeling complete, so you cling until he runs so far away that no tracking device can find him. The truth is, sometimes letting go of someone who is not right for you is the best way to find the real you again.

THE TWENTY STEPS TO A HEALTHY BREAKUP

Here is something that might surprise you: Breakups can be very healthy moments in your life. They force growth, and they are good things! Yes, they hurt, but each one is supposed to help you refine your standards and learn how to respect yourself and someone else. It is all prep work for the right relationship. Breakups are not supposed to stop your world from spinning but rather help you figure out how to make it better.

1. You talk about what is wrong and listen to each other.

2. You make an attempt to work it out one more time, just in case.

3. One, or both, of you realizes that it isn't working.

4. You follow through with the breakup, struggle, and tell your friends.

5. You separate your things and cry; losing someone close is very sad. You might make out one more time, but . . .

6. When you make peace with the breakup a few days later, you know it was for the best.

7. You respect each other and do not bad-mouth each other. You do not post anything negative or immature.

8. Since you were once so close, you occasionally check in with each other.

9. OK, you check his social media every now and then, just to see . . .

10. Eventually the check-ins get less frequent.

11. Dating other people is weird at first then *right*.

12. You cringe when you see him with someone else, but you do not do anything crazy.

13. You might feel sad and confused for a short time when it feels permanently over.

14. You talk through things with your friends and do not rehash every argument with him.

15. You do not stalk him in real life or cyber life.

16. You find new things to take up your new free time and you like it.

17. Your intuition tells you it was the right decision, and you know that you are heading in the right direction.

18. You are polite when you run into him. Feeling attracted to him is totally normal because you were once intimate, but you do not hook up; you know better.

19. You congratulate each other when you hear about the other's engagement, new job, new book, baby, lottery winning. It is tough for a moment—then you mean it.

20. You look back and might wonder, What if. But deep down you know things happened just the way that they were supposed to.

The Commitment-Phobe

While you might have a tendency to cling to someone out of your fear of abandonment, you also likely have another character living inside of you: Ms. Independent. Her voice echoes in your head when you feel pressure to commit to someone: "Don't give in. Don't give *all* of you away. You might get hurt. You need to keep one foot out, so you can run if you need to." Sound familiar? Well, there is good reason why Ms. Independent is equal parts afraid and awesome.

Lisa, thirty-four, said,

I had been in therapy for about three solid years when I started getting close to marriage with Tanner. He knew all about my dad dying when I was young and was a wonderful support for me. Our relationship was on and off for the first two years. We were always taking breaks from one another. Multiple times I gave him an ultimatum. Commit or take a hike. He chose the hillside a few times, and I let him go. I would not chase him or beg him back.

All of my friends were getting married, and Tanner could not even commit to a time frame. It was so frustrating. We both would date other people until one of us (usually him) would break down and call the other person. When we finally got on solid ground, things shifted and marriage became the goal. But once I realized he was serious, I got cold feet. I spent our entire engagement torturing myself. Would it work? Was he really The One? It seems that when I knew that I had him, I got bored. I felt as if I were going insane.

My therapist and I worked on my fear of commitment because to her it was as clear as day. I realized that marriage to me equaled boredom. My mother had never remarried. I guess for me, I had almost become too set in my ways and was too comfortable being single. My heart was telling me to move ahead, but the fear in my head was pumping the brakes. Of course, it all went back to being scared of losing him like I had lost my father. Today, we are happily married with two children.

Fatherless daughters are scared for a reason. Fully committing to someone means that you trust him or her with your heart, and with that trust comes a vulnerability that can be terrifying. You are acting out of your need for survival. You want to keep your heart alive, so you protect it by keeping it where it belongs—with *you*. When your father left, your psyche learned that men abandon you, it happens by surprise, and it is very painful. But there is a good side to all of this self-preservation: *You value yourself.* And that is awesome.

Don't let anyone beat you up for protecting your most valuable prize: your own heart. At the end of the day, something's going to give if you want to get the love that you deserve. You are strong enough to fully experience love—that is, feeling vulnerable and valued at the same time.

Fatherless daughters can get in the way of love by staying stuck in recurring patterns. Dating and committing to the wrong people at the wrong time can be two of the most unsatisfying fallouts in a fatherless daughter's quest for love. Being alone can be both comfortable and lonely. It is important to periodically stop and think: Am I in this relationship to avoid being alone? Am I holding on to something that is not what I want in life? In your gut, you know the answers. You may be in the midst of yet another breakup as you are reading this book or perhaps you have stayed single because relationships are not in your comfort zone. If you are like the rest of us, you have tried just about everything from intuitives to online dating to hanging out in coffee shops to find the right person. He or she may be right in front of you, behind you, or on the way. Are you ready?

If you are serious about committing, do some personal inventory.

Understand what it is that you want and need. Is your ideal-partner checklist old and based on unrealistic expectations? Or are you not expecting enough? Does your list need to be revamped? Take some time to get ready by putting thought to your true authentic needs and desires.

The Men Tell All

In marriages or relationships, fatherless daughters can be a handful for the men who love them. They can be hard to read and, at times, expect a lot. We interviewed some men who love fatherless daughters because we wanted to understand how they experience their relationship. We discovered that these men must draw on their own exceptional qualities of patience, compassion, strength, self-confidence, and faithfulness. That's why we love them.

We would like to say, bravo! to all of the men who were brave enough to Tell All. The consensus of the research is that those who love fatherless daughters see these women as survivors. They also see them as proactive, get-it-done types of people. They love that they love deeply, have strong spirits, and are loyal partners.

John, thirty-one, believes that all fatherless daughters need a secure man who is tough enough to handle some criticism. "My wife constantly questions our relationship. She feels the need to critique me and direct me on how to handle her needs. She is definitely vocal. You know where you stand because she will tell you all that is or is not working. It can be exhausting at times. There are moments when I don't want to be schooled."

Almost all of the guys interviewed agreed that their partners need to be in control. "The less control she has, the more controlling she can become," admitted Jet, one of the husbands who confessed to taking a backseat to some of the family decisions. He continued, "I don't mind. I kind of like her taking control. I have to be in charge fifty hours a week at work. Letting someone else do it at home works for us."

Martin, married five years, talks about the struggles with a fatherless wife who has a catastrophizing mind-set. She lost her father to cancer when she was eighteen and is highly anxious about medical issues in the family. He gets very frustrated when she starts to panic. "She always sees the glass as half-empty. I just don't think she needs to worry this much. Honestly she goes off the deep end. Here's an example: Her dermatologist was concerned about a spot on her back and she was sure that she had cancer, which she didn't. She was up all night and had to be admitted to the ER with a panic attack. I am trying to help, but I don't like to worry about something until I know the facts. She worries *before* the facts and makes herself sick. What am I supposed to do?" We talked to Martin about how daughters who lost a father to illness tend to think about worst-case scenarios because of their history. We helped him understand the importance of validating her feelings and not dismissing them. He should reassure her, stand by her, and ride out her anxiety. While Martin can help his wife feel safe, it is up to her to work on recognizing and intercepting her negative thought patterns before they can turn irrational and hurt her psyche and her body. A supportive (not critical) spouse can go a long way to helping her do this.

A few of the men who have daughters themselves shared how their wives did not like them to travel much. Robb, forty-one, said, "My wife is adamant that I not be away from our daughter for long periods of time. I used to slip out of the house while my daughter was watching cartoons to go for a run. My wife put a stop to that. She said, 'Don't leave her without telling her where you are going. She starts crying and thinks that you left her.'" He went on to say, "I know it sounds like a bit of overkill. It did to me, yet I get it. My wife's father left to go on a business trip and was killed by a drunk driver when she was in second grade." Robb has learned to call if he is going to be late. He said he feels like a better father because his wife has helped him understand how vital his role is in his daughter's life. Jon, Denna's husband, talked about how dating and marrying a fatherless daughter keeps him on his feet. "She is tried and tested and is more emotionally mature than other women, which means her expectations of me are higher. That means she expects me to do what I say I am going to do. If we have a disagreement, she wants to talk it over and find resolution immediately."

One thing most of the men agreed on was that their girlfriends or wives were fiercely independent. If he is Mr. Right, he will learn that it is imperative to understand his partner's background, feelings, and needs. Most of the spouses we interviewed thought it would be helpful for the men getting into these relationships to discuss their partner's needs and expectations of them. If they knew the trigger points early on, then they would be better prepared for her reactions and know how to contend with the fallout or, better yet, learn how to keep conflict from happening.

Wes, married to a fatherless daughter for nine years, lamented, "You have to get over the fact that you have to deal with what happened to her. It wasn't her fault. I have learned over the years that reminding her that she is complicated only pisses her off. It's just not helpful. What she needs most is acceptance, and a man that is not going to hurt her again. It took me a long time to figure that out. For years I was clueless and would say things that got her upset or forget that she needed reassurance—not knowing how deep her pain was.

"One day, after one of our fights, I thought I was going to lose it. Her mother called me, calmed me down, and explained some things. It was like a lightbulb went off because she knew how dramatic my wife could get. I got a better picture about why she acts the way she does. My mother-in-law insisted that we get into counseling and that I stop thinking that everything is about me. I had to put down my pride and do what it took to save our marriage. We have three kids, and I love her. I wanted to make it work. It took a while for me to get it, but now we are so much closer."

Most of the men agreed on a few points when dating or marrying a fatherless daughter (feel free to show this list to the significant other in your life):

- Encourage and compliment her.
- Appreciate that she is the counselor to all of her friends and yours.
- If her father cheated, she thinks you will, too.
- If her father died, she will be hypervigilant about health issues or safety.
- She will catastrophize and often expect the worst-case scenario.
- She will remind you that she can leave you at any time, so you need thick skin.
- She acts like she can take care of everything, but she deeply wants to feel protected—you can be her knight in shining armor.
- Give her unconditional love and she will give it back.
- Hug her, tend to her, and help mend her broken heart—even if she acts tough.
- Remind her that you are not going to leave her.
- Be open and strong enough to listen to her story.
- Enjoy the fact that she is a strong, mature woman, and knows what she wants.

Overall, we found that the right partner will love you despite all of your old wounds. You just have to let them. He needs to be strong, but not selfish; protective, but not controlling; and sensitive, but not coddling. He doesn't want to be blamed for what your father did or did not do in your childhood. He doesn't want to father you. What he wants is to love you and be your partner. He picked you because he was drawn to your strength, caretaking, and resilience, but he needs to feel like he can help you heal. It is your job to let him in on your fears and triggers. There are some amazing partners out there. If you already have one, thank him. Tell him how much you appreciate his love and acceptance.

Marriage and Motherhood

You have said "I do" or maybe you are contemplating commitment. Studies have shown that daughters with unstable father figures are about 50 percent more likely to marry as teenagers and are 92 percent more likely to divorce than those raised with their fathers. They are likely to marry more than once, with a higher divorce rate with each subsequent marriage.

Fatherless daughters have to take the time to get to know themselves and what they want before they commit. For many of us, marriage becomes our salvation. If you do not feel love and security at home, you are likely to settle on someone who shows you some semblance of both, even if you are not in love with that person.

In her marriage, a fatherless daughter is likely to take on the caretaker role, particularly if she had to mother her father or become a caretaker when young. It's what she knows, but it becomes a role that she can both love and loathe. Her resulting martyrdom, taking on all responsibilities while resenting it at the same time, can become poison to a relationship.

A good, successful marriage requires an equal partnership of two people who not only love each other but actually *like* each other. They want to be together not out of necessity, but out of respect and love. If one person is pulling all of the weight, the marriage will eventually tip and falter.

A fatherless daughter may have to do a little more work than other women. She has to heal from losing the first real love of her life and learn to understand what a healthy thriving intimate relationship requires. If she doesn't do this work before marriage, she may have difficulty determining when/if she should stay or go if her marriage experiences trouble. She may face the desire to run when things get tough to escape prematurely before someone else can hurt her. Fatherless daughters usually have to work hard to not assume a victim role by taking charge of their love lives and deciding to build a relationship in which both partners are equal. You are capable of creating something that you have never had before.

If You Are in an Unhealthy Marriage

If you are in an unfulfilling marriage, you might have erred toward the part of you that does not feel worthy of love and put yourself on the back burner—especially if children are involved. Be sure you are loving your true self first, then ask if you are loved for your true self by your partner. See if your partner will read some of this book and try to better understand and love you. If you see no hope for that, talk to those who support you about your feelings and options. Take a hard look at your family and what the long-term effects of your decisions are for all of you. The memory of losing your dad weighs heavily on how you move through troubles or insecurity in your marriage. You do not want your children to experience the pain you did. That does not mean that you should stay in an unhealthy situation that can potentially cause psychological damage to all of you. As you know, even if you need to move on, your children need their father in their lives so he can remain a loving presence.

If you are unhappy, constantly worried, or carrying ongoing resentment, your children can feel it on some level. They certainly are listening, even when you think they are not. Children have an innate ability to pick up on their parents' inadequacies. They know if you are miserable, just like you knew if your mother was. Watch your words, pay attention to your energy, and use good judgment about how you treat their father in front of them. Be wary of repeating any unhealthy patterns that might have been a part of your childhood home. Demonstrate an effort to work through conflict with calmness, respect, and collaboration. Seek counseling, whether it be pastoral or clinical (couples or family). Make an effort to keep your family unit together if the situation is hopeful.

If you need to leave the relationship, do not make the children pawns in the process. Making children choose sides or painting a negative picture of their father can be detrimental and could lead to another fatherless situation. Guard their hearts. Be wise about the timing of your next relationship, making sure the children know that they are your first priority.

Be aware that if you are in a loveless marriage, you might attempt to make up for the lack of spousal affection and attention by seeking it from your kids. Soak in their hugs, remain affectionate, and nurture them—just make sure that you are focused on their needs first, without expecting them to take care of you. You might overcorrect some mistakes that were made by your parents. For example, be wary of trying to become more of a pal than a parent. They need parental structure and direction and will feel vulnerable if you communicate that you are on the same level. Remain in charge. They need that stability from you.

You are responsible for building your own support network. You are worth it and should ask for it. Do not put yourself on an island or expect your kids to sustain you. Be a healthy role model for coping with change.

When You Become a Mother

It may have happened unexpectedly in your early twenties, with family planning in your thirties, or through fertility treatments in your mid-forties. However you found yourself holding your first child, becoming a mother leaves you feeling blessed and scared at the same time. For fatherless daughters, picking the right man to father your child is something to take very seriously. You look for stability, healthy DNA, and his willingness to become a father (something your own father may not have given you).

If she can, a fatherless daughter usually starts early, planning and plotting the future to ensure that her child will have a better childhood than her own. She is looking ahead like a survivor and considering resources, security, and protection for her child in a different way from someone who has never experienced loss. During pregnancy, you are hormonal and sensitive, and you may find yourself emotional because your father is not there from the beginning. You might spend many hours in tears, grieving the grandfather that will not be.

Have faith, there are other people who can be there for your child. If there are any other grandparents in the picture, you are blessed and should encourage those relationships. Aunts, uncles, siblings, cousins, and friends can all step in for a game of catch as time goes on. If you ask them, they will come. Remember, friends can be your chosen family.

Then there is your husband. Likely, you questioned him on his beliefs, values, and his own childhood to troubleshoot any unforeseen problems. You crave predictability, permanence, and reassurance. Many of us try not to repeat the same unhealthy patterns as our parents—we strive to make things right. If your father was a drug addict, and you have done your daddy work, you do your best to stay away from a user. If your father withheld his emotions or affection, you will most likely look for a man who will shower you and your children with both. Fatherless daughters tend to be super observant when watching their partners with children. Becoming a mother is one of the most serious roles in their lives, and they want to give their children all of the love and support they may not have received themselves.

As a mother, the dynamics of your childhood home will likely find their way into your adult home. Your parenting will tend to be based on what you wish to repeat or avoid from your youth. If your favorite memory of your family before your dad was gone involved camping, you have probably already been scanning the Internet for that camper. If you were sent to boarding school because your father was emotionally absent and didn't know how to handle you, you know you would never consider the same for your child. If your mother became incredibly overprotective and smothering after your father died, you will try to be a more laid-back mother—the opposite is true as well. As mothers, we tend to re-create for our children what we loved about childhood and reject what we didn't.

It is rare to have everything figured out before entering motherhood. It is OK and common to not be completely ready financially or emotionally (who really is?). Denna shared the emotional experience she had when she became a mother:

> I waited a long time to get married, so there was a rush when it came to deciding to have children. I wanted them, but it wasn't something that I ever felt a hundred percent ready for. I got pregnant with the help of fertility treatments and was due to give birth on almost the exact day my father had died at almost the exact age I was then. In many ways it seemed like a cosmic gift from both

my dad and God. The fact that I was close to the same age as my father was when he died was surreal. I guess this caused me to have anxiety, and I was scared something would go wrong with my pregnancy or the birth. Because of my age, my OB/GYN scheduled to induce me a week earlier. My labor lasted almost eighteen hours before I had an emergency C-section. Exhausted, I lost it emotionally. My vital signs went awry in the operating room, and my daughter and I both landed in critical condition, where I stayed for the next week. I was in and out of consciousness, leaving my husband with all of the work. I think I gave up. The timing of my first child's birth was so emotionally draining; I think I expected to die. My body just gave out.

When I started coming out of it, I knew I was experiencing postpartum depression. Watching the bond my husband so naturally had with our daughter made me both jealous and extremely proud. On my first night alone with our daughter, I held her in my arms. Sitting in my hospital bed, I looked down into her swollen face and saw my father in the shape of her eyes. I told her how sorry I was for almost giving up. I promised her that I would be the best mom I could be to her and thanked her for coming to be my daughter. No one will ever know how profoundly I was affected by becoming a mother. Not even I realized how much the death of my father would affect me having my own child. Knowing what my dad left behind made me mourn my own childhood in an entirely different way. I felt sorry for what he would never experience and for my mother having to go at it alone. I was never so proud of my mother and what she accomplished on her own. I was never so thankful to know that I did not have to go it alone as a single parent.

Fatherless daughters have big shoes to fill after realizing what their own mothers went through. They want to be seen as good mothers, and they want their husbands to be good fathers. The need to be supermom can be draining and confusing for them and those around them. They are likely to spoil their children with whatever their resources allow— gifts, experiences, and birthday parties. Giving children something that a parent never had can be a point of pride, but it's important not to over-indulge them. Parenthood is a dance and an opportunity for them to put their childhoods into loving balance (even if with a misstep now and again).

Fatherless daughters might mother their boys and girls differently. They can usually see themselves in their daughters and might feel much more protective of them, especially around men. They also might push them to be independent and tough—traits they want to pass on to help them lead resilient lives. They are looking out for their futures, but must do so without overriding their natural personalities. A fatherless mother can be a phenomenal role model for her daughter, instilling in her the self-confidence and wisdom to go into the world knowing how to love and be loved in a healthy way.

With boys, to satisfy the need for male comfort, motherless daugh-ters may seek affection and encourage their sons to cling, which can be a subconscious effort to feel adored. Do not feel bad if you find yourself doing this. Be sure, however, that you don't put unhealthy expectations on him or make him feel responsible for your self-worth. Fatherless mothers can be incredible teachers for their sons, raising them to love others, respect women, and balance strength with emotion. Love them, let them love you, and find joy in who they are as boys and men.

Age Matching

Parents often reminisce about their childhoods and begin stories with "When I was your age . . ." That phrase becomes more charged when your child becomes the age you were when you lost your father. We call this the Age-Matching Stage, which can be a time of reflection and sensitivity. Likewise, you will experience Age Matching when you become the age that your mother or father were when your dad became absent.

The Age-Matching Stage allows you to see parenting from a new perspective. Perhaps you find yourself looking in the mirror intently or staring at yourself or them in old photographs, realizing you *are* that age and wondering who you, or they, are and were. You contemplate what could have been going through your mother's or your father's mind back then. Be gentle with yourself during this time, expect this to bring up feelings, and talk to someone who has experienced the same thing.

Age Matching can be a surprisingly poignant time. You are likely to become overprotective, hyperaware of your children's well-being, and very intentional about keeping them secure. You may be seeing things in a new way that both enlightens and worries you. You are pushing against the fear that your own children could ever experience what you went through. Part of you wants to wrap them up and hide them away from the world where nothing can harm them because you wish someone had done that for you. Another part of you wants to start uncovering the past again and more deeply understand exactly what happened.

Do not be surprised to find yourself emotional, even re-grieving, during this time. While it can be uncomfortable, this stage can be a place of reconciliation and newfound clarity. Increase your self-care, including being open with those close to you about what you are going through and how raw you might be feeling. Increased closeness can be protective.

This is also a good time to build some healthy new coping skills. Practice mindfulness—stay grounded in the present. Keep reminding yourself that you are living a different life now and are not going to relive the same story. When Karin went through this period with her own daughter, she used EMDR (eye movement desensitization and reprocessing) therapy and spiritual counseling to help her heal some of her painful memories. This stage can be a bridge to a place of deeper understanding about your parents, yourself, and your child.

Mourning your own childhood is something that will continue to ebb and flow as you grow as a woman and mother. There will be times when you might forget about your past with the busyness of the day and the demands of motherhood. Staying in the moment and dismissing negative memories or thoughts gives your body and spirit reprieve and grounding.

Telling Your Children

Sooner or later, you will ask yourself: Do I tell my kids what happened with my dad? When and how? How do you explain who Grandpa is and why Grandpa is not around when they ask? As they grow, they will ask more questions about your dad and your childhood. As time goes by, they might reach out to other family members in a search for answers and wonder why they don't have the same kind of family as their friends.

Consult a family counselor or someone who has walked this road about how to approach these conversations. As with anything, there are gentle, age-appropriate ways to explain issues so that the answers satisfy everyone. No, you should not tell your children the entire, detailed story when they are five. You can add in specifics over the years, but be careful not to give them too much information, worrying them or giving them negative feelings about family members they love. Trust your gut and remember to take care not to put an expectation on them to soothe your emotions. When the time is right, and they are becoming young adults, being more truthful can help them piece together their history in a meaningful way. When they are ready, seeing Mom shed authentic tears over something that was painful can be a wonderful way to model emotional expression and deepen family intimacy.

As a mother, you are blessed with the promise of future generations through the lessons that you are now passing along. Knowing that you have the chance to influence, protect, and love your child is one of the most meaningful blessings of parenthood. You, more than anyone, know how much a parent means to a child's life. They are going to need *you*. Above all, remember that the best gift that you can give your children is a healthy, happy mother.

Maternal Resilience

The path of motherhood will have many peaks and valleys. Your history informs your emotional reaction to the world, especially to your family. You are resilient, but you can be deeply sensitive and sentimental. Know your strong and soft spots and keep an open dialogue with those closest to you so that your family can be aware of your process. It can be very difficult when the going gets tough; you can feel inadequate, resentful, angry, sad, and even fearful that you were not meant to be a mother at all. It is OK to doubt this enormous responsibility—most women do. This is a time when you can find great meaning in creating new patterns in your family by being in charge of what you now know in your heart and passing on that healing knowledge to your children.

Your Spouse

Your relationship with your spouse or partner is an integral part of the mothering dynamic. All being well, you are sharing parenting responsibilities. It is hoped that your partner is aware of all that you have been through. Maybe he has been through something similar himself. Because you are parents, discussions about your histories and needs should be ongoing. Your partnership will benefit from open communication of each of your challenges, joys, and fears. You will deepen your relationship if you include him in the journey, and vice versa. Be honest and conscious of your own stuff that might interfere with your relationship. This usually shows up in issues of control, trust, and stability. You are apt to be triggered by situations in which you feel unstable financially, physically, medically, or emotionally. You have a responsibility to reach a new level of self-awareness so that you *can* do this right.

Remember, as a fatherless daughter, you have a tendency to go to extremes. This holds true with your spouse as well. As a survivor, you carry fear and the need to control as your front linemen, and both can react in unhealthy ways when faced with crises. While you expect a great deal from your husband as a father to overcompensate for what you did not receive from your dad, you also hold the remnants of how your father and mother treated each other inside you. You learned about partnership by watching them, and this will affect your own relationship dynamic.

Ask your spouse if you ever become unreasonable, what that looks like, and how it makes him feel. Then listen to what he says and be brave enough to want to grow. At the same time, explain to him openly what is behind your fears and what your triggers are. Have this conversation when there is not a crisis and your emotions are calm. Strive to reach an agreement that you will both work harder at understanding each other and avoiding those reactions that hurt each other. Remember, you are now the role model through which your children learn about their future relationships. Teach them about respect, communication, and responsibility.

Be grateful to the universe, your spouse, and yourself if you married Mr. Right. If it took work, you have broken a negative cycle and are doing things right. It means you value yourself and have made a decision to honor your authentic need for love. You looked for love in the right place, and you received what you deserved. Now go and give that man a kiss!

CHAPTER 6

Coping Mechanisms: Finding Healthy Ways to Handle Your Pain

You need to spend time crawling alone through the shadows
to truly appreciate what it is to stand in the sun.

~Shaun Hick

Sometimes life seems to give us more than we can handle. Sometimes life takes away more than we can bear. In those times, pain threatens to wrap itself around us in a paralyzing cocoon unless we do something to keep from feeling suffocated. And so we do.

Our society has become used to the quick fix. We want instant gratification to feel better. If we can't handle the pain, we find a way to silence it. In order not to feel, you, like other fatherless daughters, may have tried to self-prescribe, self-harm, or self-indulge to keep yourself disconnected from your emotions. Because of the circumstances of her childhood, a fatherless daughter may not have been armed with the right coping skills. The ones learned in her childhood may have been tainted or simply not been the best tools to carry her through adulthood.

If you are struggling with any addictive tendencies today, it could be due to a combination of genetics, learned behaviors, and a lack of effective coping skills.

Over 60 percent of the fatherless daughters who responded to our surveys coped with their loss by using food, alcohol, isolation, sex, self-harming, avoidance, or drugs to try to escape their pain. The depth and breadth of father loss on daughters' lives as they mature can create an overwhelming and complicated array of aftereffects. Fatherless daughters are especially vulnerable to adapting negative coping mechanisms unless they were taught how to handle stress and care for themselves in a loving, nurturing way. They often blame it on their current situations, like the loss of a relationship or job, instead of the real reason they are not coping well, which often is the loss of their father being the root of their pain.

A wonderful finding was that 90 percent of our respondents found healthy, positive ways to cope with their pain, such as listening to music, reading inspirational books, or journaling. It is important to address those things that have inhibited your reaching for healing experiences by looking at how and why you might have taken a different path.

You may have done some of these things to keep yourself from feeling the emotions that rise up inside of you when you remember (again) that your father is gone. You may not have considered if his loss is at the root of many of your ongoing struggles, so you blame it on the here-and-now things—the job you hate, the guy you love, or the friend you have discovered you can't trust. Situations that bring up your fear can unleash the anxiety you have spent a lifetime trying to contain. All you know for sure is that you don't want to hurt anymore, so you might order another drink or go home with another guy just to feel better, if only for one night.

Research has shown that girls who grow up without their fathers are much more likely to develop rebellious behavior patterns or negative coping skills in an effort to handle their situations. These include aggression, drug and alcohol abuse, and sexual promiscuity. In fact, the majority of girls who have behavioral problems, become pregnant as teens, and serve time as juveniles come from fatherless homes. When a girl is deprived of paternal physical and emotional support, the family structure can shortchange her, and she can be left without the skill set to be self-confident and handle social pressures.

Gabriella Gobbi's research team at McGill University conducted a study on young mice that showed something extraordinary about females who were raised without a father. Like humans, California mice are monogamous creatures and are reared by both parents. Studies found that when compared to fathered female mice, the fatherless female mice displayed significant developmental differences in the prefrontal cortex, the part of the brain that manages cognitive and social activity. They also showed much more abnormal social interactions than the male mice raised without fathers, including aggression, trouble relating to others, and antisocial behavior. These female fatherless mice also showed a greater sensitivity to the stimulant drug amphetamine, creating in their bodies a higher risk for substance abuse. Gobbi asserted, "The behavioral deficits we observed are consistent with human studies of children raised without a father. These children have been shown to have an increased risk for deviant behavior and in particular, girls have been shown to be at risk for substance abuse. This suggests that these mice are a good model for understanding how these effects arise in humans."

Research has also shown that girls who are raised without their father's love usually feel more anxious and insecure when handling an emotionally stressful situation than their counterparts who had fathers in their lives. While she tends to be afraid on the inside, she might have learned how to put up a good front and appear to have everything under control. She can appear accomplished on the outside but insecure on the inside. This can become problematic if she consistently hides her feelings, burying them in a secret place and never exploring the root cause of her emotional state. The mind and body have a strong connection, and brain studies have shown that if a daughter feels rejected, the emotional pain registers in the same part of the brain as physical pain. That pain can be triggered over and over again throughout her life showing up in many physical ways like headaches, gastrointestinal issues, exhaustion, and more.

Science has shown that experience alters the way the brain functions. Because specific brain pathways may not develop normally in fatherless daughters, these women are less able to analyze, react, and emote in the same way fathered women are. Basically, without paternal guidance, she was put on life's stage without having the chance to review the script, practice the scenes, and get comfortable in front of a live audience. Her self-confidence and coping skills most likely became compromised, along with her feelings of competency and ability to form lasting, satisfying relationships. To overcompensate, she might push forward, trying to be as independent and self-reliant as possible, but the problem is that she was probably not given the tools she needed. This struggle may have left her searching for ways to fill the voids in her life.

Living with self-doubt can leave a fatherless daughter feeling very different from others. Her confusion and pain are her normal. If she lost her father while young, she may not have learned how to help herself with such techniques as positive self-talk, looking for her strengths when she has been knocked down, or asserting herself in relationships and work. She aches to feel strong, loved, and accepted and missed feeling that from her dad. Likely this has left her wondering where to learn about the world from a masculine point of view. Rather than rely on herself to find healing, she is more likely to look outside of herself for relief.

On the other extreme, she may withdraw from the world. Perhaps she is angry with God or her family and isolates herself to avoid feeling vulnerable again. In whatever way the fatherless daughter decides to escape—drugs, alcohol, sex, eating, self-harming, isolating, or acting out—she can develop a pattern of returning to that escape when she faces stress or conflict. It's possible that she is engaging in learned behavior; perhaps she saw her mother or father using substances to escape, and she is merely repeating what she witnessed. Maybe her self-worth is so underdeveloped that she has compromised herself to fit in and to punish those who say they love her. This should never be the end of the story. She can turn the page and reclaim her life through recovery, restoration, and regenerating her own strength. The possibility is always inside of her.

Mirror, Mirror on the Wall

Have you lost your way? Is it time for a change? A great way to bring yourself back to a healthier path is through self-reflection. We are not here to judge you, criticize you, or make you feel ashamed about anything you have done or are doing. And we ask you to do the same—for yourself. This is the most important lesson for you to learn at this stage of your journey. Seeing yourself in a different light and gaining insight into your behavior will help build your strength. Then you can regain power over your life and whatever it is that has been hurting you.

As you learn more about yourself and the fatherless daughters who have walked a similar path, you can find relief, wisdom, and resilience in their stories. Some of the stories are yours. You have what it takes to be your own inspiration, even if you need to ask for help to stand back up. You may also find it helpful to have another fatherless daughter read this book at the same time as you. Having a sisterhood of support can be a new way to explore what you are feeling.

Checking in with Your Emotions

The following exercise will allow you to look at your emotions (even those you may not have been able to easily identify in the past). Looking back to the time when you lost your father, is it easier to name the emotions you were feeling then? Stop for a few moments and say out loud those feelings that were inside of you when life started to change in your family. Write them down in the space provided. Seeing them on paper should validate what you could not validate back then. Name three of them. Sadness? Anger? Relief? Confusion? Lack of self-worth? Inadequacy? Isolation? Abandonment? Fear? Write exactly what you felt, no matter how normal or distant it sounds now.

1. _____

2. _____

3. _____

Now that you have recognized and named what you were feeling, it should be helpful to take a look at how you reacted to those emotions. Looking back, you will notice the times that you chose positive coping behaviors that helped you stay resilient, and the times you did things that ended up depleting your strength. For the moment, let's examine negative coping behaviors. When you were confused or hurt, what did you run *toward* for relief? What made you feel temporarily in control, or without a care, only to face reality later? Be honest with yourself; it is the only way you can forgive yourself for any behaviors that were not best for your body, mind, and soul. We want to help you bring honor back to those places that bear scars. Write down three ineffective coping skills that you have used. Sexual promiscuity? Overeating? Alcohol? Drugs? Prescription drugs? Shopping? Cutting? Isolating? The Internet? Write down whatever you think helped you cope, if any.

1. _____

2. _____

3. _____

Now think back to a time in your life when you successfully used good coping skills to get through difficult times. How did you find the strength to move forward? What helped you take care of yourself and your relationships?

Perhaps you had a falling out with a girlfriend, so you decided to open up and discuss your true feelings instead of shutting down or running away. Your reward became a friendship that has lasted for years. How about a time when you realized you were partying a bit too much after a heartbreak so you decided to release your energy through yoga or your favorite music and not happy hour? How did that feel? What were the skills you were using to forge ahead? How can you get back to that place? Name three positive coping skills that have helped you find your feet again. Sports? Meditation? Journaling? Sharing your emotions? Reading? Painting?

1. _____

2. _____

3. _____

As you read this chapter, spend time on the sections that discuss the behaviors that resonate with you. Be honest with yourself as you read and write and let this be a time of transformation.

Jacquie opened up to us about how she tried to handle her emotions after her father left:

I was already in such a difficult time in life, going from girl to adult, getting close to finishing high school. Dad had threatened to leave Mom many times, but finally did it a week before my graduation. I had to hold it together because I was the oldest. There I was, trying to take care of my mom and my two younger brothers in the middle of what was supposed to be the happiest time in my life. It was like a sinkhole opened up in front of our house and just swallowed us whole. Still, no one understood the depth of that hole. I kept it in for a long time.

Dad had been abusive and emotionally unavailable to me since I was much younger. His lack of connection put a wedge between us as I started coming into puberty, which resulted in me hanging out with the wrong crowd out of rebellion.

Throughout college, I had regular bouts with smoking pot, bulimia, binge drinking, diet pills, promiscuity, unprotected sex—just so much reckless behavior. It took me many years of regretful behavior to finally start seeing that I was messing up my life.

It is truly a miracle I did not end up in jail or dead. I am so grateful for the help of an angel that came into my life my senior year who steered me back in the right direction—a professor who saw great potential in me and took me under her wing. She helped me remember how bright I was and encouraged me to start playing piano again, in the music hall between classes. I finally mattered, and I began to regroup and thrive. It was in me. I just did not know it. It took me a full decade to forgive myself and to accept that I was doing the best that I could until I learned better. Thank God I learned better.

Fatherlessness can send a young girl out into a world having faced a very adult problem without the skills to cope with it and very little realization of how it can impact many aspects of her life. She is served a plate of emotions that she cannot make sense of, and so she looks for other ingredients to try to bring a sweeter feeling to a life that has turned bitter. The confusion about how to find answers leaves her searching high and low for something to hold on to. She might be unaware that she is trying to get away from something. All she knows is that what she has found makes her feel better—for a time. But times can change, and she has the power to make a decision to change herself.

If you have felt trapped at any point in your life, you deserve compassion and assistance to find your way out. Perhaps you have overindulged in partying so that you could check out for hours. Maybe you have isolated yourself from becoming close to anyone to protect yourself. Or maybe your daily companion has become the Internet and your nightly one a sleeping pill.

Maybe the glass of wine with dinner has turned into an entire bottle every night. Or, prescription meds seem to provide you with an escape. Perhaps you have not learned to love your body and have tried to control what you do not like about it through anorexia or bulimia. Or maybe you have filled your void with eating—overindulging in the pleasure and escape of food—so that you can feel satiated. Not all women who have lost their fathers get stuck in negative coping cycles, and none of us have to.

What Makes Your Spirit Smile?

Are you happy with how things are going, or is happiness what you are searching for? Here is an easy clue to where to find it: Pay attention to that feeling in your body. It is your intuition. What is it telling you? Your spirit smiles when it is granted those things that are good for it. Your spirit retracts when it is not comfortable with negative experiences or situations. You want to start bringing things into your life that will heal, not hurt. Search your heart and listen to your inner voice. You have the guide to your happiness within you.

Contentment comes when we can make peace with what is happening in our lives. Some things are in our control, and some aren't. Part of reaching a higher level of self-understanding is differentiating the two—especially as a fatherless daughter. It has been long proven that addictive behavior is part hereditary, part the environment we grew up in, part the company that we keep. Nature. Nurture. Environment.

If you realize that you are prone to addiction, it is vital to understand the pitfalls and learn that you can find a way to bring back personal power over your choices. Certain situations create risk such as a family history of substance abuse, neglect by parents or caregivers, and a lack of support or resources. The key risk periods for substance abuse for the fatherless daughter are during major transitions, such as losing a parent, times of crisis, experiencing family divorce, or changing schools. By looking at your family history and your personal journey, you might clearly see when you were the most vulnerable. Have compassion on yourself for all of the things that were—and were not—in place in your life that compounded to create your using drugs or alcohol to cope.

Tesha, thirty-two, says,

I started dating and realized that I was not lovable. I doubted my friends, my family, and myself. How could it be that if my real dad did not love me or my mother, that someone else could love me? I became distant and withdrawn from my family. I stopped going to church and went down a very difficult road for the next ten years. I was mad that my real father had never cared to meet me. I asked my mom where he lived, and I found out that he only lived one mile from my home. I drove to his house and knocked on his door. He answered the door with a cigarette hanging out of his mouth and said, "Well, hell, if it isn't Tesha. Come on in."

He sat down in a chair and asked me if I wanted a drink. I said no. I asked him a bunch of dumb questions about the weather and

TV, and then I left. I didn't speak to him again until three years later when one of my older brothers was getting put in rehab for the third time for drugs and alcohol. We had learned that drinking was the way to deal with things. I went down that road myself.

For years I had tried to minimize my feelings about my father by drinking, doing drugs, and sabotaging all my relationships with men. I hated myself. I did not want to be like him, yet I was acting just like him. I cannot believe how easy it was to just slip into the same patterns. Years later, I had a bad accident and got a huge wakeup call. It's like God was saying, "Tesha, you have to take responsibility for your own life." And so I did. I got a second chance and realized I was here for a much bigger purpose. So I got some support and found the strength to make some huge changes. I had to let the love in that was around me. My life completely changed.

What a beautiful second chance Tesha got at life, but before that she was a prime example of how addiction can follow generational patterns. If that is what is happening in your life, it should feel *good* to be able to change history. You can step out of the victim role and change your thoughts and behaviors. It takes time to change addictive habits, but the long-term gains are worth it—it's your life.

How Fatherless Daughters Have Coped

How do you distract yourself from feeling your pain? There are both positive and negative coping skills that can be used to deal with emotional issues. The following list shows different forms of negative coping that the women we surveyed used. We asked the respondents to check off as many as were applicable to them, and most selected multiple coping behaviors. You should know that over 38 percent of those surveyed responded that they *did not* use negative methods to cope. Their positive approaches are included later in the chapter.

Isolation	41 percent
Sexual promiscuity	33 percent
Alcohol	30 percent
Suicidal thoughts	24 percent
Food	28 percent
Illegal drugs	19 percent
Shopping	16 percent
Running away from home	12 percent
Anorexia/bulimia	11 percent
Internet	11 percent
Sexual avoidance	10 percent
Suicide attempts	10 percent
Prescription drugs	9 percent
Cutting	9 percent
Committing crime(s)	4 percent
Over-the-counter drugs	3 percent

Isolation

If you have felt misunderstood, like you didn't fit in, or simply have not had the energy or desire to be social, you may have isolated yourself from others. Do you avoid spending your energy on other people and don't want to let anyone around your own bad energy? Depriving others of your company may be an attempt to punish yourself, them, your father, your mother, or whomever else you feel has hurt you. Pulling inward can feel much easier than reaching out.

Spending time alone is not necessarily bad. In fact, it can be a tremendously healing experience if you are turning inward to seek guidance, self-awareness, and clarity in your life. Self-awareness is a necessary part of learning to love yourself and be loved by others. However, if you are spending time in isolation because you are feeling depressed, overly anxious, or outcast, that is another story. When separating yourself from the world becomes a persistent, long-term way to cope with your pain, it can be a precursor to depression and warrants seeking support. Remember, you are not alone—isolating was the most common coping behavior reported by women like you in our studies.

Jill, thirty-one, spoke about her dear friend Tracy, who lovingly forced her out of continuously isolating herself while going through a difficult divorce. "After my husband and I broke up, I was in a very dark place. I called out of work routinely and survived on pizza deliveries. Tracy was my neighbor in my condo complex. For about six months she would bang on my door both day and night and force me to go places with her. Although I tried to scream back at the door and tell her to go away she would always ignore my pleas. She saw me at my very worst and taught me how to get out of my own cocoon and back into the light of day. Turns out she was also fatherless. Our friendship is going twenty years strong. I am so thankful she was persistent in that season of my life."

We grow through our relationships, find joy in the company of others, and build community through our connections. When we deprive our bodies and souls of that affection, parts of us stop growing, and we will most likely become sadder, more stagnant, and feel less worthy of being loved. While a healing retreat can be the best medicine for your soul, the body should find a way to reengage in life with renewed hope over time, even if the process is slow.

If you have been isolating yourself for more than a few weeks, it is time to go out and engage in the world. Take your time, but put a toe in the pool. There are others who want to be in your life, and you need to reach out to them. Tell them how you are feeling. Ask for help. If you are not ready for that type of vulnerability, start small. Invite someone to come over and visit for a short time or to join you on a walk.

When you feel stronger, you can take the next step. By getting into therapy, group counseling, or joining any social activity you are engaging your courage in empowering ways. You will find out others have felt just the way that you do and that you are far from alone. The consequences of your father loss do not need to include living life disconnected from the world. Be your own hero, look yourself in the eye and say, "I am going to take a chance." Know that doing so is evidence of your bravery and progress.

Sexual Promiscuity

In previous chapters, we talked at length about the impact that fatherlessness has on a young woman's sexual behavior.

Studies have shown that fatherless daughters are prone to entering adolescence with a deficit in coping behaviors. They often act out sexually. You might believe that your body is not worth protecting or you may not have learned how to honor it. In the compelling 2014 Oprah's Lifeclass series "Daddyless Daughters," Steve Perry called sexual promiscuity by fatherless daughters "a form of self-mutilation." Iyanla Vanzant immediately agreed, saying, "Absolutely. It's violence against the self."

In a study published by the National Institutes of Health, researchers found that daughters who suffered father absence were much more likely than their fathered peers to have early sexual experiences and teenage pregnancy, making early onset of sexual activity the most common coping behavior for fatherless daughters in this age group. Not having a father can greatly skew a young woman's perception of herself, her body, and her role in intimate relationships. In our study, half of all fatherless daughters said that losing their fathers affected their decisions about intimacy and sex. One-third used sexual promiscuity as a coping mechanism.

Sex can give a young woman a feeling of power, connection, and a sense of being loved and needed. And it can be nothing short of intoxicating. But in the long run, does it really make her feel empowered? For most fatherless daughters, the answer is no.

Charlie, twenty-nine, said that she has had more sexual partners than she cared to admit. She got into therapy because she said she was just too tired to keep living the life she was living.

I thought my issues were based on the fact that I was just a wild child that needed to mature. I had a lot of secrets and felt pretty guilty about my sexual past. In therapy, I learned that almost everything I was doing with men was directly linked back to my father's emotional avoidance of me. I could get a guy to have sex with me, yet I could rarely get them to stay past daylight the next day. It took a whole lot of self-work to admit that my promiscuity was a self-fulfilled prophecy. I was repeating in my adulthood what I felt in my childhood.

This came when I had to take a long, hard look at my past. My therapist could sense that I was keeping secrets and shame about my sexual choices, and that I was really aching to get them out. I really just wanted to tell someone, just spit out all that I had done so I could move forward. He knew me well enough to know that the truth would bring me freedom. One day after beating myself up in therapy, he asked me to go home and write down every guy's name that I had slept with. Then he said, "Tear it up and let it go. It is time to forgive yourself, and start loving yourself." This became the major turning point in life that I desperately needed—it was why I was really there. I went on a one-year sabbatical from sex. I have to admit, it was one of the best years of my life. I got right with myself and ended up meeting my husband at the nine-month mark. We waited three months to consummate our relationship. By then, we were madly in love and married just six months later. I would never have been able to have a healthy marriage if I had not dealt with the demons of my past. Thank God I did.

Sex can be used as a coping mechanism to fill a void, and although true intimacy might seem foreign and terrifying, it is never too late to change the way sex is viewed and experienced. It is meant to be enjoyed and to deepen the closeness between two people. Perhaps like Charlie, you have never learned how to be truly vulnerable or deeply intimate with a partner beyond the physical, but you can learn. Sex is supposed to be a beautiful, sensual part of a relationship that feels safe, loving, and wonderful.

Becoming oversexual and undersexual can both be coping mechanisms to handle the same deep-rooted fears. In fact, 19 percent of fatherless daughters in our survey said they coped with their emotions by avoiding sex all together. Because promiscuity and avoidance can both be an attempt to deal with an internal void or sexual confusion, we could view them in the same vein. Fatherless daughters use them to compensate for a lack of understanding of and comfort with giving and receiving love from a partner. If you feel like you are using sexual promiscuity to fill a void in your life, this would be the perfect time for you to take a sabbatical, just as Charlie did.

If you are avoiding sex while doing your own mental work, it may be a good way to stay focused on yourself self while you are trying to make changes. One of the goals of a fatherless daughter's journey is to decide how intimacy is going to have a meaningful and fulfilling place in her life.

Alcohol

Drinking can be inviting for someone who is struggling because of the immediate relief and gratification it seems to bring. Alcohol is a fairly socially acceptable coping mechanism; however, we know that while alcohol can be a feel-good substance at first, it is actually a depressant. The fact is, alcohol abuse alters the body chemically, making the drinker more prone to depression, anxiety, and fear. The mind does not work as well as it could, and the body gets depleted of healthy energy. Relationships can be negatively impacted, including the relationship with the self.

There is a way out of alcohol abuse, and it starts with admitting that there might be a problem, seeking the support to learn more, and developing alternate, healthy, coping skills.

Elizabeth Vargas, of ABC News, was interviewed on *The View* in 2014 about her stint in rehab. When Barbara Walters asked her why she thought she had become an alcoholic, she responded, "When I was six years old, my dad left for the Vietnam War. From that moment on I began suffering from anxiety [every time my Mom would leave]. In order to cope, I turned to alcohol." Because of her father's absence, she was afraid of being abandoned, and coping with that anxiety by drinking stayed with her into adulthood.

Her story shows that even those who seem to have it all together on the outside could be crumbling on the inside. The good news is that there is a way out. Vargas told George Stephanopoulos in a 2014 interview how she has been learning to cope in healthy ways. "What I learned to do when I was away [in rehab] was to feel the feelings. You know what? They're not going to kill you. You have to experience them. I never learned that skill and (it) makes it tough some days. Alcohol for me is no longer an option." She now lets herself deal with her emotions more mindfully by calling a friend, meditating, or praying.

If you think you may have a problem with alcohol try to take the next two weeks off from drinking. Go about your daily and weekend routines. If you can't make it through the two weeks without a drink you may need to take closer look at your relationship with alcohol. There are multiple resources and groups ready to welcome you with open arms. Call a therapist's office and ask for a referral based on your needs. Google resources in your area, searching for specialists, treatment options, and open groups. Alcoholics Anonymous (AA) and Adult Children of Alcoholics (ACA) likely have weekly meetings in your community that are welcoming and supportive.

Suicidal Thoughts

About 24 percent of fatherless daughters in our survey have contemplated suicide. This is one of the more heartbreaking statistics that we uncovered. Depression is real, and unfortunately some people are in so much pain that suicide seems like their only option. It. Is. Not. Suicide is not the ideal way to escape or solve pain. It is not a method to punish others. Suicide tears a hole in the world of those left behind. If you are engaging in or contemplating self-harm, you are in pain so deep that you probably do not think anyone understands. Please seek help if you are feeling like taking your life or harming yourself.

Tell someone who loves you the truth. Ask for trust and a space free of judgment, and let him or her know how you are feeling. Ask for support and resources. People will want to help you, especially if you are vulnerable enough to ask. Find a therapist who specializes in depression. Grief counselors are skilled at helping people through these dark times. Sometimes admitting to a specialized treatment facility is the best way for an individual to build a bridge back to recovery, hope, and a healthy life. If you are in crisis, contact someone at the National Suicide Prevention Lifeline (1-800-273-8255) at any hour, and he or she will help you with whatever level of assistance you need. (See the resources section for additional organizations and their contact information.)

Food

What do you reach for when you are down? Is food your companion? Food is social, it is acceptable, and we need to eat to maintain our bodies. So while it might not appear to be an unhealthy way to find solace, when we overindulge, negative feelings frequently follow. What happened last time you were heartbroken? Did you order and devour an entire pizza? Did you lock yourself in your room with a pint of rocky road ice cream? Did you continue to search for that fill night after night, only to feel worse and worse? Occasional indulging is not the issue, because it's OK to treat yourself. The problem is the self-loathing and disappointment that can be triggered in the cycle of overeating. Gorging on food overfills your tummy while leaving your soul empty.

For many women, eating is attached to feelings because food literally fills a void in their bodies. Emotional eating involves consuming large amounts of food (usually junk or comfort food) because of emotional triggers instead of true hunger. Experts estimate that 75 percent of overeating is due to emotions. We turn to food for comfort because of feelings of anger, depression, anxiety, boredom, loneliness, low self-esteem, or stress.

As a fatherless daughter, you might already have body issues. Perhaps you saw your mother use food for comfort when your father was gone, and the coping mechanism became ingrained in you at a young age.

Phelicia recounts:

I remember before Dad left, he was always criticizing how much Mom ate and how she looked. She was the type who would taste the ice cream when she got home from the grocery store, watch a TV show with a bag of chips, and sample from each serving platter when clearing the table. Dad would embarrass her in front of us kids every night by calling her out for dipping back into the mashed potatoes. "Fat ass Shirley," he would say, and we would all laugh, including my mom, although I could see the pain on her face. I felt terrible for her.

I find myself doing the same things: trying to look good for my husband but feeling impulsive about opening the cake container when he goes to bed. I go up and down with my weight, and he says he can tell with each pound. It's like I've married my dad. He constantly tells me that I look the best when I am skinny, which takes so much work. Then I try to stop eating, but I cannot help myself in the evenings when I am most sad. In the morning, I hate myself for what I did the night before. Then I deprive myself. It's a horrible cycle. I never feel adequate, no matter what.

There is a true link between overeating and childhood abuse. In the Nurses' Health Study II, researchers studied 57,321 adult participants. "Women who had experienced physical or sexual abuse before the age of eighteen years were almost twice as likely to have a food addiction in middle adulthood compared to women without a history of childhood abuse." If you have been abused, seek support by talking to someone who understands. Don't feed your pain to the point that it not only takes over your mind but also your body. Your body needs to be nourished by healthy food so that your mind and body have the energy to thrive. Do an online search in your community for "child abuse survivor therapy" and find a therapist, resource, or hotline that can assist you. We know this topic is delicate, so take your time to look around and see what or who looks right for you. You can also turn to someone you trust in the field of healthcare or counseling to find a referral for you. When you start advocating for your own well-being and sending messages to your body that you are valuable, you can start heading toward a happier life.

Eating well isn't simply for maintaining your physical appearance; it is for maintaining a lifestyle of psychological, spiritual, and physical health. You are not helping your body thrive if you are overindulging in unhealthy, overprocessed foods. They can clog not only your digestive track and arteries but your emotions as well. Deciding to make a change is about taking care of your body and your mind. Make the decision today to be accountable for what you are eating. A positive coping tool like keeping a food diary, connecting with an accountability buddy, or participating in a healthy weight loss plan can be the kick starter you need to get healthy both physically and emotionally.

Illegal Drugs

Avoidance, sadness, and fear are usually at the root of addictive behavior. Fatherless daughters are significantly more likely to use drugs at a young age than those who have fathers. The feelings that drugs deliver can seem to provide a complete escape from depression, angst, and self-doubt. When one starts life with a higher chance of using drugs than those around her, she also has a higher chance of progressing into addiction.

If you have abused drugs, you may be unsure what initially brought you to that point. Perhaps you thought it was a breakup or losing a job. Understanding the true impetus for your behavior is the real question. Were you angry, depressed, or both, about the unfairness of your life? You did the best you could to cope, but now you might need to help yourself. Dealing with those old wounds can take a great deal of effort, and numbing yourself through drug use can be an easy, but tremendously costly option.

The road to recovery takes work, support, and the courage to face emotions that may hit full force once they are allowed to be expressed. This is a powerful part of your passage to becoming strong, clean, and beautiful. You can learn to tap in to the resilience inside of you, treat your body with love, and reclaim yourself.

There are many people who have experienced the same cycle of addiction and can help you through recovery. Groups like Narcotics Anonymous (NA) can be phenomenally life changing and supportive of your reinventing your life and coming out a much stronger, more purposeful person. Every person has a different recovery, just like every person has a different history. If you have attempted to become sober and then relapsed, it is OK. Relapsing can be part of the process. Don't look at it as failure; look at it as a reminder of the life you do not want. Just choose to start over. Today.

Shopping

Retail therapy seems like an innocuous way to beat the blues. But what happens when you do it time after time, spending more money than you should to get that immediate gratification of the buy that soon turns into regret and emptiness? Once you open all of the packages what happens?

We are not saying that pulling a Carrie Bradshaw (from *Sex and the City*) and buying that pair of shoes that has been talking to you through the store window is a bad thing. It is OK to treat yourself! There is joy in having beautiful things. We are talking about a persistent need to shop out of an emotional need to feel the temporary shopper's high. Shopping to fill a void in your life with things is not going to work because your soul needs something deeper. The need you are seeking to fill cannot be soothed with the season's latest styles. It needs to be soothed with love, support, and experiences that make you feel alive, not guilty that you have reached your credit limit.

By realizing that you are relying on a behavior to satisfy something on the inside, you can begin to regain your authority. Find support by telling your friends you need help with your shopaholic tendencies. Learn to be accountable to yourself, to them, and to your creditors. One of the fatherless daughters who contacted us through our website said that to cure her overspending, she put her credit cards into a large container of water and froze them. She keeps them in the freezer and when she has an impulse to buy something, she pulls out the container and waits for the ice to melt. If she still wants to make the purchase after the ice has melted, she does so. For her, taking the time she needs to examine why she is spending has given her the insight into what triggered the urge to shop and allows her to evaluate if the item is necessary or just an impulse buy.

We understand the desire to shop, but we also understand the huge hole that it can create—not only in your credit but in your heart. Recent studies have shown that people who save and spend their money on experiences or trips were happier in the long run than those who continued to accumulate *things*. Look for ways to fill your shopping bags with adventures and moments that make you feel good. Your pocketbook and heart will thank you.

Anorexia/Bulimia

As a fatherless daughter there is a strong likelihood that you have struggled with fear and instability in your life. What do we do when we feel like we do not have any control? We focus on something that *is* in our control and hypermanage it. Many women seek to gain control over their bodies by regulating the food they eat. They strive to maintain a certain weight, strictly limit what they eat, and associate food with control rather than nourishment.

Bethenny Frankel, who initially rose to fame on *The Real Housewives of New York City*, was estranged from her father right up to the day he died. Frankel told *US Weekly* in 2011, "I spent my entire life being obsessed with dieting. Bingeing and then fasting or starving. Forbidding everything."

If you are struggling with an eating disorder, your friends and family most likely know. What you may not know is that you could be struggling with body dysmorphia. What you see in the mirror may not be an accurate representation of the reality of how you look. Body dysmorphia can take over your thoughts with an imagined physical defect that is just not there. For a reality check, ask someone who loves you what they see when they look at you. Compare that with what you tell yourself when you see your body. If you are struggling with pervasive negative body image, it is important to seek out specialized treatment. There is a clinic, therapist, or support group in your area that can be found through an Internet search or request for a referral. The National Eating Disorders Association (NEDA) has a confidential Helpline (1-800-931-2237) that offers you the support you deserve.

The goal is to look in the mirror, say to yourself, "I love my body," and get to where you can believe it—cellulite, scars, and all. You are beautiful just the way you are.

Childhood Pain and Body Image

When a girl is abused, abandoned, or betrayed by her father, the wound left behind can be like a jagged cut that refuses to heal. If she was treated as if she were inadequate, unlovable, or burdensome, her young brain may have been programmed to carry those beliefs about herself and her body into adulthood. Quite often the father–daughter relationship is so powerful in a daughter's life that she develops an insatiable need to obtain approval about her looks from her father, which can be especially detrimental if she knows that being thin is preferable to him. Perhaps he told her mother and her that their thighs were getting too big or berated their curves. Those negative life experiences can become the blueprint by which she directs the shape of her body, which can morph into self-loathing, feelings of inferiority, and a complete lack of confidence that she is an exquisite creature both inside and out.

In an effort to try to transform herself into something lovable, a fatherless daughter might restrict her own needs to feel a sense of control and acceptance in an otherwise unstable environment. Looking in the mirror, she sees something very different from what others see, and she has learned that she somehow needs to change it to be loved and to love herself. By restricting her diet, overexercising, forcing her body to regurgitate food, or taking laxatives, she victimizes her body. The source of the behavior warrants compassion, but you now can make the choice to regain control over it.

Start by reaching out to someone you love and talking honestly about what you are doing and how you wish to change. Decide to be the one to love your body more than anyone in the world and show it that it is a temple of light in its natural shape. Love your body by feeding it what it needs to thrive and get the help to learn how to do that. When you are honoring your body's needs for healthy nourishment, your outward beauty will radiate like never before because it will reflect the true you.

Internet

There can be many reasons why the World Wide Web is comforting. For one, it is easy and available; two, you don't have to gussy up to spend the evening with it; and three, you can be anyone you want, looking at anything you want. You can post, comment, share, and feel gratified by doing so much more, and it's easier than having to do so face-to-face. And before you know it, hours, nights, and an entire weekend have gone by with you staring at the screen.

What emotional rewards are you getting from your interactions online? Is the exchange truly authentic to who you are and as fulfilling as real, face-to-face experiences with people? The web is an amazing thing. But is it getting in the way of your real life? Are you bowing out of commitments because of the time you want to spend gaming, or are you checking your messages every time you look at your phone? Is your use of the Internet interfering with your possibility for loving relationships with real people?

Do you want to change? Are you aware that you are missing real interaction with others because of your relationship with your screens? If so, you are like millions of other people in the world who are missing out on a mindful life. Ask for accountability from someone who lives with you or tell your friends that you are trying to make this change and need to see them more. Put your computer in the kitchen so you are accountable to your family or roommates. Post a Signing Off For Now message on your favorite social networking sites, and be proud of your hiatus. Engage in the real world; learn that your connections can become stronger when you show up in person.

Prescription Drugs

The day might come when you realize that getting drugs might not be as difficult or as wrong as you thought. After all, prescription drugs can be obtained from your doctor, mother's medicine cabinet, or online.

There is no secret about their accessibility. Therein lies one of our nation's biggest addiction problems, especially for those without the support and knowledge about the risks they pose to mind and body.

One of the fatherless daughters that we interviewed said it was a running joke to give a friend in her circle a bottle of prescription sleeping pills after a breakup. But there is no joke in sedative addiction. Taking prescription medication can seem harmless, but it can quickly lead to a real issue. In fact, accidental overdoses are on the rise because most people don't know the dangers of combining certain drugs—especially selective serotonin reuptake inhibitors (SSRIs), opioids, benzodiazepines, and alcohol. Mixing prescribed and/or illegal drugs can be deadly.

Prescription pill addiction is a real risk for women like fatherless daughters because of their lack of paternal guidance, effective coping skills, and feelings of self-worth. For example, Nina's father moved overseas for a job when she was five, ended up falling in love with a man, and never came back. She was devastated, feeling completely unlovable and abandoned. In her early twenties, she became addicted to prescription drugs.

When Mom and Dad divorced, my world fell apart. He just never looked back, and I still cannot understand why. Was he gay? He never even mentioned this to us once. When I was twenty-one, I had been out drinking and had a bad car accident, resulting in some major nerve and neck damage. I had several surgeries and ended up going on oxycodone. It was complete euphoria. It took the edge off of the pain and helped me detach emotionally. It was the first time that I realized I was not feeling all of the pain over my dad leaving, and it felt good.

No one knew, but I ended up getting several doctors to write prescriptions for me over the years for some pretty heavy stuff.

Before long I was on more oxycodone, Xanax, Adderall, and Ambien than anyone knew—not to mention my drinking. I spent years in a daze. I had to take pills to wake up and pills to go to sleep. I hid it from everyone, especially family.

When I was twenty-four I found out Daddy died, and I hit an all-time low. I was taking so many pills, I could not keep up. My tolerance had just gotten so high. I got in a fist fight with my brother, lost my job, got a DUI, and just started losing hope. So I would take more. The next week I ran out of all of the pills because two of my doctors had cut me off. I started to detox, and it was unbearable. After two years of this vicious circle, my family checked me into rehab for my third treatment. Finally, it hit home. One special counselor stayed late to talk to me every night—she had also lost her father. She helped me understand what I was doing to my body and why. I felt like someone finally understood my pain. I wanted to love myself again and find a way to feel joy instead of disconnection. I decided to change and become the artist I always wanted to be. I am still a work in progress, but I am determined to get back to who I am.

Are you asking for or taking more prescription medications than you really need to avoid the issues in your life? If you are, start by telling someone the real truth, preferably your prescribing physician. He or she can help you taper your habit in a safe way. Don't try to go it alone. This is not the time to continue your quest for isolation and independence. You need to decide for yourself that you want to change, but it also helps to have an advocate for your sobriety. You need someone to gauge your BS meter so you don't get into trouble again and again. We can lie to ourselves, but our friends or family can help hold us accountable if we let them in. Once the problem has been identified you can find a good therapist or a program with sponsors to help you become sober.

Self-Harm (Cutting)

Self-harm is one of the most controversial and misunderstood coping behaviors. Some wonder why anyone would heap pain on top of pain or see it as an attention-getting behavior. Fatherless daughters can be left with intense grief that makes them feel so isolated, so out of control and worthless, that they want to find a way out. The physical sensation of bodily pain (as from cutting) can eclipse the emotional pain and create an outlet, a sense of control, or even a trance experience, however temporary. Nearly 10 percent of fatherless daughters that we surveyed have confessed to cutting.

First, we could not be more adamant about this behavior being harmful. We understand it, but we want to be clear that hurting your body is not the way to solve pain. If you are experiencing these thoughts or actions take the first step and tell someone that you trust. Ask for the empathy and support that you need to get through this. The Adolescent Self Injury Foundation (adolescentselfinjuryfoundation.com) is a wonderful place to start getting the help that you need.

Over-the-Counter Drugs

Over-the-counter drugs are accessible and marketed to us daily. For many women, they are a hidden little secret. It can be the path of least resistance to getting the result you desire, whether it be a reduced appetite or more sleep. Renee, thirty-two, has always wanted to lose the twenty pounds she thinks is standing in her way of happiness. She had a family friend for an internist, which made things easy. He trusted her and gave her amphetamines to help her lose weight until he realized that she was also giving them to her friends. He immediately told her she had a problem and she should not take this type of pill again.

Desperate to lose more weight, Renee started taking over-the-counter diuretics and cold medicine because it subdued her appetite. When we asked her more about her history, we learned that although her father was in the home, he was not emotionally available. She shared with us that the only time he seemed to notice her was when she lost weight. Renee revealed, "I remember the one and only time Dad told me I was pretty. I had lost like twenty-five pounds on a crash diet, and he noticed me. He said, 'You look great, Renee—so skinny!' Finally, I felt like he loved me."

Whatever the reason, if you are relying on an over-the-counter drug, make no mistake: It is still a drug. The medications that women seem to struggle with most are those that help them sleep, such as nighttime pain killers and cough syrup. Adele recalled, "After I turned thirty, I was looking around, realizing that I still did not have a man and all of my friends were married. I was exhausted from going from man to man, and I couldn't figure out what I was doing wrong. I was over the whole scene and fell into depression. For about a year, when I got home from work, all I wanted to do was sleep, so I would take two Tylenol PMs after dinner and fall asleep. When I became tolerant to the two Tylenol PMs I added in a few glasses of wine to rock me to sleep. It became a habit, and I could not sleep without it. Who knows what I did to my liver that year."

If you are like Adele and are taking a sleep aid on a nightly basis, it is time to take a look at why you are having insomnia. Are you anxious? It is important to see a medical doctor to address what could be causing your sleeplessness. Are you carrying too much mental stress? Are you trying to avoid feeling by sleeping? Oversleeping can be an act of avoidance, and, you guessed it, isolation. Neither are healthy coping mechanisms to get you better in the long run. Try avoiding caffeine and strenuous exercise for a few hours before bed. Let your body know it is time for rest. Breathe slowly and deeply into gentle stretching movements. Massage your muscles with a foam roller on the floor. Enjoy a long bath. Turn off the noise. Unplug. Read. Journal. Consider natural therapies like chamomile, lemon balm, or valerian root. Do some research and find what is safe and effective for you. Make a promise to yourself to figure out what it is that is keeping you awake. There are times and situations that warrant a little help with your sleep for periods of time. If you have begun to abuse over-the-counter medication to mask another problem, that problem will still be there when you wake up.

Recent studies on sleep show that seven to nine hours a night are a good gauge for healthy rest. If you are regularly sleeping much more or much less a night (or day), you are disrupting your body's natural circadian rhythms. This compromises your immune system and further contributes to feelings of depression, instability, and anxiety.

Finding a balance of exercise, routine, stress relief, diet, and self-care can help you regulate sleep without overusing medication. Consult a physician, homeopathic doctor, or sleep specialist for guidance on what is best for you.

Healthy Coping

There are healthy ways to cope and heal.

Facing your feelings is the first step toward coping with something that is painful. Psychiatrist Carl Jung said, "What you resist, persists." When a fatherless daughter decides to take a deep breath, pull her real feelings up from hiding, and acknowledge what is inside of her, she is taking a huge step in learning how to cope. Once she knows what she is dealing with and decides to seek support from others (and from within herself), she then can decide how long she is going to stay in those emotions. This part is up to each woman individually. Yes, finding the roots of the emotions can become an integral part of healing. Going back is sometimes the best thing about moving forward.

Coping comes to us in response to different stressors or issues.

1. Acute triggers: specific short-term situations, which require coping by engaging in a healthy response in the moment. This can mean using deep breathing, removing yourself from the situation, or responding to the other person with "I" statements. Using "I" statements is a way of communicating your position without putting the other person on the defensive. You state your feelings honestly by beginning your statements with *I* instead of *you*. For example, instead of saying, *"You* are always so flirtatious with other women!" you say, *"I* feel very insecure when I see someone I am committed to touching another woman—even if it is casual affection." This keeps the focus on your feelings instead of making an accusation that the other person immediately feels the need to defend. "I" statements dismantle the need to argue and instead focus on the feelings that were triggered by the situation.

2. Occasional patterns of hurt: encountering new relationships or situations that may last a limited amount of time. When something about an experience or person pulls at your nerves, you need a way to handle it and continue on. Coping could mean being clear about boundaries or finding release by doing something physical like running or something relaxing like listening to classical music. You find your best methods of refueling and repairing the emotional and mental wear and tear you experience in a given situation.

3. Long-term pain and suffering: most likely rooted in a pain suffered in childhood, perhaps father loss, that will likely always affect you on some level. When exposed to a trigger, you must learn to remind yourself of your own strengths and hope. Positive coping methods are those that lower your stress level and increase your sense of well-being naturally. You may have to go through some trial and error to hit on the ideal coping mechanisms that work for you, whether it be a cleansing visualization, positive self-talk, or physical activity. Understanding where the emotions are coming from, how they feel, and why you are reacting are necessary steps to coping with long-term pain.

By building up a collection of coping skills, a fatherless daughter has a host of positive techniques at the ready, which also helps free up some of the mental space she had been using to dwell on old issues. It's likely that she developed her habitual negative coping and distracting skills as a way to avoid (knowingly or unknowingly) facing her issues. Many fatherless daughters turn to hobbies as a seemingly healthy distraction, but this replacement activity generally works for only a short time. To achieve long-term results, she must commit to long-term changes. Stepping onto the road of self-discovery and resilient healing is key to becoming fully engaged in living the life you want.

To break free from unhealthy patterns you can begin to determine how to fill the time that you formerly spent on unhealthy coping with healthier choices. Start by becoming aware of the situations or stressors that send you down the path of negative coping. Your body has established a habit—a pattern of behavior—and you need to teach it how to intervene on its own behalf with a new code of conduct.

After you have increased your awareness, you will be ready to deal with your feelings by choosing new, healthier ways of dealing with life. With this growth can come the restoration of your stronger, happier

self. In order to find what might help, ask yourself, "When was I completely happy in my life? What was I doing? What was I really good at?
What made me feel joyful?"

Denna remembers signing up to complete her first and only mara-
thon after about six months of doing her self-work.

> I decided that I needed a goal. I wanted to do something that would
> both help me and benefit others—so I ran for the Leukemia and
> Lymphoma Society. Through stress fractures, blisters, missing toe-
> nails, and the companionship of my friend Traci, I ran every day
> and ended up raising almost $20K for the Leukemia and Lymphoma
> Society. We honored Traci's mother, Carlene, and my paternal grand-
> mother, Heida, both of whom had battled cancer. Every time I wanted
> to give up while on a hard run, I would talk to my dad in my head.
> I would hear him along with my mom and uncle telling me that I
> could do it. On the day of the marathon, around mile sixteen, my
> stress fractures were killing me, and I thought about quitting. I told
> myself not to give up and began talking to my dad again. I said,
> "OK, I need you to meet me at the finish line." Tears started to fall.
> I saw my husband, who was my boyfriend at the time, standing
> proudly at the finish line. I quietly started thanking him, my dad,
> my mom, my brother, my uncle, my friends, and everyone for help-
> ing me while I got to this glorious point in my life. I tore through
> the finish line and felt a euphoria that I had never experienced. I had
> finished a marathon and started to let go of my past. I was replacing
> everything in my life with love. Life was opening itself up to me,
> and boy was I ready to take it!

Going back to school at age thirty became the most life-changing
decision in Karin's journey. It was her therapists who suggested she take
the leap of faith after coming through a series of losses in her life.

Becoming a counselor and an educator became Karin's life calling, and a decade later, she completed her doctorate.

> Walking across that stage—by then a mother of three—I felt like I had earned the biggest prize in the world. I had gotten myself back . . . and in the meantime left a legacy of resilience for my own children. It was the persistent drive to prove so many people wrong who had hurt me in the past that I had what it took to earn a PhD. And now, those old voices don't even matter anymore—it is the purpose of my journey that has moved front and center.

Go toward what you love, what is healthy, and what is *good*. Sing that old-school song to yourself, find that book that once made you feel powerful, set up something to look forward to this weekend. Surround yourself with people and situations that inspire you, not diminish you.

If you need to, remember to use a lifeline for any addictive behavior. You can find help through organizations that specialize in prevention and treatment for your specific issues, such as Alcoholics Anonymous (AA), Narcotics Anonymous (NA), Cocaine Anonymous (CA), the National Clearinghouse for Alcohol and Drug Abuse Information Line (800-729-6686), or the Eating Disorders Awareness and Prevention Helpline (800-931-2237). Speaking to someone who has been in your shoes can help you ride out your urges and triggers.

Positive Coping

The fatherless women we surveyed engaged in a range of activities that helped them cope when they were faced with life's challenges. We asked respondents to select from a list all of the positive coping skills that they had used in the years following their father loss. As you can see, fatherless daughters relied on a range and combination of creative coping skills. Looking at the list below, it might be a nice surprise to see that you have already implemented positive coping skills in your own life—maybe without even knowing it.

Listening to music	50 percent
Laughter and humor	40 percent
Journaling or writing	33 percent
Time with animals	30 percent
Religious or spiritual practices	27 percent
Self-help/inspirational reading	26 percent
Time in nature	25 percent
Physical health	21 percent
Traveling/adventure	17 percent
Therapy	17 percent

Other healthy coping experiences included dancing, volunteering, painting, drawing, playing an instrument, and meditation. We also found that once many of these fatherless daughters did their work and began handling stress differently, more lifelong changes took place in their lives, from getting sober to starting a business. The possibilities are boundless.

Now that you have plenty to pick from, write down three coping mechanisms that you can begin to use. Which ones make you smile? (Feel free to list more than three if you wish!)

1. _____

2. _____

3. _____

Here is your homework for the week. Put reminders in your phone or on your calendar to do at least one of these positive coping mechanisms every day. Schedule it as an appointment and honor it. By doing so, you will give yourself a healthy dose of feel-good neurotransmitters (chemicals your brain releases to your body's systems), leading to an instant boost. The body releases chemicals like dopamine and serotonin into your system to let you know when you are doing things that are beneficial to your well-being. They are your rewards. So go ahead, dose yourself! By doing this every day, you are reeducating your body on how to cope with life by medicating itself with its own chemicals, which will put you on the right track to a happier life—naturally.

Not every fatherless daughter has succumbed to bad habits. Some have been able to find better ways and healthier choices by filling up their time early on using many of the ideas listed in this chapter. We are each on our own path, and the desire to live a purely happy life is inside of each of us.

Lolo Jones is an Olympian with three gold medals who was raised by a single mother. She discovered her interest in track while attending day camps at the church where she and her family resided in the basement. She turned her circumstances into blessings and didn't let herself slide into victimhood.

Misty Copeland is a dancer for the American Ballet Theatre, and only the third African American soloist to dance for the company. Copeland was estranged from her biological father between the ages of two and twenty-two and was raised by her mother and a series of stepfathers. She was first introduced to ballet at her local Boys & Girls Club, where she spent her afternoons after school. It was there that she met her mentor, Cynthia Bradley, whom she eventually moved in with and who coached her to becoming a professional dancer.

Both of these women are a true testament to rising above tremendous losses as children. They both used physical activity as a distraction and a coping mechanism to make it through childhoods that otherwise could have pushed them in an entirely different direction.

Barbra Streisand, Mary J. Blige, and Mariah Carey sang through their childhoods. All three singers are fatherless. Mother Teresa's father was murdered, and she became the ultimate example of living a meaningful life. The fatherless daughter who inspires you may be that woman who you admire most at work, the funniest one in your book club, or the mom next door who seems to roll with life, no matter the obstacles.

Remind yourself to see the survivors around you as inspiration, but also remember that there is always more to the story than what you see on the outside. There is a balance that we must strike when we look at others, just as when we look at ourselves. Part compassion, part push, part deal, part drive.

For each success, every laugh, there might have been twenty failures and a hundred tears. Watch what makes these women rise above. You have that in you. It is called resilience.

There is life beyond the mess you feel inside. You may be both driven and discouraged at the same time. The takeaway here is to tackle the ghosts of the past so that they no longer claim your future.

CHAPTER 7

Missing Your Dad

If I'd had someone, anyone, to guide me through those years, to
tell me that what I felt was normal, that I wasn't alone, maybe
it would have been different. But if you haven't been through
a major loss, then the truth is that you just don't know
what to say to someone who has.

~Claire Bidwell Smith, *The Rules of Inheritance*

Certain days on the calendar can wreak havoc on your psyche. If you are like other fatherless daughters there is usually one day that is particularly arduous because of what it brings up for you. Overwhelmingly, fatherless daughters queried in our surveys reported Father's Day as the hardest day to get through. It is the one day that they feel the most alone and the saddest about their loss.

Studies show that daughters whose fathers have passed carry the most sadness. They usually mourn their father loss over and over again. There can be an unwritten expectation that these daughters preserve their fathers' memory. Sabrina, twenty-five, told us, "My dad died in November. However, it was not until I was in college when I saw the exact date. Maybe

I buried it in my subconscious, but when I pulled out his death certificate from my safe, I saw the date glaring back at me in bold print. He had died on November 16th. I made myself internalize it into my memory. What kind of daughter was I for not 'mourning appropriately' for him on the date of his death? From that moment on, I started to regress at the beginning of every November. Thanksgiving was blown for me—for life. I made sure that all my friends and loved ones recognized the day as well, not because I wanted the attention, but because I thought that he deserved it."

Sabrina dearly loved her father. Remembering the date of his death became important to her. Grief is as unique as the person going through it. If your father died, consider letting those close to you know the days that are the most difficult for you so that they can understand you better and know how to help you. Open up. Explain what happens when you are triggered and tell them the importance of someone calling to say they care. If, after a substantial amount of time your grief becomes over-whelming and is interfering with your daily activities, it may be time to think about getting some help to deal with his loss. Grief counselors and support groups can facilitate beautiful bridges to peace and acceptance.

For some, it is the anniversary of his death; others the day he walked out the door. You might grieve in silence so you don't make everyone around you feel uncomfortable, or you might get together with a sibling to talk through the day. Some women's upset is more apparent. They may snap at their significant others or curse the poor table that gets in their way as they stand up to stomp out of the room. We've hosted our own pity parties, so we totally get it. Not having your dad around isn't fair. It is not fair that you had to have your brother walk you down the aisle. It is not fair that your father did not tell you how proud he was at your graduation. It is not fair that your child does not have a maternal grandfather. And while it may sound childish and petulant to bemoan the "unfairness" of life, sometimes fatherless daughters (no matter how old) feel like the child who just lost her dad.

It may take friends or significant others a few years to understand the wide range of emotions that you regularly face missing your father. Fatherless daughters whose fathers are still living wonder, Do I mourn him? Do I get angry? Do I try to forge ahead and ignore that he has not called me in years to wish me a happy birthday? Even if you choose to try to ignore your loss, major milestones and holidays can be surprising reminders of his absence. These are the days when a fatherless daughter might recognize that she is different from everyone else. Her father is gone. She stands in line with her children to visit Santa and feels like every single person has a gray-haired grandpa with them except her family. If he is still alive, she has probably come to believe that she is not important to him or loved by him. It is downright heartbreaking. If a father has died, not only does she keenly miss him, but she mourns that he is missing out on a celebration or seeing his grandchild. Even the happiest events can be tinged with sadness.

Once your dad is gone there will be significant moments in your life that will hold new meaning. You may miss him on Passover or be sad on the day you go for your first job interview because he is not there to give you a pep talk. You may have become overly emotional or irritated in any given situation without being aware of the root cause of your anger or upset—your dad isn't there.

There are so many moments when you can feel his loss. Some days are common to other fatherless daughters (holidays, birthdays), some days are specific to you and are not necessarily an anniversary or annual holiday. Something as ordinary as trying to push a sofa up your new apartment building's stairwell can make you feel more alone than any-one could ever imagine. Maria, twenty-one, told us how it is for her. "I cringe when I hear my roommate on the phone with her dad. Some-times I literally have to put my fingers in my ears so I don't have to hear their playful banter. I am glad she will never have to know what it is like to have no one to call. If her tire is flat, he is her mechanic. If she feels lonely, he is there to hug her. If her bank account is low, he is her lender. She has no idea the pain that I carry. She has no idea how sad it makes me, and I don't want her to. But I walk around with this jealousy in my gut because I wish that he were my dad too."

Envying other father–daughter relationships is not something that a fatherless daughter likes to admit; she tries to learn to live with it. Although major milestones bring your loss front and center, everyday small reminders can continue to stir feelings that are a part of your normal. Going to a game and sitting next to a father with his daughters cheering for your team might put a lump in your throat. Watching a father and daughter have lunch at a nearby table could make you choke back tears. Seeing your daughter being carried around on your husband's shoulders can take you back to your childhood yard all of those years ago. His loss is always there, following you around like your own shadow.

What can you do to feel better? How do you mourn him while continuing to live your own life? How do you shed the pain of the past in order to move ahead? If he is still alive, do you contact him? If so, when should you reach out to him, and when should you make the decision not to? These are all questions that we cover later in this chapter.

Your Father Passed Away

If you lost your father through death when you were a child, having someone to help you through this process can be both validating and gratifying. Although you grieved for him when you were a child, it can be helpful to explore your childhood loss from an adult perspective.

If you feel better handling things on your own, a book called *The Inner Child Workbook* by Cathryn L. Taylor has helped many people get to the root of their lost childhood. The point is, there are resources out there for you, and all you have to do is reach out. Ask a connection in the healthcare field to help you find a referral to a therapist who specializes in your specific needs, such as grief, loss, or trauma. With support and guidance you can learn some wonderful things about yourself that you were not expecting. Give yourself that gift.

Twice Lost

If you were estranged from your father or hardly knew him before his death, finding out who he really was and how he lived can be challenging. If you have tried to find out more about him, you probably had to depend on other family members, friends, or photographs to help you fill in the blanks about his life. If a long period of time has lapsed, people may not remember the specific details about him or his life, which can be discouraging. The people you most need to speak to may have passed on or you have long since lost contact with them. If there is some secret about what happened to him, people might not open up and give you the answers that you need.

In the case of divorce, your mom might not want to speak of your father or may have only negative things to say about him. Asking about him might put you in an especially vulnerable place and might leave you disappointed by what you discover. Sometimes the story that you believe you need and seek is not the story that you find. These stories are what fill in the blanks to what you are missing and when you are missing it. They will change according to where you are in your process of grieving and what you are going through in your life. You will want to know different things about your father when you are fifteen, twenty-five, thirty-five, and so on. Perspectives change and curiosity opens up as life experience unfolds.

Discussing your dad with your siblings can be helpful for all of you. Although you shared him, you will realize that each of you has different memories and perceptions of him. Share specific moments or stories that stand out to you—no matter how silly, small, or emotional they might feel to you—you can help one another fill in your memories. Putting the pieces back together is not an easy undertaking. Let those close to you know what you are attempting to do and ask for help. Gaining an understanding of the past in order to move forward can have huge emotional benefits. You will be free to move toward your future while living in the moment; you will be able to recognize your feelings and curiosities as your truths, tending to them when needed. As you move forward, you will be creating a rhythm of healing for yourself.

For some fatherless daughters, the process of going back can be much more difficult. If your father suffered from his own demons, finding peace yourself can be challenging. Trying to make sense of his problems can turn your heart and mind upside down. It can make you wonder if you are doomed by your DNA as well as question your own tendencies. No matter what, it is always up to you to decide how deep to dig.

By researching who he really was and what his life entailed, you will get to know your father in a new way. Be ready and open. As you speak to others, you might find yourself defending who he was in order to bring some honor to his life and put his memory to rest. Keep in mind that your relationship with your dad was unique. At the same time, you will have to figure out how seeing his history through the eyes of others can benefit you and help you live a meaningful life.

During the times that you reflect on your fatherless story, keep yourself grounded in the present while you thoughtfully look back. Keep reminding yourself that you are living a different life now and are not going to relive the same story. It is possible to use the insight that you are gaining as building blocks to help you reach a new, freer place in your life from here forward.

Keeping His Memory Alive

There are many ways to keep your father's memory alive. Talk about him with family and friends. Remind them to ask you questions as well. Tell them it does not upset you to talk about your father, in fact, it helps you to keep him present in your life. Incorporate your dad into your own life experiences, like during a big move, when you turn thirty, or when you go on an important interview. Look at photos, watch old home movies, carry his vintage watch in your pocket, or spray some of his cologne on your arm. These physical symbols of him are confirmation of your connection. If you have something on your heart, talk to him. Write him a letter. Get it all out. It will help you become clearer and release so much that is still inside of you. These are all forms of communication and confirmation of the ongoing relationship that you have with him. You can bet that many people (including us) would tell you that he can indeed feel and hear you.

Remember your dad in whatever way feels right to you, and make it unique to you and your family. One young woman we spoke with talked about the memorial and celebration her family holds each year on her father's birthday. All of his children put on one of his many fedora hats and take silly, wonderful pictures together. (Don't you love that?) Another young lady we interviewed revealed that on her wedding day she wore her father's wedding ring to feel close to him. The Kardashians' father was Armenian American, so every year on the anniversary of their father's death they go to a local Armenian restaurant and have a family meal.

Sadie, ten, was two years old when her father passed away in his sleep while only in his mid-twenties. He was cremated and his ashes are contained in one side of a beautiful mahogany box. The other side holds years of letters that Sadie had penned to her father. One such letter simply says, "Dear Daddy, I like spaghetti. Do you? It is my favorite meal that Mommy makes for me. What is your favorite meal?" Sadie has found a way to continue conversations with her father. As she ages, her relationship with him and to his loss will continue to change and deepen.

The way we grieve may seem random to some and meaningful to others. You may find yourself stopping by the cemetery every Tuesday or never at all. A bag of boiled peanuts or a Motown song may bring tears to your eyes and a smile to your face. Perusing old letters or videos might make you cry one day and laugh the next. He was and will always be your father. You miss him. Countless fatherless daughters have described to us how they often talk to their dad and believe that his spirit helps guide them in their life. Some look for signs that he might leave along the way—a ladybug, a cardinal, or a penny—and they treasure these gifts each time they find one. Your way of remembering is just as special as you are. Trust whatever feels right to you and claim it as your own.

Your Father Is Absent and Still Living

If her father left by choice and is still alive, a fatherless daughter will feel something very different from a daughter whose father is deceased. He is out there somewhere and there is still a possibility that she will have contact. Perhaps she will find him or he will come searching for her. Maybe she finds herself perpetually on the look-out for him as she shops, strolls through the park, or attends a crowded event. She may envision one day running into him in public and often have an internal dialogue about what she might say. Some fatherless daughters have googled their dad or found him on Facebook. It can be particularly painful to see his life play out on the Internet through relatives who are still in touch with him when she is not.

Maybe you want to confront him, but you cannot. Maybe you want
to hold him closer, but you can't seem to figure out how. Ask yourself,
How big of a place does my father deserve to have in my life? Look at
your expectations compared to reality and sit down with someone who
can see things objectively and help you figure out what is realistic and
best for you. Balance what is good for your heart against what is causing
you pain (or *could* cause you pain), and move toward those things that
help you feel more balanced. Seek out that place where you stop putting
yourself in a position of being a victim. It is time to stop being consumed
by something that is out of your control and instead start claiming
power over your life and self-worth. What do you really and truly want?
Where can you find that if your father is unavailable? What have others
told you that you deserve? What is realistic and what is false hope?
Which direction has your spirit been tugging you?

Look at the truth of your life and his life. How do you want this relationship to look in six months? A year? Where do you want to be as a
woman at peace? Create a plan of action for what you need to do to get
there, and value your own life enough to release your mind from painful
thought cycles. It was not your fault. You are valuable. You can do this.

Phoebe, twenty-one, knows all too well how it feels to be continuously let down by her biological father.

My dad won a few hundred thousand dollars on a scratch-off lottery
ticket. Someone in his family slipped up and told me. They made
me promise not to tell him that I knew. I sat quiet right through my
twenty-first birthday with no call and no present from him. A few
of my friends had gotten new cars and beautiful jewelry from their
dads. Not me—it really hurt.

I got extremely depressed and worked myself up so much that I
had to go to the ER with an ulcer. He went crazy with his new
money buying a boat, a new truck, and a Jet Ski. A month later my

college tuition and hospital bill were due. My mom was helping as much as she could. I was working a full-time job. Still, I needed money. I decided to do something I had never done before. I confronted him. It did not go over well. He yelled at me, saying, "You and your mother want to take everything from me!" before slamming down the phone. We barely talk now. Not that we spoke much before. I knew that if I ever crossed him he would desert me. What little relationship we once had is now done for good.

If you are a fatherless daughter whose father is absent by choice, you will probably have to work extra hard to manage your expectations regarding him. It can be difficult to strike a balance between being bitter and holding on to hope. There is no crystal ball to see into the future of your relationship, so there is no telling what could happen. However, keep in mind: Past behavior is the best predictor of future behavior. You can count on people being who they are unless they have experienced a major life shift out of the desire to change. For you, that may mean that you need to take yourself by the hand, steel yourself for what is ahead, and acknowledge reality, based on his past performance: "I know what to expect. Either my dad is capable or he is not. Nothing I can do can change who he is. I won't set myself up for disappointment by expecting him to be someone he is not. I will draw on my inner strength and trust my own wisdom and resilience." Repeat this over and over again. Over time, you will absorb that truth and feel stronger about your decisions.

Elle, thirty, looks back on her childhood and remembers asking her mother questions about her emotionally unavailable father. "I would say, 'Mom, why doesn't Dad ever go to any of my tennis matches?' 'Mom, why doesn't Daddy sit down and eat dinner with us at night?' 'Mom, why is Daddy always on the phone?' 'Mom, why does Daddy stay inside his office and never come out and spend time with us?' Over time, Mom's excuses became transparent, and I learned that there was nothing endearing enough that I could do to make him choose me over his computer and phone. It just was what it was. I never understood him or really knew him. And he definitely doesn't know me. I don't know why he had children, to be honest."

Being repeatedly neglected and abandoned never gets easy. It is unnatural. Deciding between letting go of having a real relationship with your father or reaching out to try once more can be an overwhelming choice. Daughters are not meant to be put in this position, but all too often, they are. While time can deepen the wound, sometimes time and space can bring clarity.

Angelina Jolie Pitt has spoken publicly about her estrangement from her father. It has been reported that their disconnection was because he had an extramarital affair while still married to her mother. After her parents divorced in 1976, their single mother raised Jolie and her brother. Jolie has admitted to suffering from depression, drug use, and self-harming along the way.

Her father, actor Jon Voight, told *Access Hollywood* that Jolie had mental problems and needed help. As a result, in 2002, the actress dropped "Voight" from her name and distanced herself from her father. They were estranged off and on for the next decade before reconciling. Jolie, just like many other fatherless daughters, suffered through a lot of uncertainties and emotional pain trying to put herself back together again. Later, Voight admitted to not realizing the suffering that his daughter was going through after the family broke up. He stated, "She was a baby when we were divorced. So it surprised me when she said it affected her as severely as it did. But, looking back, I can see that there were times when perhaps she expressed her anger in different ways."

Your experience and your father's experience of the past are bound to be very different. Understanding if and when you want to separate from or reconcile with your father is a personal choice and one that is a part of your own growth and self-awareness.

If your dad is out there somewhere, when it comes to him it might be difficult to find a place to rest emotionally. Some days, you might feel at peace to think of him never being in your life, only to question it the next. If you have unresolved issues with your dad, you will be more sensitive to triggers and likely have a difficult time getting clear on how you really feel and what you can truly expect. Figuring out how to let go of or hold onto your father isn't easy, but it can be a significant stepping-stone on your path. Claim your truth, your needs, and your emotions. Then find a healthy way to speak them, feel them, act on them, and continue living. With the right support, you will find the answers and growth that your life deserves.

Yes, this takes time, and there is not one timetable that fits every situation. Karin shares that she did not figure out things until she faced some personal struggles after having three young children of her own. Relationships took on a different meaning to her then. She had a difficult time determining what would be best for her in regard to each of her fathers because of what the truth might mean. She went back and forth about what to say to her birth father, whether or not to contact her stepfather, and how to handle the situation with the rest of the family. It took years of reflection, spiritual work, and therapy for her to find peace. As her natural father became more integrated in her life as her dad and her children's grandpa, she got honest with him and embraced the relationship for what it was. This was a great reward for her, as she never had a close relationship with a grandfather and to see her children have that gift was beautiful. After seldom seeing him as a child, he now visits her and her children more than anyone else in the family—quite the miracle. Over time, Karin chose not to reach out to the adoptive father who raised her. They had been estranged for half of her life at that point, and she had to let go of the hope that he would be who she needed him to be. Ultimately, she felt sadness and loss alongside freedom and peace that she had never felt before, and all were healing. You truly never know how your story is going to play out.

Take responsibility for where you are in life right now—are you blaming your father for everything or are you being accountable for yourself? Do you set yourself up to be hurt? Are you constantly feeling like a victim? Have you looked at the control you have in making decisions? As Lynne Forrest explains in her transformational book *Guiding Principles for Life beyond Victim Consciousness*, "We automatically assume that our discomfort and misery come from outside causes or circumstances. . . . [B]ut the true reason for our unhappiness is always what we are thinking about an event, never the event itself."

It is time to stop being consumed by something that is out of your control and instead start claiming your own power over your life and self-worth. Staying in the victim role only relinquishes your power. It gives it to something or someone outside of you. Something that is not supposed to define you.

To help you determine what you should do, ask yourself these questions:

- What do I really and truly want from the relationship?
- Does my father wish to become available to me or has he shown me otherwise?
- What have others told me that I deserve or what I might expect from him?
- What is realistic and what is false hope?

Tune into the direction that your spirit (not your wounded self) has been tugging you toward; we can promise you it's not in the direction of victimhood. Create a plan of action for what you need to do to get to a place of strength and prioritize the happiness that you seek in your life.

An action plan could include therapy for learning how to reconcile unanswered questions or praying over the decision about whether or not to contact your father. Perhaps contacting him is not an option, so set a goal of finding more peace with letting go of the relationship with your father. Ask for work to do outside of therapy, examining the pros and cons in your decisions and implementing your own power. Harness what is already inside of you and feed it until it grows.

Making Contact

However your father left your life, there is something that almost all of us have in common: We have some things we wish we could say to him. You may need clarification from him or more information from family.

In our survey, an overwhelming 91 percent of fatherless daughters revealed that they had something they wished to say to their dads. Almost half of fatherless daughters interviewed would say, "I wish we had more time together" or "I needed you." A large number of women would tell their dads, "You have no idea how much pain I have been in," while others would say, "I wish I could have helped you." Only 7 percent of fatherless daughters would tell their fathers that they do not forgive them, whereas 28 percent wanted to say, "I forgive you."

You might have questions for your dad too. Many of the fatherless daughters we spoke to said they would ask their fathers why they didn't love them or exactly why they left. You might have the same yearning to hear answers directly from the source. Whatever you are feeling, whatever you want to say, is exactly right for you. Only you know what the voice inside of you needs to speak. This is about finding a way to let it out, however that is for you.

We have heard many stories about fathers who failed to contact their daughters because they thought it was too late, were scared, or felt completely inadequate. We have also seen many fathers who try to make up for their lack of good fathering with being a loving and present grandfather. Fathers are human after all, and a man's—a father's—ego can be a very fragile thing. Sometimes a new connection can bring healing, but be realistic, because setting yourself up for more disappointment can cause you to backslide into the victim role or reopen still-raw wounds. Prepare yourself for any outcome and have your healthy coping mechanisms and support network in place.

The reason and way that he left will help you to resolve the question of whether your relationship is over. The circumstances of his leaving speak volumes about his character and the possibility for his making efforts toward recovering a relationship with you.

Five Reasons You Might Want to Give Your Dad Another Chance

1. He has tried at some point in your life to have contact with you without asking for anything in return.
2. Your mother has only said bad things about him and not let you find out about him yourself.
3. He gave you up for adoption or never knew about you to begin with.
4. He has successfully completed therapy, a twelve-step program, or had a spiritual renewal.
5. He has not had a chance to do anything right with you and you truly believe he deserves that.

At the end of the day, while it is his choice whether to respond to you, you also have a choice to pursue the relationship or let it go. If your gut tells you that you might not know the whole story and if you won't be putting yourself at risk, then maybe it is time to reach out to him.

Maybe you have heard only one side of the story (likely your mom's or grandmother's), and he has been demonized all of these years. Their experiences have left them feeling the way that they feel, but you have your own road to walk.

Has it been weighing on you to sit down with your father and hear him out? First, get yourself in a healthy place before you pursue interacting with him. Make sure that you are ready for any outcome, and by all means see what may come of it. Tell yourself that you are seeking the truth, and be very careful about any expectations you might have. Be as prepared as possible, protect yourself, and ask for support. Then go where your heart leads, and take somebody you trust with you.

On the other hand, is there something in your past that has kept you from contacting him? Pay attention to that feeling in your gut. Kim, forty-five, said that one of the best pieces of advice she has ever received about her dad was from a therapist. When she was dealing with her daddy issues at age thirty, her wise psychoanalyst looked up at her and said, "The sad part about acceptance is that there really are *just purely bad people* out there. And your dad is one of them. He's a bad person, Kim. He abused you and is not a healthy person. He is not going to change. Narcissists feel entitled to their behavior. This is a very sad story. I am so sorry you went through this." After Kim took in what her therapist was saying, she surprised herself and felt validated and lighter! Somebody had finally given her permission to speak the truth about her dad and stop feeling guilty—and then replied to her with more truth. After years of carrying around the burden of thinking she needed to do something, anything, to make things better, to make him change, to make him love her, she was released. The fact is, we cannot change other people. People change only when two conditions are met: they want to and they have the capacity to. *Period.*

If your dad was a bad egg, you have suffered. The miracle is that you are here, but the tragedy is that to stay healthy, he cannot be an intimate part of your life. It is OK to grieve the loss of hope of reconciliation. Giving up and mourning what you were supposed to have is important. Most people have never been through what you have experienced, so it may be difficult for them to understand this part of your loss, asking, "Why would you want to have someone so toxic in your life?" What they may not understand is that you are mourning *the idea* of having a father as well as being sad about the circumstances of your life. Part of letting go is realizing and releasing that thing that you might be holding on to so tightly while resisting at the same time. It is a Buddhist principle that resistance of unpleasant things is the root of suffering. It is time for the suffering to end. We want *you* to thrive and feed the hope for your own life by letting go of those things that weigh you down.

If you have a bad feeling in your gut and are confused about contacting your dad because part of you knows that you will be hurt, here are some things to think about regarding healthy boundaries.

Five Reasons You Might Want to Keep a Healthy Distance from Your Dad

1. He abused or traumatized you sexually, physically, or emotionally.
2. He molested you, your siblings, your friends, or other children.
3. He has continued to engage in criminal activities, including substance abuse, violence, theft, or fraud that could put you at risk.
4. He has stolen from you or otherwise betrayed your trust.
5. He is an eternal victim, blaming everyone but himself, demanding that everyone meet his needs while he refuses to change.

The biggest rule of thumb here is to follow your instincts and not let your little-girl needs lead you astray. You are an adult, you are wise, and you can make an intelligent choice. Listen to the reflections of others, the truth from family members, and the wisdom of your own intuition. While the decision is your own to make, that doesn't mean that you have to make it alone. Don't forget about your stand-ins and the other amazing people who have stepped up in your life and continue to do so. They are wonderful souls who came into your world for moments such as these.

A Few Tips for When You Miss Your Dad

Self-acceptance and love can be significant ways to keep yourself grounded and strong. Stay in the moment, resist self-judgment, and dismiss negative thoughts and memories about yourself. Give your body, mind, and spirit time to rejuvenate themselves and rebuild the weak spots that yearn to strengthen.

During the times that awareness of your loss floods in, the void can feel like it is as big as the room. When you feel the time is right, let it go in a safe place. It can be a good idea to have a cue word that your spouse or partner knows so that he or she understands when you get flooded with grief or need to be left alone. By saying something like "space," you grant yourself permission to honor your emotions in privacy, without worrying about anyone else's needs. Karin's spiritual mentor recently told her, "Cry. Cry. Cry. Crying is like giving birth to your emotions." With release comes healing. Listen to your body. Listen to your heart. Take your time in the way that feels right to you.

Sometimes the missing can be lessened when you revere your father's memory in some way. This can allow you to maintain a connection with him. Some women find comfort in engaging in an activity that they did with their dads, such as visiting a ball park, going to a show, or taking a day trip to a special spot. Others may find purpose and peace by volunteering, fund-raising, or donating to a cause he supported or one that has special meaning for him. Find your way of connecting and prioritize this time with him as part of your healing.

CHAPTER 8

Moving Forward: Mentally, Physically, and Spiritually

The body heals with play, the mind heals with laughter,
and the spirit heals with joy.

~Proverb

Attracting and living the good life means you will have to make some shifts in the way you think, act, and expect life to be. This means deciding that you are not going to let pain and resentment hold you down anymore because that keeps you in the victim role. You are allowed to feel, cry, and ask for TLC on Father's Day. Claiming and expressing emotions are a part of being in charge of this process. However, holding on to pain and keeping your life stuck in old patterns do not foster change. Let the positive in and make room for growth.

Most people resist change because it can be scary. There is risk that you will fail. In order to move ahead you have to let go of your security blanket. Your fatherless story will now change because you view it with a different perspective. Perhaps you have held tightly to the identity of being fatherless, and you are ready to shed that piece of how you present yourself to the world. You decide to lead with what you have gained in your life rather than what you have lost. You have to learn and practice a new way of doing things and venture down an unfamiliar road. There may be some people in your world who are not on board with the New You. Because you are ready to change your path, as you start putting thoughts to actions, your energy will shift and people will pick up on it. You will give off a glow that others will start to notice.

Within a short time, you will see growth, and that should be something to embrace. You will have clearer mental wisdom, deeper emotional insight, and more purposeful spiritual direction. You might feel yourself opening up so fully that you sense you are going through a deeper transformation. Things will become lighter; the world will become more beautiful. Old hurts will begin to fade away and peace and forgiveness will begin to take root. You can become so much more than you once believed.

Claiming It

Begin to feel pride in how far you have come on your journey. Even if you are in a rough spot in life, your childhood is behind you; you made it. You did the best you could at each hour along the way. To grant yourself the growth that you are looking for, you need to pull yourself out of living in any other moment than the present.

Even if you did not face as many challenges that other fatherless daughters have, you may be in a place where you want more knowledge and strive to understand your life and the impact that your past might have had on your present. Be proud of yourself for taking the steps toward gaining insight and growth and becoming your highest self. Self-awareness elevates your potential in life, as you relate with a richer consciousness to the world and yourself.

Part of healing is knowing oneself more deeply and accepting the emotions and reactions that are felt on the inside, while moving forward with purpose on the outside. Sometimes, you have to stop and tend to a part of you that might feel rebroken, but each time you do this, you are not the same person as you were the last time. You are stronger all the way around. Healing means learning to assimilate the painful parts into the growing parts and allowing the self to be human alongside being a stronger divine being. When you allow all of these parts to join together with acceptance, nonjudgment, and love for who you are completely, you begin to shift all areas of your life.

By accepting that you have power over your life, things can start to transform on every level. Begin by purging old clutter, including mental blockages, relationships that cause you pain, and unnecessary material possessions.

Cleaning house (mentally and physically) can be an important step in the growth process. However, we recommend that you think before you toss. There may be photos and mementos that bring pain now, but it might be worth packing them away until you can review them from a less emotional perspective. Deidre, thirty-two, told us about how glad she was that she found something unexpected twenty years after her dad's departure. "My dad left my family when I was twelve because of gambling issues. He said he just was not meant to be a family man. It was such a terrible time. I wanted to get rid of everything that reminded me of him.

"My mom hid away a dollhouse he had made when I was six, before things got really bad. Just this year, I was visiting Mom with my three-year-old daughter, and Mom pulled the dollhouse out of the attic. I was shocked. I would have trashed it had she not hidden it, but I realized that it was very healing for me to still have it. My daughter started playing with it, and I remembered those few good years when Dad was attentive. Touching it brought me back, reminding me that there were some memories that I should value. He did love me at this time, and finding that out came at just the right time. I was ready to let that in, and I am so grateful Mom had the wisdom to save it even when she was in pain. I would tell any girl whose father has left *not* to throw everything away."

Put some things that represent good memories in a box at the top of a closet until you are ready to hold them again. If you treasure memories and mementos of your dad, hold on to those things that remind you of that. Don't forget that the memory and energy attached to the object stays around you too. Positive attachments to objects, memories, or people help you remember the truth in a way that, while they might make you feel emotional, ultimately enhance your life and self-acceptance. Negative attachments make you feel bad about yourself or your story. If your gut reaction is to retreat to a place of anger, resentment, or shame when you see, feel, or smell a certain thing, then it's probably best to get rid of it. Purging the things that cause you pain can be a very deliberate act that symbolizes your movement to a cleaner life. Remember: Every time you get rid of something old, you are creating a space for something new.

The new objects and activities you add to your life are yours for the choosing. What makes you happy? What makes you feel good about yourself? Who makes you want to be a better person? What activity makes you feel alive, silly, or strong? That is what should be filling your life. Add people to your circle who build you up, support you, and share your interests. Growth comes with change, and change comes with movement. Enjoy following your heart!

Your Mental Self

Your mind has a significant amount of power over the rest of your body and plays a much more powerful role in your life than you may know. What do you say when you talk to yourself? The dialogue in your head is something that you create due to your physical, emotional, and spiritual reactions to the world that you have lived in—past and present. You translate your interpretation of situations into words in your head, and you label, or mislabel, them to suit your internal needs or fears. Each thought is put into your body like instructions for how life is going to play out for you, and so it does.

Changing Your Thoughts

Our thoughts are very powerful and can impact our emotions, behavior, and attitudes. They are the first place that you can establish new power in your life because you are taking charge of your mind. Many of us carry a running dialogue in our heads that is negative and judgmental. You can intercept your usual internal messages by creating a dialogue that is encouraging and not critical. The trick is to replace one thought with the other.

1. First, think about a person or situation in your life who has hurt you. Got the image in your head?
2. Now take a deep breath . . . and another . . . and when you breathe out picture that emotion being exhaled from your body.
3. On your next deep breath, take a moment, close your eyes and say, "Happy." Think about the last time that you were in a joyful moment. Hold the picture in your mind and allow those feelings to bathe your spirit again. Feel that? You made that happen.

You took charge of your focus and thus received a dose of mood-boosting neurotransmitters in your system that lifted your spirits immediately. Those yummy feelings linger as long as you let them. Your body actually rewards you when it gets what it needs.

You just started your new practice of replacing one thought with another and taking charge of your mood. In fact, you not only replaced emotions by changing your thoughts but you completely shifted your energy. Your change in attitude impacts how you are experienced by others—your family, your friends, your spouse, your children, and your colleagues, even the stranger who passes you on the street. Emanate what you wish to attract.

To heal as a fatherless daughter, you must know that your thoughts play a major role in how you see the world. They command how you feel. What you tell yourself, what you believe, and what you say about your loss and yourself all hold the power to keep you stuck in the past or moving *forward*. Here's a little mental homework. Sit quietly, and ask yourself a series of questions and note the first thing that comes to your mind:

1. What do I say to myself about my dad leaving?
2. What did his leaving/dying make me feel about myself?
3. What do I tell people about him being gone?

Look at those three questions. Are your desires, thoughts, and voice all in alignment? Remember, thought + desire = voice. Over time, your thoughts learn to follow the truth, which should be directed toward love, compassion, and hope. Judgment, dread, and negative remarks should fall to the wayside as you learn to speak with positivity and power. This takes practice but is entirely possible and is a step toward authentic living.

If you are practicing alignment, you are working on a critical step on your road to restoration. If not, get honest with yourself. Set some time in the coming weeks or months to work on getting those mental blocks out of your system. Spend some time alone and figure out what *you* are feeling without other opinions swirling around you.

Once you are tuned into what you are telling yourself on a daily basis, then you can do the psychological work to transform those irrational thoughts and develop positive cognitive patterns to treat yourself with love. You can train your brain and transform the way you feel physically and emotionally.

Physical Self

Think of your major body entities as forming a triangle. What you think (mental), influences how you feel (physical), influences what you believe (spiritual), influences what you think (mental), and so on. What we think, we feel, and what we feel, we believe.

We have to be purposeful about striving to get every part of ourselves in working order so that all systems support moving forward in a positive direction.

Thankfully, modern science is catching up to what some cultures have known for centuries: Our thoughts are powerful enough to heal us both mentally and physically. Emotions such as fear, anger, and depression can absolutely make us physically ill. Studies have shown that women tend to suffer more physical symptoms from stress than men do because we process emotions and experiences differently.

Think of yourself, or a friend you may know, who is always sick. Is she struggling with a stressful life change or holding on to something that she should let go? We have all been there or know someone who constantly has an upset stomach, cold, or migraine headache. Maybe you are losing your hair, grinding your teeth, or experiencing insomnia. The body might be manifesting what the soul will not release. The American Psychological Association reports that one-third of Americans say they have had an illness that was primarily caused by stress. There is substantial evidence that emotional pain can manifest as illness. What we hold in will find its way out.

Some of us are keenly aware of how stress can lead to headaches and nausea, but it goes much deeper than that. Depression can affect nearly every part of your body. Stress brought on by underlying depression can drive your blood pressure up and your immune system down.

It has been well-established that women are much more likely to suffer from anxiety and depression than men, and that these two disorders often coexist. Anxiety can lead to depression, which can lead to physical ailments. Depression has long been linked to heart disease, which is the leading cause of death for women in the United States. The *Journal of the American Heart Association* reports, "Young women who are moderately or severely depressed have a significantly higher heart disease death risk compared to women who are mentally healthy." Heartache can start as an emotional issue that can transform into a physical one.

It has been well substantiated in medical literature that myriad other physical illnesses are linked to depression including fibromyalgia, cancer, and chronic neck and back pain. Researchers at the Johns Hopkins School of Public Health conducted a longitudinal study to see if depression and cancer were linked. What researchers found was that participants with a history of depression were four times more likely to develop breast cancer. No such link was found with other cancer types.

There are multiple studies connecting depression with neck and back pain in both adolescent and adult women. Angelica, twenty-six, who was given up for adoption by her biological father only to be abandoned by the man who adopted her was diagnosed in adolescence with scoliosis, which required surgery. She had a metal rod placed into her spine and had to wear a brace twenty-three hours a day for a year. Since then, she has researched some of the factors that can contribute to back pain. In an article on scoliosis and alternative medicine, Angelica found something that resonated with her. From the perspective of energy medicine, the spine, as the support of the body, can be negatively affected by feeling a lack of support or by experiences of pain and anger as a child. Angelica tells us what she believes happened in her life, "I now know that scoliosis is something that is carried in your genetic line, but it does not seem to manifest unless something triggers the gene to turn on—especially in childhood. When I read that, I immediately made the connection between my back pain beginning and the year, around age thirteen, that I started feeling overburdened and tremendously insecure in most areas of my life. I felt that I had to be a mother to my sister and mom, and it got to be too much to bear. I literally had the weight of the world on my shoulders, and my spine twisted. To this day, I can feel that when I start to stress about the same issues, I get pain in my back in the exact same place."

Many Americans are looking into how the three parts of the triangle have affected their physical health and are looking for answers beyond the traditional standards of care. Holistic and complimentary treatments are on the rise. When surveyed, most women believe that, in regard to their health, it is important to be cognizant of the mind, body, and soul connection.

As a nurse, Denna has seen the physical problems that can be brought on by emotional distress. "The patients who have the best attitudes and outlooks seem to heal the quickest, whereas patients with family or emotional strife tend to have more setbacks on the road to recovery." Many of the women we surveyed have integrated alternative medicine, energy healing, and modern medicine to heal their minds, bodies, and spirits.

The body is clearly affected by the tug-of-war of past emotional issues and present-day thinking. Holding on to resentment can lead to headaches, gastrointestinal issues, and body aches. For example, lower back pain can come from feeling a lack of security and stability. Middle backaches can indicate a lack of support and guilt. Upper backaches or shoulder pain might arise when you feel you are carrying a load that is too heavy. Where in your life are you not feeling supported? What are you holding on to or being burdened with for someone else? Does your stomach get upset when you are thinking or worrying about certain things? Anxiety and a feeling of fear about what is happening in your life can make you sick. Consider massage and meditation while you are getting your head in the right place. Learn to work the stress out and let go of what is creating pain in your body.

Your body craves balance, so pay attention to the signs and look for areas in your life where you are feeling spread thin or overworked. Seek harmony and health in your life by being authentic to your own needs, truth, and capacities.

Patrice was hoarse for almost six months without knowing why. She was engaged to a guy who was cheating on her but continuously made her feel as if it were all in her head. She had no voice in the relationship and her body responded. If you frequently suffer from asthma, bronchitis, or the common cold, is it likely that you are feeling completely worn out and your body is reacting.

Many people who have blood pressure issues seem to be wrestling with unresolved grief or emotional issues in their lives. Heartburn can flare up when we feel a loss of control. Be open to the changes that are coming your way and make happiness and peace priorities in your mental and spiritual life. Your physical body will follow your lead.

"In researching this book," Denna says, "it dawned on me just how many physical ailments happened on the left side of my body. I broke my left arm three separate times. I suffered a serious cut on the bottom of my left foot, severing a few tendons and narrowly missing the ligaments.

It took me a few months of rehab to learn how to walk again. It turns out that unresolved emotional pain from childhood tends to show up as ailments specifically on the left side of your body—it's a part of what Louise Hay teaches. When I was in the thick of my transformation and healing, I had to have spine surgery. For a long time I had neck issues and refused to let it get the best of me. In other words, I was being a typical nurse and trying to fix myself although I could no longer run and was in constant, unbearable pain. During the time when my neck seemed to be at the point of needing surgery, I was making big, positive changes in my own personal life but having a hard time letting go of my old fears.

"Neck problems are known to arise when a person is being inflexible and stubborn. I was engaged to be married and scared to death to commit. I did not want to make a mistake even though my heart knew he was the right person. My head, however, was working overtime trying to make sure I was ready. Truth be told, I went back to my therapist and worked through the final daddy issue that seemed to be standing in my way of true love. Three months before I walked down the aisle, I had a cervical fusion. The cervical spine in particular represents flexibility and having the ability to see what is in the past. It still amazes me just how much the loss of my father has taken a toll on my life and body." Karin also reflected back on her own history with recurrent bronchitis, chronic sciatica, and scoliosis. Studying the mind-body-spirit connection to illness and disease, she believes there is great credibility to the notion that her physical body manifested the effects of stress and trauma in very specific ways.

Take charge of your body. Get a comprehensive physical exam. Understand your family's medical history, both physical and mental. Be armed with knowledge so that you can be proactive. Nourish your body with the mental and nutritional needs that it is craving. Regulate the systems in your body so you can help them communicate with one another effectively. Think about how you are helping or hindering this process. If you are dealing with a physical health issue, see the appropriate medical professional. If you are plagued with anxiety or pains from the past, consider seeing a therapist. If you can't seem to get relief from traditional medicine, seek a holistic physician or look into integrative treatments. Get to the bottom of what is causing the problem. Your body will thank you for it by blessing you right back.

Spiritual Self

Now that you are letting go of the past, it is time to really think about your spirit, the essence of *you*. When you are ready, ask yourself some real questions: Why am I here? What am I here to do? What would I do if I stopped doing what everyone else thought I should do?

If you do not yet know the answers, keep asking. Gabrielle Bernstein is a best-selling author and new thought leader in the field of spirituality. She is a master at training others to meditate and listen to what is coming from within. She says, "Much of our anxiety and stress comes when we're focused on fear and disconnected from the voice of our inner guide." Find a moment to be still and write down what comes to mind. Keep a journal handy to jot down your thoughts, scribble on a sticky note and place it on your bathroom mirror, make a note in your smartphone or tablet. What keeps coming up as your true passion? What is getting in the way of you pursuing it and feeling peace? What are some old negative thoughts that are blocking your happiness?

Best-selling author and neuropsychologist Rick Hanson delivered a TED Talk in 2013 about this topic. He realized he could change his own brain by choosing to linger on positive feelings for longer periods of time and letting go of the negative thoughts that had been inside of him since childhood. He stated, "Now, many years later, as a neural psychologist, I began to understand what I was actually doing. I wasn't just changing my mind; I was actually changing my brain. That's because, as the neuroscientists say, 'Neurons that fire together, wire together. Passing mental states become lasting neural traits.' The mind can change the brain to change the mind."

Although our minds are biased toward focusing on negative experiences, Hanson teaches us how to hardwire happiness into our brains by recalling and enriching wonderful memories into our thought patterns. The gradual accumulation of directing our thoughts and emotions toward the positive builds up to an actual change in our brain's functioning, and therefore influences our well-being and happiness. You can do this by reducing the time spent reflecting on those things that have hurt you and increasing your awareness of those things that have shown you love.

The next time a feeling creates negative thoughts, which in turn create more feelings, establishing an internal message that says you are unlovable or not worth holding on to, you can choose to redirect your thoughts. Gently choose to turn your focus to a moment with someone who deeply cares about you and then enjoy how that memory makes you feel. Then sit with that memory and feeling for ten, twenty, thirty seconds. Enjoy it. Teach your system to avoid the path of pain and redirect itself to the path of joy.

Tara Brach, Western teacher of Buddhist meditation and emotional healing and author of the best-selling book *Radical Acceptance*, believes that by keeping ourselves trapped in negative thinking, or self-criticism, we keep the emotion of fear front and center, which limits our interactions with the world. She says, "Perhaps the biggest tragedy of our lives is that freedom is possible, yet we can pass our years trapped in the same old patterns. . . . We may want to love other people without holding back, to feel authentic, to breathe in the beauty around us, to dance and sing. Yet each day we listen to inner voices that keep our life small."

No matter the messages that a daughter received when she was young, or those she created all on her own, she can exercise control over where she is focused, and what grows inside of her. By diminishing her potential joy with internal reminders of flaws, she is holding (and growing) negative beliefs inside of her spiritual, mental, and physical self. Her body will respond to what she is telling it. Thoughts are the power cords into our bodies. If we accept that as humans we can experience doubt, shame, or fear and not judge ourselves for those feelings, we loosen their hold on us and bring more awareness to those things about ourselves that feel loved, harmonious, and talented. Each time we do this, we are teaching ourselves how to find happiness and fulfillment, no matter the old memories that threaten it.

When you are ready to focus on a positive future, ask yourself what you most desire. Be still and listen for what makes your heart beat with excitement. Dream *big*—your spirit wouldn't pull you if you weren't capable. What do *you* want? What path calls you most often but gets drowned out by fear? When you picture yourself being the *real you*, authentic to yourself and no one else, what are you doing? If you had a million dollars right this moment to do anything in the world that you want, what would you do? Don't think about it, weighing the options; what is the first thing that comes to your mind? Write it down now. There is your answer.

Do you want to travel? Write down the places you want to go. Do you wish you could transform your hobby into your career? Make a list of people you know who could help you find an open door to a new possibility. Do you want to be a mother? Record the baby names you like and stick them up on your mirror. Start saving things that move you: pictures of breathtaking beaches or landscapes, words of affirmation from a fortune cookie, or an inspirational article from a magazine that seems written just for you. Make a vision board: a collage of pictures, words, or items that you envision for your life. Speak out loud what you want. Stop using words like *never, won't, impossible.* Remember that when you say "I am _____," you are predicting your own future.

Create a strong message to the universe that what you want is actually going to happen, and declare it in every way until it does. Start making room for all of the good that can come into your life.

Many people wake up feeling anxious because life is stressful. We tend to focus on the negative instead of the positive. We stress ourselves out, sending and resending our minds and bodies messages of stress, dread, and fear. You can change this. Tomorrow, when you wake up, say something out loud that inspires you. Keep a motivational book by your bed and read a page of it as soon as you wake up. Repeat the words to your favorite happy song. Declare who you really are or who you are striving to be. Begin to believe that all things are possible. Give yourself the power to manifest the life you want. Continue speaking positively until it becomes second nature to replace negative thoughts with positive ones. Find time in each day for yourself. Create a place for meditation in a comfy corner of your office or private part of the yard. Place fresh flowers in a hand-painted vase by your bed. Take a walk in nature on the grass, under the trees—and go barefoot if you can. Surround yourself with beautiful things. Give yourself permission to use the good candles and the real china. Widen your field of view by surrounding yourself with successful people who are living out their dreams. Seeing other people's dreams come true will show you that it can happen for you too.

Wherever you are, allow the gift of mindful silence to permeate your being long enough for you to become settled and free of the noise of life. Life will meet you where you are, and it can be as beautiful as you choose to see it.

The Gifts of Your Loss

Have you taken a look back at your life with awe at your own resilience? You should. You are here because something inside of you has refused to give up and has been drawn toward restoring the parts of you that have been wounded. You are doing this work and that is something to be proud of. We know your road has not been without speed bumps, potholes, and wrong turns—all of ours have—but in the midst of the long journey, you have created your own miracles. You are willing to grow and reach for something better, which takes inner strength and hope, and that is what we want you to celebrate. Your foundation is so much more solid than when you were younger. Claim it.

As one fatherless daughter put it, "I want to create purpose out of my pain." Yes, there can be a purpose and meaning to all that once felt insurmountable. You have received gifts that you may not be aware of, and they have helped form you into a strong, intuitive woman even if you have not claimed her yet.

In our survey of over a thousand fatherless daughters, we asked women to write one word that they would use to describe themselves. The word that was overwhelmingly used was *strong*. Strength does not show up in our bodies unless we have been required to flex our muscles and push against something that has its own power. Mentally, with each act of perseverance, we gain might and ability—fortitude that would not have been there if our road had not required it of us. While you may have wished that some of the circumstances in your life had been different, this gives you the opportunity to claim and be grateful for the strength that you have gained because of what you have been through.

By acknowledging that you have received other blessings along the way, such as intuition, passion, or success, you are giving yourself and the divine (however you honor or perceive it) well-deserved gratitude. This is the grateful part of your journey! You get to wrap your arms around yourself and your gifts and say, "I am standing because I am strong." Don't dismiss all of the things that you have done to survive, because what you have done can serve as an inspiration to others.

Throw open the doors of your achievements, allow yourself to feel proud of your work, and share what you have earned along the way.

What Other Fatherless Daughters Have Gained

In our fatherless daughters' survey, we asked women to share what they have gained in their lives while learning to cope with their loss. So often, we stay focused on what we have missed instead of looking at how rising above painful circumstances actually gave us some traits, experiences, and relationships that blessed us along the way. Take time to complete this statement: "If I had never gone through _____, then I never would have gotten/met/learned _____."

As you read, reflect on your life and think outside of the box in looking at your gifts. Give yourself credit for your resilience and decisions that countered your feeling unworthy or hurt. Can you see how strong you were to keep going in the middle of all that happened? Can you think of an example of when you may have helped someone else who was experiencing the same pain? Have you found wisdom, spiritual fortitude, or creative abilities, or formed deep relationships that you otherwise might not have had? See the times when you got through the darkest days and validate the strength and connections that you found to hang on to. Therein lie your blessings. We offered more than twenty traits for fatherless daughters to choose from, and we loved what we learned.

The following is a list of those things that fatherless daughters told us they believed were gifts in their lives, despite losing their dads. Take a few moments to check off the gifts that you have been given and see what you share with your sisters.

GIFTS

Resilience	
Deep friendships	
Soul of a survivor	
Forgiveness	
Closer relationship with my mom	
Deeper self-awareness	
Closer relationship with God or a higher power	
Closer relationship with my sibling(s)	
Meaning in life	
Fulfillment through giving back	
Artistic or creative talents	
Professional success	

This list shows you what is possible, what other fatherless daughters are achieving as they move toward healing. When we are grateful, the sun shines through the clouds with rays that are suddenly brighter than before. Be mindful about staying in the light of gratitude. Think about any other gifts that you have received along the way. No matter how big or small, serious or silly, if it comes to your mind as a gift, honor it by writing it down in the margins of this page. Fill them up!

The Resilient One

It was no surprise to us that our research revealed the most common gift for fatherless daughters was resilience. Resilience develops through facing, and surviving, adversity. You know what the worst feels like, and you have learned how to rise above challenges, reminding yourself that you have a proven capacity for toughness.

Your resilience is a product of strength and self-empowerment, even if it has been formed around some potentially debilitating experiences. Circumstances of your past cannot be changed, but know that you can access emotions and experiences that someone who has not walked in your shoes cannot. *You* are a survivor whose story can encourage others and potentially help them to create positive change as well.

Natalia Vodianova, an internationally successful model, was born in the Soviet Union and grew up very poor. Her father walked out on her family when she was two, leaving her mother and two sisters, one of whom had cerebral palsy, facing poverty. Her mother refused to turn the girls over to anyone else, committing her life to the family, working odd jobs, and opening a fruit stand to keep them afloat. It was *resilience* and hard work that kept them going. Witnessing her mother's love for her and her sisters, despite the conditions they were living in, inspired Natalia. By the age of seventeen, after having her own successful fruit stand business, she started modeling in Paris and rose to stardom quickly. Not one to forget her roots, at age twenty-two, Natalia started the Naked Heart Foundation to build playgrounds and parks for children in Russia and Ukraine—especially for those with disabilities. Natalia explains, "My childhood gave me resilience, and there's little that can surprise me in life."

The Truth Teller

The odds are that you have had to keep family secrets, whether about your father's death, your mother's struggles, something your grandmother told you, or your own life. You might have been taught to keep things hidden in an effort to hold together what was falling apart. But as life continued, you may have realized that secrets are not the healthiest glue to bind families, or any relationship. As a result, you have had a choice: continue the secret-keeping pattern because it is familiar or pursue a different path by speaking the truth. By *speaking the truth*, we mean being emotionally honest and having reverence for the past, not revealing secrets out of revenge. Your motives must be the highest good. This requires genuine love and acceptance for what is and what was, letting the truth bring unifying freedom to something that has been painfully hidden.

The truth gives you (and others) permission to use your voice without shame. And because you might feel compelled to be your own warrior and perhaps an advocate for others seeking to escape the shadows of painful secrets, your life can find a renewed dimension of purpose. There is a trickle-down effect with truth. It empowers others to follow suit. Although truth can be painful at first, its energy unfetters the shackles of lies and shame, granting the soul freedom to be its true self.

Maybe you have decided to tell the truth, becoming the brave one in the family, choosing to look behind the curtain and find out what has been hidden for so many years. Perhaps you started asking questions that have been avoided for decades, searching documents or questioning people to finally get the real story. You have spoken up. You have spoken out.

As a girl, you did not know how to handle such a task, but now that you are a woman, you have the gift of knowing the power of the truth. You can find release for yourself, your family, and for future generations so that they do not become bound by secrets.

Jackie, forty, tells us a story about her decision to speak up.

I grew up in a home that held secrets behind its doors. On the outside, we were expected to portray this perfect family, never speak of the abuse or dysfunction that was going on inside, and so I learned how to be a great pretender. We would show up at church with smiles on our faces, acting as if we had it all together when we had just come from a home with intense fighting. Dad would shove Mom into walls or throw things at her, and then we were instructed that everything was to remain "within the family."

Over time, Mom kept discovering more empty bottles and evidence of affairs. Dad became more of an angry, controlling ruler—when he was home. He started hitting us kids more. I believed he hated me and that I had to earn love—after being hit. I buried those beliefs and later ended up marrying someone a lot like him.

When I went through my own abusive marriage, I finally heard something that changed my life. God did not intend on us being abused—love was supposed to be given without expectation or abuse. I did not have to stay in that environment! It was an extremely difficult decision, but I got out, and I decided I was over all of the lies, and it was so liberating.

I told my friends about what was really happening at home, and I confronted my husband with my lawyers about the issues. I wrote my father (whom I had become estranged from) a long letter, naming his actions and telling him my feelings. I sent a copy of that letter to every family member so that the secret would be out. The process of truth telling changed my life forever. It gave me a voice that I had never been allowed to use before.

Even though Jackie grew up with a negative inner voice that eventually played into her adult marriage, she took that lie and flipped it on its head, repositioning her adult life on strong, positive grounding by speaking her truth.

The Power of Writing

At the beginning of the book we asked you to write your own fatherless story. We asked you to write how you view the world and how these beliefs may still play out in your adult life.

Tara Parker-Pope wrote an insightful article in the *New York Times*, "Writing Your Way to Happiness," about the amazing benefits of expressive writing. The idea was based on the premise that we all have a personal narrative that can shape our views of the world and ourselves, and we can actually rewrite our own stories to shape our worldview, which Parker-Pope points out "can change our perceptions of ourselves and identify obstacles that stand in the way of better health." Just like our experiences writing this book, our narratives transformed along the way—through talking to others, retelling our stories, and gaining perspective, we continued to reshape the way our stories were written. This is a tangible way to see real evidence of your growth . . . in your own words.

Stop here and add anything you might have discovered about yourself and your journey. Explore how you feel about what happened to you and why. Reach into your truth, think about everything we have talked about in the book, and write from your heart. Ask yourself, Have I become any more aware of what happened to me? Is my truth clearer than it was before? Can I see growth in myself and my story? It is important to acknowledge, validate, and celebrate each step in your new awareness. The more you validate your own evolving energy, the more you will continue to draw it into your life. A life of celebration is a life on fire!

The Support Sister

By surviving all that you have faced, you have become an expert on the subject. You have earned the gifts of wisdom and insight in supporting yourself, and others, through crisis. These are extraordinarily strong traits to possess.

Because you have been an observer of how others have handled, or mishandled, crises, you have developed a proficiency in seeing things from a broader perspective. You likely watched others when you were young, tucking information into your mental file cabinets. You saw family members handle things in very different ways, and you paid attention to how things played out. You may have developed a heightened ability to read people and situations, sense energy, and give advice based on what you see playing out in the future as a result of the dynamics currently in place. You may have gained clearer intuition and the ability to trust your sixth sense.

Your friends come to you because they know you have developed a knack for dealing with people. You may not have perfected this in your own life (yet), but you can sure call it like it is in someone else's. You have probably learned how to spot truth, pain, dysfunction, and need, and you have a pretty good idea of what needs to happen for the welfare of those you love. Your history has made you wiser. Your friends trust that they can get the truth from you and feel safe unburdening themselves to you.

Many fatherless daughters have told us the same two things when it comes to their friends:

1. They tend to be the ones who friends come to when they need support.
2. Their friends feel more like family.

You have the ability to comfort those who are starting to take steps on their fatherless journey. Because of your history, you have gained genuine expertise that does not depend on any degree, licensure, or income. This wisdom is drawn from experience and could provide you with a beautiful opportunity to help someone else. By passing along empathy and guidance, you are blessing not only others but also yourself. You are honoring your gifts by paying them forward, reforming the energy of loss into an energy of support.

Be proud that you are one of the best travel companions that life has to offer, but never forget to protect your energy resources as well by not giving too much of it away. You first. Always.

The Funny Girl

Believe it or not, some of your favorite comedians grew up fatherless. The late beloved Gilda Radner, who was very close to her father, lost him to brain cancer when she was just fourteen years old. She went on to star in *Saturday Night Live* and, just as some of us do, used comedy to cope with her pain. Comedian, actress, and cohost of *The Talk*, Sheryl Underwood, opened up on the show in 2014, revealing the pain that she experienced as a child losing the relationship with her father for years because her abusive mother lied to her, telling her that he had killed her twin sister at only a few days old. Sheryl said that she witnessed her mother stab her father when she was five, after becoming angry that Sheryl had tried to become close to him. Luckily, he survived, but her experiences influenced the trajectory of her life.

"People ask where does the 'funny' come from," Sheryl said when talking about her talent. "For me it comes from my desire to never have anyone feel what I felt throughout my childhood and certain periods of my life. So I try to make everybody laugh and everybody happy."

Laughter in the face of adversity helps us lighten the load, even if just for a time. Fatherless daughters know that seeing humor in situations indeed makes things more tolerable. You might have become the one with excellent comedic timing, refined your storytelling talents, or gravitated toward people who are incredibly funny. However you find your laughter, your soul seeks it because it gives the mind–body–spirit the break and reboot that it craves. As women, it can be tough to allow ourselves to let loose at times—we are too stressed out, don't want to be immature, or have a tough time letting humor in. One of the most mature, loving gifts you can give your body is a good laugh.

Is it any surprise that in our fatherless daughter survey, the most common reported healthy coping mechanism was "Laughter/A Sense of Humor"? Not to us. It is one of the biggest reasons we, Denna and Karin, became quick friends.

In 2014, a young girl bravely spoke at Jane Fonda's Georgia Campaign for Adolescent Power & Potential (GCAPP) Empower Party in Atlanta. She spoke about her tumultuous childhood and how she made the decision to get away from a very abusive home early in her adolescence. Through GCAPP's resources she found not only a safe place to live and feel secure but a rewarding place to thrive. She ended her speech with a very moving statement: "What I needed was a hand up, not a hand out." Isn't that exactly what we all need in times of despair? Because she got the hand up she needed, she not only went on to receive a college scholarship but had set a goal to open up her own home in the future to help children in need.

In the week that we organized this part of the book, we found it no coincidence that we heard a message that applied directly to it. Andy Stanley, nationally syndicated pastor of North Point Community Church in Atlanta, seemed to speak directly to us when he said in a sermon, "When you have walked through the same experience as someone, you have the special ability to help them like no one else can. I call this the

Fellowship of Suffering. It means that those who have suffered are uniquely qualified to comfort those who are suffering." That is *you*. When and if you want to be a comfort to someone else, ask for opportunities. Believe us, they will show up. Then trust yourself. Accept gratitude when others thank you for your help and thank your higher power for the wisdom, compassion, and humor that you have inside of you.

Forgiveness for Good

Have you experienced the gift of forgiveness? Forgiveness might be at the top of your list when it comes to certain people. Karin's mom, a Presbyterian pastor, has taught her through the years that forgiveness is really about letting go of something that is not hers to carry. The word *forgive* comes from the words "give" and "forth." To *give forth* a pain that does not belong to you. To *give forth* something that you no longer want to hold because it is poisoning your body. To *give forth* the heavy cloak of victimhood and leave it in the road behind you. We all have people in our lives who we could choose to forgive, and that can be a heavy weight to bear. Whether it is your father, your mother, your friend, your sibling, your ex, or yourself—forgiveness is a powerful tool in healing the soul. Forgiveness is not easy for many reasons. It might feel like you are giving up your power if you let go. When you weigh the positive and negative feelings associated with the idea of forgiveness, you are faced with trying to figure out if you can truly release what you've held on to for so long.

By forgiving, you are making the choice to move forward. Forgiveness is a process with its own challenges, but it is quite possibly one of the greatest gifts you can give *yourself*. In fact, if you have digested the true meaning of forgiveness, you have realized that it is not about the other person, but rather about you.

By forgiving, you unpack the suitcase of negativity and hand back the pain to the person or situation that caused it. You are not saying you are OK with what happened. You are not saying that the person does not need to be accountable. You are not taking responsibility for causing a situation or fixing it. By forgiving, you are no longer going to allow your life to be weighed down by carrying around a burden that you did not create. By giving it back, you will gain lightness and freedom.

Getting to this place of clarity is monumental. Sometimes you have to go it alone while other family members choose to stay in the place you no longer want to reside. If you are already there, good for you. You do not deserve the dis-ease of carrying these toxins or bitterness in your body. By releasing them, you can let go of what can continue to harm you.

Finding Forgiveness

Here are some steps to help you find your way to heart-mind-body forgiveness.

First, identify and speak the name of the person and the action that you wish to forgive. By doing this, you are voicing your intention and your body is made aware that release is coming. This declaration helps you create a shift from weakness to power, as you call out something that once had ownership of you and are now claiming ownership over it.

Next, recognize the presence of an old emotion tied to the person or action you wish to forgive. One of the most important pieces of a healing journey is to look at how recognizing an emotion affects your life holistically: mind, body, and spirit. Often emotions can be held as pain or discomfort in the body. Take a moment to locate where the pain resides in your body—that is your physical representation of the memory. You might feel the pain hiding in your gut, your neck and shoulders, or deep down when you hold your breath. Now that you have located it, tell it that you are giving it back. You are no longer letting it reside inside of you, creating a heaviness that is not yours to carry. Let it out.

Then, as you start to feel yourself pulling the unforgiven pain from its hiding place, remind your heart that it is protected. You are not saying that what happened to you was OK. You are not absolving the other person of responsibility for causing you pain. You are taking control over how it affects you. This is a new place of growth and strength and a major turning point in your life. Say these words out loud (if it feels right to do so): "I am no longer going to be burdened or identified by what [insert name] did to hurt me. I am done with feeling weak and am now going to feel strong. There is no longer room for this in my body, and I am giving it back now." Visualize the pain leaving that place in your body. See it leaving anywhere that you have carried it—your heart, your soul, your gut, your core, your mind—watch it go out into the air and leave the space around you, never to return again.

Finally, create the place where you want the feeling to go—a closed box in a faraway closet, into the hands of the person who gave it to you, or hurled into space where you will never see it again.

Repeat this visualization as many times as you wish, with whatever symbolism or ritual that feels good to you. Some women have created a letting-go ceremony by lighting candles or safely burning a piece of paper with the pain written on it. You are in charge now. Create a meaningful rite of passage for this transition in your life. Reinforce your achievement of forgiveness as the days pass by, making positive statements that speak about your healing. Resist the urge to speak badly about the person who hurt you, understanding that words are energy and that they will create new growth in whatever form they are spoken. Let those close to you know that you are going through this process and ask for their help getting to the other side. Let them know what kinds of things you will be changing about your life and ask them to help you by loving you through it and reminding you of the goodness of this forgiveness.

As you heal, expect to have triggers or to reexperience negative old emotions that can threaten to weaken you. Have a plan in place so that when something or someone tries to pull you back to that place of hurt, you know exactly what you are going to do. Be compassionate with yourself by remembering the Buddhist tradition of full acceptance by allowing the feelings to exist without judgment as they come toward you and then move through you and away from you. Repeat your visualization of letting go as much as you need to; achieving forgiveness is going to be a process. Soon, you will have established a new, stronger way of reacting to the old hurt, and your thoughts, feelings, and physical reactions will be retrained to travel down a different path to one of vibrancy, hope, and power.

By practicing these steps, you will teach yourself how to let go of toxic energy in your body and open yourself up to new thinking, internal belief structures, and life potential. Holding on tightly to not forgiving takes up space in your life. Reclaim that space and fill it with something wonderful.

Closer Relationship with Your Mom, Grandparents, or Siblings

If your mother is still in your life, there is a big chance that, like almost half of our women surveyed, you two have become closer over the years. If your grandparent(s) raised you, this is a gift that you have given each other. And if you have worked through things with your sibling(s), you have likely become tighter because of the experiences you have shared.

Your strong family relationships are the big glasses of lemonade that were made from life's lemons. As you all grow older, the connections have deepened as you understand them more fully than when you were a child. If you have found a way to be honest, open, and flexible with your relatives along the way, you have been able to find a healthy balance with them that has helped sustain you all.

Karin relates, "I am closer now to my older brother than I ever was when I was young. We had a run of some very difficult years, as we both dealt with our childhood losses very differently. As time went on, and I went through a very painful public divorce (reexperiencing my father abandonment fears), he was the one who stepped in; I got my big brother back. He started protecting me, trusting me, and fighting for me—something I had never received from a father. We are extremely close to this day, and I know that he always has my back.

"I have also gotten closer to my little brother as we have discussed our family's history over the years and listened to each other's experiences and feelings as adults. Time and parenting have given us deeper insight and perspective, and I relish the time that I get to spend alone with him. We listen more intently these days and offer each other a great deal of compassion for our personal losses. My brothers are my rainbows after the storms."

Denna says, "For years I gave my mom a card on Father's Day. In countless ways she was both parents to me. When I fell she was always there to catch me, but the most amazing thing is she has always met me where I am. A testament to that is during the time I was in therapy about my father. She sat on the other end of the phone while I relayed every painstakingly revelation to her. She never insisted on me seeing her point. She and my brother walked with me on my journey even though I know much of it was not easy for either of them. My mom is the definition of what a mother should be. Selfless. Protective. Encouraging. Loving. Giving.

"I have spent a good portion of my adulthood trying to give her back some of the things she gave to me. When I look back on the tragedy of my childhood I now see that God had a wonderful plan for me and my brother. He knew that our mom could not only handle it alone, she would rise to the occasion. I hope that one day when I finally make it to the stage for my first TED talk, she and my brother will be front row and center."

Deeper Self-Awareness

Through your willingness to look at yourself with sharper lenses, reflecting, adjusting, and finding the truth inside of you, you have deepened your self-awareness. Being willing to ask yourself the tough questions, you are getting to know yourself better. By searching your life for its patterns and being accountable to your own power, you wisely and strongly can claim the life that you were meant to lead. By making decisions based on your heart's needs, you honor yourself in the way that you were meant to. And through that, you understand who you are.

Self-awareness is the catalyst to living a life of meaning and fulfillment. You will learn that life comes with losses, recoveries, and lessons, and you are becoming aware of what yours are. You are understanding your weaknesses and strengths, and you accept that you are a work in progress. The most wonderful thing about this level of self-understanding is the power and peace that you emanate. We all have energy that we give off when we enter a room. Whether you call it vibration, aura, spirit, vibes, or mood, people can feel it. By reaching deeper self-awareness, we carry light with us because we have learned not to let anger, retaliation, or judgment lead the way. We accept who we are, so we have an easier time accepting others—faults and all. People can feel it, and it makes them trust us. And the beautiful part about this is that we also learn to trust *ourselves*.

The Gift of You

Tuck away the knowledge that although you have had your share of pain, you've also gained a greater knowledge of who you really are.

Whatever you went through when you lost your relationship with your father was nothing short of painful, traumatic, or perhaps even paralyzing for a while. It takes time to work through the reality that he is gone and figure out how you are going to live without him. It takes tears and a lot of soul-searching if questions remain unanswered. It takes faith to step outside of your pain when the time is right and discover what you have also gained. One of the most amazing gifts of being a survivor is discovering a side to yourself that you may not have known existed.

Tomorrow does not have to be as painful as yesterday. In fact, it can be more fulfilling than you ever dreamed possible. It is your choice. Your dreams are waiting.

EPILOGUE

Typing the word *epilogue* is bittersweet. It means that we have finished writing this labor of love. A dream of ours has finally come to fruition. It also means that we, along with many other brave fatherless daughters, have shared our secrets, insecurities, and lives. Along the way, we have prayed to have the wisdom to help you, as well as ourselves. The redeeming thing about secrets is that, once they are out, they no longer hold power over our lives. In letting go, we grant ourselves a freedom that is brand new.

Writing is cathartic and magical in the way that it transforms unspoken emotions from inside the heart into voices on the page. These words begin the quiet conversation among all of us in an effort to reach deeper and understand ourselves and one another more. It is our hope that you have experienced some of your own revelations here and can feel yourself growing. When you start shedding your grief and anger, inner peace is waiting for you. Each of us gets there in her own time. We hope that by picking up this book, it is your time.

Denna says,

For me, my father will eternally be a forty-two-year-old man. It still takes my breath away that I will never hear him say my name again or see him hold my children, but I can find him in the photographs that I keep. I can see by looking at them that he was once vibrant and full of life. Oh, and that he was handsome. The pictures tell a story of my youth and innocence in a time before it all changed. I have a photo in my wallet of my father holding my brother and me in his lap. In it I see a man lovingly squeezing his children close to him. He stares back at me with his signature tinted sunglasses and wide smile. He is happy. We all are. For years it was hard for me to look at this photo. It was too powerful and made me feel too raw, but I kept it near me. I wanted him with me although I was not ready to be with him.

Over the years, I have often told people that I did not really know my father because he died so young. The truth is that this book allowed me to go looking for him. What I found was us. Writing brought him back to me, which is why it is a little hard for me to let go again now. I see him differently now. I understand him more. More important, I understand myself even more and why it all happened to me. I was meant to be here for you. Yes, there is still pain. I still cry like a baby some days, but now I also smile. I smile at the memories and the magic of how life has perfectly come full circle.

The first real memory I have of my father was centered on magic, or what a toddler would maybe refer to as magic. It was in the early 1970s when the car radio would turn off as a car was going under a bridge. We were riding down the interstate singing along with "Love Will Keep Us Together" by the Captain and Tennille when my dad pointed out that a bridge was coming up. He announced that he could make the music stop by snapping his fingers. "Daddy, can I do it too?" I asked. "Why, yes, darling, you can do anything that you want to do," he said confidentially. As the bridge appeared we snapped in unison, and just like that the music stopped. Quickly he encouraged me to snap again to bring the music back. Snap!

Snap! And just like magic the music was back. Without either of us knowing, his encouragement would have to last me a lifetime.

For some fatherless daughters, our time with our dads was cut short. We needed more. For others, the time we spent with him was a disappointment. No matter what the situation is or was, we usually want to make sense of what happened and grow as women with that understanding. Use the past as a point of reference. Go back and visit when you need to, but don't stay, because you don't live there anymore. Suffering is no longer necessary for you to grow.

Being a fatherless daughter means having the strength to learn how to let go *and* stay connected. It is an intricate dance. In our survey and on our social media pages, we have heard from thousands of daughters, fathers, and mothers. Usually, the daughters are looking for a place where they can feel at home sharing their stories. The stories come from all over the world with the same underlying message: They want answers and they want to know how to feel better. It is our hope that through this book, daughters can find peace in knowing that they are not alone and that they do not need to stay stuck. There is so much room for growth around all of us, and all we have to do is lean in and breathe it into our cells until we learn how to do it on our own. It is a learning process, and each step is growth.

The fathers who contact us want the same thing. They want to feel heard and show that there are many of them who want desperately to be a part of their daughters' lives. They are willing to take the steps, yet they are not sure how. It is our biggest hope that these fathers and their daughters all find connection and peace. Our message to fathers is "Stay in your daughter's life. If you are not there, go back and get her. Show her that you love her. Show her that she is worth coming back for."

Mothers have come to us wanting to know how to help their own daughters whose fathers have either left or passed away too young.

Many mothers are struggling with their own fatherless stories and praying to be purposeful about stopping the pattern of pain and doing things right. They search for direction and inspiration on how to fill the empty spaces in their girls' lives. They are looking for education on what can happen down the road and want to equip themselves with the knowledge and compassion needed to help their daughters. And they can.

Karin says,

Writing this book with one of my best friends [Denna] has been more than a growing experience—it has been life changing. This journey has helped us fully embrace ourselves and each other as lovable, perfectly imperfect, strong women (and both Leos at that). The synchronicity that has transpired in our lives while writing this manuscript has made us cheer, cry, laugh, retreat, push forward, and choose to speak the truth, even if it hurt. Amazing how this creative process has spread the wings of our friendship and individual identities to such beautiful places. I am so grateful.

I started this journey as a therapist who was in therapy herself, trying to unravel pain from my childhood that kept manifesting in my relationships. I found myself writing *to myself* many times. The therapy of writing—voicing—what I knew to be true became one of the most healing seasons of my life. Denna and I often called each other crying about a revelation while tackling a topic or pointing it out clearly for the other one. The lessons came often. I needed to keep growing, and that meant speaking my truth, trusting my instincts, and putting my needs at the forefront, something that I had not learned to do yet. I learned it right here with you.

And so my relationships with my fathers transformed along the way. I had to come to terms with holding on or letting go—both made me feel vulnerable. What was the best thing for my life? What was worth my energy and love? I know that so many of you are dealing with the same conflict while you read this book, and I hope that you have gained the clarity that I have from our time together.

I had to look deeply at what I knew from the past and what I could truly expect in the future. I had to look at the purpose or pain of other relationships in my life and get honest about which ones were truly for my highest good. In doing so, I paid attention to what my body was telling me about the now. I was continuing to let secrets and hurt reside inside my body, muffle my voice, and keep me floating without a feeling of security. And I was allowing it to re-create over and over again in my life.

Coming to terms with the pain of not being in the life of the father who raised me was extremely difficult. I have carried a little girl around inside of me who has always hoped she would be rescued because she was too good to let go. That never happened, and I have had to release that hope. A deep moat had formed between us, and I had to stare at the moat for a long time before accepting that it was there for a reason. I had to find peace with the comfort that I was not weakened by letting go, but instead empowered. I would not be a victim any longer but a strong woman who knew what was best for her life and her own children.

With the release of that relationship, I learned to hug my real father again. We had become closer since I was adult, but I had never felt a safe space to tell him how I really felt. The truth is raw when it breaks to the surface, and it carried a tremendous fear of rejection. But my dad did not reject me when I finally spoke up. He tolerated the shifting current and listened. I could not stay in the pattern of denial about the past any longer, and I needed him in my life in a real way.

It took me over forty years to tell my birth father that I had felt abandoned by him. I told him I needed him to say he was sorry.

That day, our relationship changed dramatically. We have gotten closer and I realize more each time I see him how much I need him and that other part of me. I am not sure if either of us would have had the courage to break to the surface had it not been for my writing this book. And all along the way, my mom has listened to and encouraged each step I have taken and each word I have typed onto these pages, even when it has meant facing difficult truths. That has taken bravery, and I respect and love her for it deeply.

We all have our own story. We hope you have learned how you want your fatherless story to play out with your positive self in the lead. You must trust the voice inside of you. The universe and those who love you are rooting for you to grow.

Wonderful change can come from pain. We hope we have helped you progress from being stuck to moving forward, feeling confident in your stride. We are in this together and can thrive with the support of one another—first for ourselves, and then for our sisters. Now that we have initiated you into the sisterhood we hope that you too are inspired to pay it forward. Find your truth, recover your voice, and restore your strength. Understand your loss and reclaim your life. The answers are in you just as much as they were in us, and now are in this book. Trust what you have taught yourself along the way as you take a step into the wonder of tomorrow.

ACKNOWLEDGMENTS

Writing a book is no easy task. Along the way, we were challenged by our own major life transitions, losses of loved ones, serious family illnesses, full-time jobs, careers, technical mishaps, personal struggles, family changes, and raising five children between the two of us. One never knows what each year will bring, alter, or take away from one's life, and we have been forever changed during this process. We have written in coffee shops, playgrounds, hospital waiting rooms, museums, carpool lines, and in every room of our homes with children (and one crazy dog) crawling over our feet. We have lost sleep, gained a few wrinkles, and endured dark roots all with one goal in mind: to help *you* in this mission of helping fatherless daughters.

Although the tears sometimes overtook us, it was our passion for this book that always brought us back to the keyboard, at each new stage, with fresh insight, vigor, and inspiration. We would not trade the experience for anything because it taught us more about ourselves than we ever expected. But it was not just about us.

When we mention this book in the company of friends and strangers, something magical happens—women and men become brave and transparent. Stories ache to be shared and emotions fill up the room. People pass along memories that they have never shared or talk about relationships that have yet to heal. They ask how they can help a best friend come to peace with her father's death, look for insight raising children as a single mother, or express how meaningful it is to find out that they are not alone. People want to listen to what we have learned, and they want to be heard for what they know.

Karin often talks about how life meets us where we are, sending us messages if we are open to receiving them. While doing our final edits, the two of us practically lived at one another's homes. One night, we were editing Chapter 7 when something beautiful happened to Denna: "I asked Karin's son, West, to get me a Diet Coke. Karin and I were sitting side by side in her office when we got into an emotional conversation about how much I was missing my dad. I had watched her grow closer to her father during our writing process, and while it made my heart full to see, it also made me miss what could never happen with my own father. I poured the last drop of Diet Coke into my glass and wiped away my tears. Karin stopped talking abruptly, looked up at me with wide eyes, saying, 'Oh my God, look at the side of the can.' (It was all the rage to find your name on a Coke can during this time.) I turned the can toward me to see the word *Dad* in bold red letters. We both just stared at the can saying, 'Oh my God.' He was with me. It is moments such as these that have made this process a truly amazing gift. Our friendship and deep understanding of one another has grown through this journey. We are sisters, and our love for one another is unbreakable."

Many of the women who worked with us on this book offered not only their expertise but, very often, their own personal stories. Your lives are why this book had to be written, and your resilience is what inspired us along the way. We hope we found the right words to tell your stories, share your tragedies and triumphs, and facilitate healing for those who read it.

First and foremost, we want to thank our agent, Wendy Sherman, for pushing us to deliver the best book we could possibly write. Wendy, you are a beautiful person with a huge heart who is doing exactly what you are meant to do. You are damn good at it. Thank you for talking to us in traffic, answering our emails at the crack of dawn, and helping us find our way. You are a mentor, a friend, and an inspiration to us both.

Thank you, Caroline Sutton, our editor at Penguin Random House, for believing in us and knowing that this book needed to be written. Your insight and guidance have been key to the completion of this project. Sheila Curry Oakes, we are so happy you came on board with your talent and wisdom—you helped us mold the manuscript into exactly what it needed to be. Stephanie Abarbanel, thank you for all of your help and expertise as we began this journey. You have a heart of gold. Thank you to our copyeditor Candace Levy, marketing expert Roshé Anderson, and public relations guru Louisa Farrar.

Many thanks to all of our unofficial editors and incredible cheerleaders: Nelie Lyman (we could not have done it without you), Jamie Pope, Dana Spinola, Cindy Itkoff, Amy Clay, Laken Radvansky, Kate Swenson, Elizabeth Wright, Jill Edgecombe, Traci Mayo, Carol Mathias, Robin Finley, Cassie DeLany, Kimberly Lusink, Melissa Fullam, Courtney Bowman, Jim Shipley, Julie Sheggrud, April Vanderpoort, Todd and Melissa Pennington, EJ Aspuru, Elizabeth Richards, Ada Lee Correll, Caroline LeFleur Loftin, Julie Longino, Lauren Fulford, Staci Delesandri Monahan, Bella Borbon, Jackie Allen, Stacey Elgin, Tiffany McNary, Kimberley Kennedy, Kristen Gibbs, Leslie McLeod, Naomi Mann, Angela Means, Nikki Fein, Stacy Galan, Monica Pearson, Kim Lape, Paula Dickey, Wanda Rogers, Tonia Kenny, Misty Clare, Lisa David, Colleen Babul, Tom Bird, Matt Ruggles, Meg Reggie, Jamie Latiolais, Deedee Glass, Charlotte Ottley, Amity Borck, Amy Stephens, Marnie Witters, Karen Rutherford, Robyn Spizman, Eileen Gordon, Brittany Wilson, Natalie Demarko, and Gaelle Philbert.

We are grateful for all of the places and spaces that we filled and that filled us: Nancy G's Café, Caribou Coffee, Seasons 52, Chops, Tootsie's,

Fab'rik, Café Jonah, the Magical Attic, the Center for Love & Light, The Lodge, and Core Studios. A special thank-you to Beth Weitzman for introducing us, and to every single daughter who picks up this book and pays it forward. We also thank our amazing board members for the Fatherless Project nonprofit. Each of you are helping us change the lives of fatherless daughters around the world.

Denna

First, I have to thank God for showing me what to do with the heartbreak of losing my father. My mother, Mary Dobbins, for her constant encouragement, beautiful love, and endless listening while I tried for years to get everyone around the world to understand the importance of both a mother and a father in a daughter's life.

My husband, Jon Babul, who is a saint for loving me perfectly for who I am. I will love you forever. I am so grateful for my two delicious children, Sophie Bleu and Weston Grey, for filling up my heart and making me whole again. Thank you to my selfless mother-in-law, Joan, for coming to my aid any time I asked.

My brother, Jim Dobbins Jr., for being my partner in crime during our childhood. You always make me laugh. Sorry for telling Mom that you caused a bruise on my leg when it was actually eye shadow applied by me.

My Dad, Jim Dobbins, I am thankful for the short time we shared together on this earth. I know you are with me and guiding me through this amazing life.

Thank you to my two best friends, Trina Winde and Denise Branham. God had a plan. I am so happy you two were there for the ride. Thank you to my brother, Jim, (again) and my uncles Bill and Albert for standing in and helping me become the confident and successful woman I am today. I am so appreciative for Nicole Ergle for taking care of my two beautiful babies from birth. Thanks to all of the babysitters from the Hawks.

Thank you to the Dobbins, Babul, Smith, Surles, and Thomas families for encouraging me to tell my story no matter what. Thank you, Dwayne. Thank you to Karin Luise for going on this journey with me and providing dark chocolate and cold Pinot along the way. Thank you to Danny Belk, Eric Honroth, Tyler Bullock, Mike McCully, Sean Ezell, Peter H'Doubler, and Pete Wellborn for all of your mentoring.

Karin

I thank God, my angels, and guides for all that has been done to protect, direct, and nurture me along my path.

To my children, West, Elise, and Hoyte—you have been the miracles that I prayed for my whole life. Daily you teach me to feel love in its deepest form with your brilliant, hilarious, exquisite souls. Thank you for helping me to remember the joy of being present to each moment.

Thank you to the special members of the Fack, Graves, Fulford, Klebe, Correll, and Smithson families who have supported me in this journey. Joe, thank you for loving our children.

To Mom, the Reverend Lisa Graves, my first advocate, champion, and friend. You ingrained in me from a young girl that God gave me a strong intuition and that prayer is the ultimate guiding light. You helped me find my voice, my strength, and my resolve—because you did it first.

To my brother Steve, thank you for coming in when the world went out. You are one of the wisest, caring, most authentic people I know. We chose to be in this life side by side . . . birthday by birthday . . . soul by soul . . . as a lifeboat for each other.

To my dad, Herb Klebe, I am so grateful for the closeness that we now share. Our story will give hope to so many fathers and daughters who read this book—thank you for letting me share it. I am so grateful my children have you for a grandpa.

To my "little" brother, Alex, who is bigger than me in so many ways. I am deeply proud of you and your family (Tava, William, Wesley, and Cora) and of the man and father that you have become. You made things right again.

To my stepfather, Brice Graves. Your patience, steadfast loyalty, and fluid acceptance are such gifts. You inspired me to become a therapist, author, and liberal thinker—no matter who is in the room. Thank you for truly loving my mother.

To the best of the best: Shana Gustafson, you have buoyed me through everything. Rebecca Holmes, your support and humor are boundless. You are my soul sisters.

Big Mama Bear hugs to the amazing women who have loved my children like they were their own: Dillia Sena, Kyra Knowles, Holly Giamfortone Fett, and Emily Osborne.

My deepest gratitude for the teachers, professors, and mentors who have helped me find my way: Eulita Dykes, Ruth Fruit, Ron Broadway, Dr. Betty Sue Newman, Dr. Bill Doverspike, Dr. Brian J. Dew, Dr. Ken Matheny, Dr. Becky Beaton, and Dr. Joanna White.

To my counselors and healers, from deep in my soul, thank you: Dr. J. Mickey Nardo, Dr. Lauren Berman, Dr. Kathleen Hall, Shelly Ruggiano, Kimberly Cook, Jamie Butler, Laura Boone, Autumn Bond-Ross, and Lisa McCardle.

To Denna Babul, you have helped me rise to find pieces of myself that I never knew existed. Your wit, insight, and depth have amazed me every step of the way. There is no one else who could have been a better yin to my yang.

RESOURCES

RECOMMENDED READING

Brach, Tara. *Radical Acceptance*. Rpt. ed. New York: Bantam, 2004.

Brizendine, Louann. *The Female Brain*. New York: Harmony, 2007.

Brown, Brené. *The Gifts of Imperfection*. Center City, MN: Hazelden, 2010.

Chopra, Deepak. *Magical Beginning, Enchanted Lives*. New York: Harmony, 2005.

Edelman, Hope. *Motherless Daughters*. 3rd ed. New York: DeCapo Lifelong Books, 2014.

Forrest, Lynne. *Guiding Principles for Life beyond Victim Consciousness*. Chattanooga, TN: Conscious Living Media, 2011.

Gilbert, Elizabeth. *Eat, Pray, Love*. New York: Riverhead, 2007.

Hanson, Rick. *Buddha's Brain*. Oakland, CA: New Harbinger, 2009.

Hanson, Rick. *Hardwiring Happiness*. New York: Harmony, 2013.

Hay, Louise. *You Can Heal Your Life*. New York: Hay House, 1984.

Herman, Judith. *Trauma and Recovery*. New York: Basic Books, 1997.

Lerner, Harriet. *The Dance of Anger*. New York: Sounderbooks, 1985.

Peck, M. Scott. *The Road Less Traveled*. New York: Touchstone, 2003.

Smith, Claire Bidwell. *The Rules of Inheritance*. New York: Plume, 2012.

Strayed, Cheryl. *Wild*. New York: Vintage, 2013.

Taylor, Catheryn L. *The Inner Child Workbook*. New York: Tarcher, 1991.

Weiss, Brian L. *Many Lives, Many Masters*. Fireside, 1988.

Woititz, Janet Geringer. *Adult Children of Alcoholics*. Deerfield Beach, FL: Health Communications, 1990.

VIDEO

A Voice for the Young Child with an Incarcerated Parent. Portland, OR: Children's Justice
Alliance, 2012. Information available at apps.americanbar.org/litigation/com
mittees/childrights/content/articles/winter2012-young-child-incarcerated
-parent.html.

SOURCES OF INFORMATION AND SUPPORT

Adolescent Self Injury Foundation www.adolescentselfinjuryfoundation.com
Adverse Childhood Experiences www.acestudy.org
Al-Anon www.al-anon.org
Alcoholics Anonymous www.aa.org
Cocaine Anonymous www.ca.org
Denna Babul, Life Coach, Writer, Speaker www.dennababul.com
Fatherless Daughter Project www.fatherlessdaughterproject.com
Karin Luise, Therapist, Educator, Speaker www.doctorkarin.com
Nar-Anon www.nar-anon.org
Narcotics Anonymous www.na.org
National Association of Adult Survivors of Child Abuse www.naasca.org
National Clearinghouse for Alcohol and Drug Information 800-729-6686
The National Eating Disorders Association 800-931-2237
National Suicide Prevention Lifeline 800-273-8255

NOTES

U.S. statistics: 67 percent of African American families: National Kids Count, "Children in Single-Parent Families by Race," data from Population Reference Bureau, analysis of data from the U.S. Census Bureau, Census 2000 Supplementary Survey, 2001 Supplementary Survey, and 2002 through 2013 American Community Survey. Available at datacenter.kidscount.org/data /tables/107-children-in-single-parent-families-by#detailed/1/any/false /36,868,867,133,38/10,168,9,12,1,13,185/432,431.

80 percent of single-parent families are father-absent households: U.S. Census Bureau, "America's Families and Living Arrangements: 2013," and "Current Population Survey 2014 Annual Social and Economic Supplement," released January 2015.

Carol Gilligan's landmark research out of Harvard University: Carol Gilligan, *In a Different Voice: Psychological Theory and Women's Development* (Cambridge: Harvard University Press, 1982).

one in two marriages will end in divorce: American Psychological Association, "Marriage & Divorce." Available at www.apa.org/topics/divorce.

three or more parental marriage breakups: F. F. Furstenberg, C. W. Nord, J. L. Peterson, and N. Zill, "The Life Course of Children of Divorce: Marital Disruption and Parental Contact," *American Sociological Review* 48 (1983): 656–668.

Author Jill Di Donato talks: Curtis M. Wong, "Why Author Jill Di Donato Wishes Her Gay Dad Had Come Out Sooner," *The Huffington Post*, August 29, 2014. Available at http://www.huffingtonpost.com/2014/08/29/daughter-gay-father -coming-out_n_5737932.html.

I am what I have lost: Riese, "Before You Know It Something's Over," *Autostraddle*, June 15, 2014. Available at http://www.autostraddle.com /before-you-know-it-somethings-over-241440.

more people die today of suicide than in car accidents: Centers for Disease Control and Prevention, "Suicide among Adults Aged 35–64 Years—United States, 1999–2010," *Morbidity and Mortality Weekly Report* 62, no. 17 (2013): 321–325. Available at www.cdc.gov/mmwr/preview/mmwrhtml/mm6217a1 .htm?s_cid=mm6217a1_w.

between the ages of twenty-five and sixty-five: National Strategy for Suicide Prevention, "Suicide: Cost to the Nation." Available at www.mentalhealth .samhsa.gov/suicideprevention/costtonation.asp.

men over forty-five who are depressed or alcoholic: Mental Health America, "Suicide." Available at www.mentalhealthamerica.net/suicide.

suicide was discovered to be twice as prevalent among divorced men compared to divorced women: Augustine J. Kposowa, "Marital Status and Suicide in the National Longitudinal Mortality Study," *Journal of Epidemiology and Community Health* 54 (2000): 254–261. Available at http://jech.bmj.com/content/54/4/254 .abstract?ijkey=0c94ef8b97c2ead0a8f99946eb310db66a38206a&keytype2=tf _ipsecsha.

about 25 percent of all U.S. adults have mental illness: Centers for Disease Control and Prevention, "Mental Illness Surveillance Among Adults in the United States." Available at http://www.cdc.gov/mentalhealthsurveillance /fact_sheet.html.

When a parent goes to prison: Lynne Reckman and Debra Rothstein, "A Voice for the Young Child with an Incarcerated Parent," *American Bar Association*, January 9, 2012. Available at http://apps.americanbar.org/litigation /committees/childrights/content/articles/winter2012-young-child-incarcerated -parent.html.

1.7 million children in the United States with an incarcerated parent: Lauren Glaze and Laura Maruschak, "Parents in Prison and Their Minor Children," Bureau of Justice Statistics, Special Report, U.S. Department of Justice, August 2009. Available at http://www.bjs.gov/content/pub/pdf/pptmc.pdf.

Many abused children cling to the hope that growing up will bring escape and freedom: Judith Herman, *Trauma and Recovery: The Aftermath of Violence—from Domestic Abuse to Political Terror* (New York: Basic Books, 1997), 110.

a girl's self-esteem and sociability are significantly higher: Claudette Wassil-Grimm, *Where's Daddy?: How Divorced, Single and Widowed Mothers Can Provide What's Missing When Dad's Missing* (Woodstock, NY: Overlook Press, 1994).

toddler girls also tend to form emotional and social connections differently: Simon Baron-Cohen, *The Essential Difference: Men, Women, and the Extreme Male Brain* (New York: Penguin Group, 2004).

healthy development can be derailed by excessive or prolonged activation of stress response systems: Center on the Developing Child at Harvard University, "Key Concepts: Toxic Stress." Available at developingchild.harvard .edu/key_concepts/toxic_stress_response.

much more likely to have "an early onset of puberty": David E. Comings, Donn Muhlemann, James P. Johnson, and James P. MacMurray, "Parent-Daughter Transmission of the Androgen Receptor Gene as an Explanation of the Effect of Father Absence on Age of Menarche," *Child Development* 73 (July–Aug. 2002): 1046.

According to psychologist Carl Pickhard: Charles E. Pickard, "The Impact of Divorce on Young Children and Adolescents: Young Children and Adolescents Can Respond Differently to Divorce," *Psychology Today*, December 19, 2011. Available at https://www.psychologytoday.com/blog/surviving-your-childs -adolescence/201112/the-impact-divorce-young-children-and-adolescents.

grief does not end at a specific time: J. William Worden, *Grief Counseling and Grief Therapy* (New York: Springer, 2009).

kids can show signs of social problems: J. William Worden and Phyllis R. Silverman, "Parental Death and the Adjustment of School-Age Children," *Omega—Journal of Death and Dying* 33 (1996): 91–102.

Elizabeth Gilbert said in a 2014 interview: "Super Soul Sunday," OWN Network, season 5, episode 528, October 5, 2014. Available at http://www.oprah.com /own-super-soul-sunday/Elizabeth-Gilbert.

women who lost their fathers after the age of nineteen: Nadine F. Marks, Heyjung Jun, and Jieun Song, "Death of Parents and Adult Psychological and Physical Well-Being: A Prospective U.S. National Study," *Journal of Family Issues* 28 (2007): 1611–1638.

Daniel Levinson's landmark study of thirteen hundred women: Daniel J. Levinson, *The Seasons of a Woman's Life* (New York: Ballantine Books, 1996).

a theory about family dynamics: The Bowen Center for the Study of the Family, "Nuclear Family Emotional Process." Available at www.thebowencenter.org /theory/eight-concepts/nuclear-family-emotional-process.

Harvard Child Bereavement Study: James W. Worden, *Children and Grief: When a Parent Dies* (New York: Guilford Press, 1996).

In general, mother loss is harder on children than father loss: Hope Edelman, *Motherless Daughters: The Legacy of Loss*, 20th ed. (Boston: Da Capo Press, 2014),

xxiii. Original source: James W. Worden, *Children and Grief: When a Parent Dies* (New York: Guilford Press, 1996).

Children of divorce do better: Diane N. Lye, "Washington State Parenting Act Study," June 1999, p. 178. Available at www.courts.wa.gov/committee/pdf /parentingplanstudy.pdf.

stepfamilies are likely to have up to three times the amount: E. Mavis Hetherington and Joan Kelly, *For Better or For Worse: Divorce Reconsidered*, (New York: W. W. Norton and Company, 2002).

experience difficulties forming lasting, intimate relationships with men: Wassil-Grimm, *Where's Daddy?*

more physical contact with males: Franklin B. Krohn and Zoe Bogan, "The Effects Absent Fathers Have on Female Development and College Attendance," *College Student Journal* 35 (2001).

girls who lost their fathers as a result of death tended to be more scared of men: Wassil-Grimm, *Where's Daddy?*

fathers are most influential in these specific areas of child development: Ibid.

Daughters need the example of what a man really is: Donna Griffin, *Fatherless Women* (Los Angeles, California: Milligan Books, 1998).

a study on young mice: Julie Robert, "Dads: How Important Are They?," McGill University Health Centre, December 4, 2013. Available at muhc.ca/newsroom /news/dads-how-important-are-they. Original study: Francis R. Bambico, Baptiste Lacoste, Patrick R. Hattan, and Gabriella Gobbi, "Father Absence in the Monogamous California Mouse Impairs Social Behavior and Modifies Dopamine and Glutamate Synapses in the Medial Prefrontal Cortex," *Cerebral Cortex* 11 (2013): 24. Available at cercor.oxfordjournals.org/content/early/2013 /11/24/cercor.bht310.abstract.

mice are a good model for understanding how these effects arise in humans: McGill University, "Dads: How Important Are They?" December 4, 2013. Available at http://www.mcgill.ca/channels/news/dads-how-important-are -they-231936.

girls who are raised without their fathers' love usually feel more anxious and insecure: Abdul Khaleque and Ronald P. Rohner, "Transnational Relations between Perceived Parental Acceptance and Personality Dispositions of Children and Adults: A Meta-Analytic Review," *Personality and Social Psychology Review* 16 (2011): 103.

daughters who suffered father absence were much more likely to have early sexual experiences: Bruce J. Ellis, John E. Bates, Kenneth A. Dodge, David M. Fergusson, L. John Horwood, Gregory S. Pettit, and Lianne Woodward,

"Does Father Absence Place Daughters at Special Risk for Early Sexual Activity and Teenage Pregnancy?" National Institutes of Health, October 20, 2009. Available at www.ncbi.nlm.nih.gov/pmc/articles/PMC2764264.

In order to cope, I turned to alcohol: Interview with Elizabeth Vargas, *The View*, January 2014. Available at http://abc.go.com/shows/the-view/video/VDKA0 _a39nckdu.

Women who had experienced physical or sexual abuse before the age of eighteen: Susan M. Mason, Alan J. Flint, Alison E. Field, S. Bryn Austin, and Janet W. Rich-Edwards, "Abuse Victimization in Childhood or Adolescence and Risk of Food Addiction in Adult Women," *Obesity* 21, no. 12 (2013): E775– E781. Available at www.ncbi.nlm.nih.gov/pmc/articles/PMC3855159.

one-third of Americans say they have had an illness that was primarily caused by stress: American Psychological Association. "Stress a Major Health Problem in the U.S., Warns APA," October 24, 2007. Available at http://www.apa.org /news/press/releases/2007/10/stress.aspx.

Young women who are moderately or severely depressed have a significantly higher heart disease death risk: American Heart Association, "Depression Linked to Higher Heart Disease Death Risk in Younger Women," American Heart Association Rapid Access Journal Report, June 18, 2014.

participants with a history of depression were four times more likely to develop breast cancer: Alden L. Gross, Joseph J. Gallo, and William W. Eaton, "Depression and Cancer Risk: 24 Years of Follow-Up of the Baltimore Epidemiologic Catchment Area Sample," *Cancer Causes Control*, 21, no. 2 (2010): 191–199. Available at http://newsroom.heart.org/news/depression -linked-to-higher-heart-disease-death-risk-in-younger-women.

It's a part of what Louise Hay teaches: Louise Hay, *You Can Heal Your Life* (New York: Hay House, 1984).

Rick Hanson delivered a TED Talk: Rick Hanson, "Hardwiring Happiness: The Hidden Power of Everyday Experiences on the Modern Brain," TEDx Marin 2013, TEDx Talks. Available at https://www.youtube.com/watch?v= jpuDyGgIeh0.

Perhaps the biggest tragedy of our lives is that freedom is possible: Tara Brach, *Radical Acceptance: Embracing Your Life with the Heart of a Buddha* (New York: Bantam Dell, 2003).

Tara Parker-Pope wrote an insightful article: Tara Parker-Pope, "Writing Your Way to Happiness," *New York Times*, January 19, 2015. Available at well.blogs .nytimes.com/2015/01/19/writing-your-way-to-happiness.

"People ask where does the 'funny' come from": Sheryl Underwood, comments on *The Talk*, CBS Television, September 14, 2013. Available at http://www

.nydailynews.com/entertainment/gossip/sheryl-underwood-talk-reveals
-childhood-tragedy-secret-twin-article-1.1455944.

girl bravely spoke at Jane Fonda's Georgia Campaign for Adolescent Power &
Potential: GCAPP Empower Party, September 11, 2014. Event information
available at http://gcapp.org/event/empower-party-0.

I call this the Fellowship of Suffering: Andy Stanley, North Point Community
Church, Atlanta, GA, Sermon "In the Meantime," September 21, 2014.
Available at http://northpoint.org/messages/in-the-meantime/comfort-zone/.

"Much of our anxiety and stress": *Miracles Now: 108 Life-Changing Tools for Less Stress,
More Flow, and Finding Your True Purpose* (Carlsbad, CA: Hay House Inc.): 19.

INDEX